THE CAVENDISH Q & A SERIES

G000135413

CRIMINAL LAW

TITLES IN THE Q&A SERIES

THE CAVENDISH Q & A SERIES

CRIMINAL LAW

Norman Baird BA BSc
Senior Lecturer
Department of Law
Thames Valley University

Cavendish
Publishing
Limited

First published in Great Britain 1993 by Cavendish Publishing Limited,
23A Countess Road, London NW5 2XH.

Telephone: 071-485 0303   Facsimile: 071-485 0304

British Library Cataloguing in Publication Data

Baird, N
Criminal Law - (Q & A Series)
I Title II Series
344.205

ISBN 1-874241-25-2

Printed and bound in Great Britain

Contents

Introduction

The purpose of this book is to assist students in their study of criminal law. It is aimed primarily at students on degree courses and courses leading to professional examinations. It is not intended to replace standard textbooks, law reports and academic journals but to complement them by providing illustrations of answers to typical examination and course assessment questions. It is anticipated that it will be of most use to the student who has acquired a good knowledge of the relevant rules and principles of criminal law but who still experiences difficulty in expressing that knowledge.

It is often not clear to students what is expected of them when answering a question in criminal law. Common difficulties include tackling problem questions where some of the relevant facts are not disclosed, the treatment of conflicting or ambiguous rules of law, the resolution of problems where there are no adequate authorities, and judging the extent to which it may be necessary to refer to the facts of previous decisions. It is hoped that this book will help to resolve these difficulties.

Where the law is in doubt reference is occasionally made to the opinions of academics expressed in the standard texts on criminal law.

The questions are modelled on those used in past examination papers from a variety of sources including the University of London (External) LLB. They include 'problem questions', 'essay questions' and 'mixed part questions'. The answers to each question are preceded by an answer plan which explains, in outline, the issues raised by the question.

I hope that this book will assist you to make the best use of your knowledge of criminal law in examinations and course assessments.

I have endeavoured to state the law as at 1 February 1993.

Norman Baird
London
February 1993

Table of Cases

Table of Statutes

General Principles of Criminal Law

Introduction

This chapter contains questions concerning some of the fundamental principles of criminal law. Also included are questions regarding the objectives of punishment and the proper scope of the criminal law.

Inevitably, because of the subject matter, the majority of the questions in this chapter are of the essay type.

Checklist

The following topics should be prepared in advance of tackling the questions:

- The competing theories of punishment
  Why do we punish? What objectives ought we to have in mind? 'Utilitarian' and 'desert' theories of punishment.
- The scope of the criminal law
  What conduct ought to be subject to the criminal sanction? Should behaviour be subject to the criminal law merely because it is considered 'immoral' or should only 'harmful' conduct be criminalised? What other considerations ought the legislature to bear in mind when deciding whether to make particular conduct unlawful?
- *Mens rea* terms - 'intention' and 'recklessness'
  What is meant by 'intention'? The current approach as expressed in the recent cases of *Moloney*, *Hancock & Shankland*, and *Nedrick*. Previous approaches to the issue.
  What is meant by 'recklessness'? '*Caldwell* recklessness' and '*Cunningham* recklessness' - the distinction between 'advertent' and 'inadvertent' recklessness.
  It is not sufficient to be able to give an account of the relevant definitions. Most examiners, when they set questions on these topics, ask for a *critical* evaluation of the current definitions.
- Liability for omissions
  The circumstances in which criminal liability may be incurred for a failure to act. The duty principle. Co-incidence of *actus reus* and *mens rea*.
- Strict liability
  What is meant by a crime of strict liability? How do the courts determine whether or not an offence requires *mens rea*? What are the justifications for imposing liability on a strict basis?

Question 1

'(For a practice to be subject to the criminal sanction) it is not enough in our submission that (it) is ... regarded as immoral. Nor is it enough that it should cause harm. Both of these are minimal conditions for action by means of the criminal law but they are not sufficient.' Clarkson and Keating 1990.

   Discuss.

Answer plan

The quotation expresses the commonly held view that immorality and harmfulness are *necessary but not sufficient* conditions of criminal liability: that the legislator ought to consider further matters when deciding whether to criminalise or legalise particular conduct. The starting point in answering this question is the well known 'debate' in the 50s and 60s between Lord Devlin and Professor Hart.

- the 'moral' theory : the Wolfenden Committee and Lord Devlin's response to the Report
- criticisms of the 'moral' theory - its irrationalism
- the 'harm' principle
- the limitations of the 'harm' principle
- considerations additional to the supposed immorality or harmfulness of the behaviour - the social effects of prohibition and enforcement
- is immorality a 'necessary' condition?

Answer

In 1959 Lord Devlin delivered the Maccabean Lecture in Jurisprudence of the British Academy under the title 'The enforcement of morals' in which he argued that the legislature are entitled to use the criminal law against behaviour which is generally condemned as immoral.

   The catalyst for Lord Devlin's thesis was the Report of the Wolfenden Committee on Homosexual Offences and Prostitution. The Committee had recommended that homosexual behaviour between consenting adults in private should no longer be a criminal offence. The Committee thought it was not the function of the law to intervene in the private lives of citizens or to enforce any particular morality *except* where it is necessary to protect the citizen from what is offensive or injurious and to provide protection against exploitation and corruption.

Lord Devlin contended that these additional criteria are unnecessary. In his opinion there are no limits to the power of the state to legislate against immoral behaviour - 'immorality' is a necessary and sufficient condition of criminalisation.

Lord Devlin based his argument upon the premise that if morality is not underwritten by the law social harmony will be jeopardised. According to this view, tolerance of immorality threatens the social fabric and, therefore, the legislature should criminalise behaviour where it is clear that there is a 'collective judgment' condemning the behaviour in question (1).

According to Lord Devlin immorality is what every 'right-minded' person considers to be immoral. If the behaviour in question provokes feelings of disgust and indignation in this 'individual' then it should be subject to the criminal sanction. Lord Devlin suggests the judiciary are particularly well placed to express the appropriate standards by virtue of their familiarity with the 'reasonable man in the jury'.

There are a number of different objections to Lord Devlin's thesis but the principal criticisms relate to its 'overt rejection of rationality' (2). That is, instead of rational argument and empirical investigation of the likely effects of criminalisation or legalisation Lord Devlin advocates that we place our reliance upon *presumptions* about the *feelings* of the right minded individual and *assumptions* about the societal effects of liberalisation and tolerance.

Opponents to Devlin's thesis argue that, although the feelings of the community are an important consideration, they cannot be the sole basis for deciding whether behaviour is to be subject to the criminal sanction.

Graham Hughes, for example, points out that if the revulsion of the ordinary person is a dangerous basis for criminalisation then reliance on judicial estimates of that disgust is even more dangerous (2). And Bentham warned us to be suspicious when officials claim that they are acting in the name of 'right minded people'. In many cases 'popular opinion' is used as a pretext to justify the prejudices of the legislators themselves (3).

With reference to Lord Devlin's assertion that morality forms a seamless web Professor Hart claims that there is no evidence that people abandon their moral views about murder, cruelty and dishonesty purely because a practice which they regard as immoral is not punished by law (4).

Professor Hart argues that the proper approach to determining whether the criminal law should intervene involves full consideration of the social consequences of the conduct in question. To this extent he is a supporter of the liberal approach which stresses the importance of rational discussion in terms of the possible harmful consequences of the conduct. The principle of democracy may require the legislator to consider the values of the 'moral' majority but the liberal tradition urges that the autonomy of the individual be respected and that individuals have rights that may override majority will.

The general approach of this tradition was expressed by John Stuart Mill in his essay *On Liberty*. He maintained that the exercise of force over an individual is justified only if it is done to prevent harm to others. The fact that the behaviour might cause harm to the person who performs it is no justification for criminalisation (5).

Professor Hart agrees that we must consider whether a practice which is generally regarded as immoral is also harmful before we take the step of criminalising the behaviour. He argues that a reasoned assessment of the harmful effects of the behaviour is a far superior approach to the question whether it should be outlawed than simple reliance on the feelings of disgust that the behaviour might cause us to feel (6).

It might be supposed that the harm theorist would be opposed to legislation controlling narcotics or compelling the use of seat belts in motor vehicles on the basis that legislation of this type involves a violation of the fundamental principle of individual autonomy. The harm theorist is opposed to legislation designed to protect the individual from himself.

In fact legislation of this type is often supported by modern harm theorists. They point out that the prohibited behaviour *is* potentially harmful to others. Kaplan explains that there are different categories of harm any one of which may be used to justify the criminalisation of behaviour that at first sight appears only to expose the actor to the risk of harm (7). The individual who drives without wearing a seat belt or the person who consumes drugs may expose others to a 'public ward harm'. That is, he may impose on others the cost of rectifying the damage he causes himself. He may be rendered incapable of discharging economic responsibilities he owes to others ('non support harm'). Or a case may be made out that if the individual is allowed to indulge in the behaviour other susceptible individuals may copy or 'model' the behaviour and suffer harm as a consequence.

This, it might be argued, reveals one of the limitations of the liberal 'harm' theory. When secondary harms are taken into account the theory appears to lack precision. As Kaplan points out, if we acknowledge the broad concept of harm, there are few actions that one can perform that threaten harm only to oneself.

Moreover, the prohibition of particular 'harmful' conduct may, in itself, result in harmful consequences. For example, the sale of certain commodities (heroin, alcohol, sugar, petrol, hamburgers etc) may directly or indirectly cause *physical* harm to consumers. However, prohibiting the sale of those commodities will cause *economic* harm to the business enterprises involved. Thus, it is often argued that, in general, we ought to weigh the harms resulting from tolerance against the harms of prohibition.

Bentham recognised that, in this process, careful consideration should be given to the general effects of prohibition. Even though certain behaviour may be regarded as immoral or harmful it should not be prohibited if punishment would be inefficacious as a deterrent or the harm caused by prohibition would be greater than that which would be suffered if the behaviour was left unpunished (8).

For example it is sometimes argued that as the demand for certain commodities and services (eg prostitution, abortion, alcohol and other drugs) is relatively inelastic, there is little point in criminalisation of the behaviour concerned. Indeed it is suggested that criminalisation may make matters worse. Prior to legalisation, back street abortions were carried out in conditions of great risk to the mother. Legalisation permits official control whereby considerations of public health might be better addressed (9).

In addition, the criminalisation of certain types of conduct (eg the possession of drugs) requires, for reasons of enforcement, intrusive forms of policing involving, for example, powers of stop and search etc. There is the danger that these powers might be used in a discriminatory and oppressive manner against particular groups. Similarly, the outlawing of homosexual behaviour meant that the police were often involved in dubious and degrading practices to catch offenders (10).

Thus the fact that behaviour is harmful to others cannot be a sufficient condition of prohibition. The virtue of the harm theory is that at least it focuses attention on the empirical issues concerning the social effects of the conduct *and* the effects of legal intervention - issues which the moral principle patently ignores.

The quotation suggests that immorality is a *necessary* condition of criminalisation. Is this correct? What importance should be attached to the moral feelings of a section of the community?

It is sometimes argued that support for the law is stronger where the prohibited conduct is perceived by a significant section of the population to be immoral (11).

It is submitted, however, that immorality ought not to be regarded as even a necessary condition of prohibition. Much of modern criminal legislation (eg road traffic laws) is concerned with conduct which would not ordinarily be termed 'immoral' but one would be hard pressed to deny the need for that legislation.

In any case, where behaviour is perceived to be immoral it is normally supported by empirical claims expressed in terms of the harmful consequences, real or imagined, that will result if the behaviour is tolerated (12). It is right that the debate should be focused on those empirical claims. It is only by insisting upon arguments articulated in terms of the social consequences of tolerance, on the one hand, and prohibition, on the other, that a rational analysis of the fairness of legal intervention can be conducted.

The fact that a section of the community *feel* that certain behaviour is immoral cannot be either a necessary or a sufficient condition of prohibition in the absence of a reasoned explanation of their feelings. Although it may be prudent *on some occasions* for the legislator to acknowledge the 'feelings' of a section of the community - to ignore those irrational sentiments may result in the harmful consequence of social unrest - he should not *rely* upon the 'stomach of the man in the street'. Disgust or revulsion ought never to replace careful investigation of the social effects of prohibition (13).

Notes

1 Lord Devlin argued that morality forms a 'seamless web'. By this metaphor Lord Devlin intended to convey the notion that 'society's morals' form a fragile interlocking structure and that if morality is not generally reinforced by legal means then 'damage' to the entire social structure will follow. Morality as a whole will be undermined.

2 Graham Hughes *Morals and the Criminal Law* in *Essays in Legal Philosophy*, ed Robert Summers (1968) p 198.

3 Theory of Legislation (1876).

4 Hart *Immorality and Treason* The Listener 30 30 1959.

5 Harm is not to be understood as restricted to 'physical harm'. As Gross points out 'harm' is caused when any recognised interest is violated. A Theory of Criminal Justice (1979).

6 Professor Hart does suggest however that Mill's thesis is perhaps too simple. Cruelty to animals, for example, should be outlawed although there is no harm caused to other people. And, it might be argued, legal intervention may be appropriate to restrain young people for example from certain activities. This is justified not on the grounds that the behaviour may cause harm to the young person but on the grounds that such a person is not sufficiently mature to be capable of appreciating the dangers of the behaviour in question.

7 See the extract from *The Role of Law in Drug Control* in Clarkson and Keating (1990) 2nd ed p 86.

8 Principles of Morals and Legislation.

9 Similarly if prostitution were decriminalised a condition of operating as a licensed or registered prostitute might be periodic health checks.

10 In addition homosexuals were exposed to the risk of blackmail.

11 H Packer *The Limits of the Criminal Sanction* (1968).

12 For example Lord Devlin believed that the tolerance of homosexuality would result in harm - ie damage to society at large. (see Note 1 above) This prediction can at least be evaluated and *if* it were true it would provide a very good argument in favour of prohibiting homosexuality. (Emperor Justinian believed that homosexual behaviour was the cause of earthquakes. Seismologists do not agree). On the other hand, the assertion that 'homosexuality should be prohibited *because it is immoral*' cannot be evaluated in the same way.

13 Graham Hughes. Ibid, p 206.

Question 2

How should 'intention' be defined?

Answer plan

It is not sufficient in answering this question to give an account of the current approach to the definition of intention in criminal law. Nor is it sufficient to add a review of previous approaches. The question asks 'how *should* intention be defined?' and, therefore, the answer should include a reasoned argument in favour of a particular definition.

The principal issues are:

- the requirements of a definition of intention
- assessment of various approaches to the issue - *Mohan; Hyam v DPP; Moloney; Hancock & Shankland; Nedrick*
- assessment of the Law Commission proposal

Answer

Introduction

For a number of offences the prosecution must prove beyond a reasonable doubt that the accused intended a particular consequence. To secure a conviction for murder, for example, it must be proved that the accused intended either to kill or cause grievous bodily harm. Recklessness will not suffice. Similarly, intention, and intention alone, is the basis of liability for the offence of wounding with intent contrary to s 18 of the Offences Against the Person Act 1861 and for offences of attempt contrary to the Criminal Attempts Act 1981.

The meaning of intention is not to be found in any statute. Its meaning is to be found in judicial decisions. Unfortunately, there has been a lack of consistency in the approach of the courts to the question of what constitutes intention.

Before reviewing those decisions it is important to consider some matters of principle.

Firstly, the fault elements most commonly encountered in the definition of offences - intention and recklessness - reflect different levels or degrees of blameworthiness. A person who kills, intending to kill is, all other things being equal, regarded as more blameworthy than a person who kills recklessly. This is reflected in the fact that the former is guilty of murder and subject to a mandatory term of life imprisonment whereas the latter is guilty of manslaughter which carries a maximum of life imprisonment (Murder (Abolition of Death Penalty) Act 1965 ; s 5 Offences Against the Person Act 1861). The concepts of intention and recklessness are distinct and stand in a hierarchical relationship one to the other. Thus, the definition of intention should not overlap with the definition of recklessness - the essence of which is unjustified risk-taking - and the boundary between the two concepts should be drawn at a point that reflects a difference in degree of moral blameworthiness.

Furthermore, as the jury will have the task of determining whether the accused did or did not intend the evil consequence in question, the judicial instruction as to the meaning of intention should be clear and should correspond as closely as possible to the ordinary meaning of the word. It is often suggested that if the legal definition of intention were quite different from ordinary usage then the risk of the jury failing to understand the judge's direction would be increased. In addition, it is often argued that the law should reflect ordinary principles of attribution of moral responsibility.

Finally, to ensure consistency of decisions the definition should be as precise as possible.

Judicial decisions

The central or core meaning of intention is aim, objective or purpose. This approach to intention was adopted by the Court of Appeal in *Mohan* (1976) in which James LJ defined intention as a decision to bring about a particular consequence irrespective of whether the defendant desired that consequence. The latter part of the definition indicates that a person can be said to intend a particular consequence even though it is not desired if it is a condition precedent to the desired consequence.

The definition in *Mohan* is generally accepted as a good one. It corresponds to the ordinary meaning of the word (1). However, it has not always been accepted as a sufficiently broad definition.

Prior to the decision of the House of Lords in *Moloney* it was generally accepted that a person could be said to have intended a result if he foresaw that the result was virtually or practically certain to result from the behaviour in question even if it was not his aim or purpose (2).

The point is commonly discussed by reference to the following hypothetical example: D places a bomb on a plane. The bomb is timed to explode when the plane is in mid-flight. His aim is to collect the insurance money on cargo he has placed on the flight. Although he hopes the passengers and crew will survive the explosion D knows that it is practically certain that they will die. Does D intend to kill in these circumstances or is he to be regarded 'merely' as reckless with respect to killing the passengers and crew?

It has been argued that a consequence is intended only where its non - occurrence would be regarded as a failure and thus, as D would not regard the survival of the passengers and crew as marking the failure of his plan, he does not intend to kill (3).

On the other hand, it has been suggested that, despite the fact that it is not D's purpose to kill the passengers, there is no *moral* distinction between D and the purposeful killer, and, although there may be philosophical objections to extending the concept of intention to include this case, D ought to be categorised as a murderer if the plan is carried out and death results. Intention, it is said, ought to include foresight of virtual certainty (4).

Until recently, intention was even more broadly defined. The leading case was *Hyam v DPP* (1975) in which it was said that a person intends a result which he foresees as a *(highly) probable result* of his actions. This decision was criticised as it blurred the distinction between intention and recklessness.

The recent cases have taken a different approach to the question of intention. In *Moloney* (1985) the House of Lords held that ordinarily the judge need not define the word 'intention' except to explain that it is not the same thing as either desire or foresight (5). In 'rare' and 'exceptional' cases, however, - those in which the primary purpose of the defendant was not to cause the defined harmful consequence - the judge may instruct the jury that if the defendant foresaw the consequence as a natural consequence of his act then they *may* infer that he intended it.

In *Hancock & Shankland* (1986) the House of Lords amended the guidelines. The House considered that reference to 'natural consequences' was potentially misleading. Lord Scarman held that it should be explained to the jury that the greater the probability of a consequence the more likely it is that the consequence was foreseen, and that if the consequence was foreseen, the more likely it is that it was intended.

In both these decisions the House of Lords state that foresight is *evidence* of intention to be considered along with all other relevant evidence.

In *Nedrick* (1986) the Court of Appeal held that the jury are entitled to draw the inference of intention only where they are sure that the defendant foresaw as a virtual certainty the consequence in question. Indeed, Lord Lane thought that, in those circumstances, the 'inference may be irresistible' (6).

The outcome of these decisions is that there is no longer a definition of intention. *Hyam* is effectively overruled. Foresight, even of a virtually certain consequence, is merely evidence of intention.

Commentary

Professors Smith and Hogan criticise the decisions. They point out that if foresight is evidence from which an intention may be inferred, then intention must be a state of mind distinct from foresight but, in the absence of an explanation of the meaning of intention, how are the jury to assess or weigh this evidence against other evidence? Furthermore, leaving the concept undefined means that different juries may return different verdicts even where the agreed facts are, in all important respects, identical (7).

Most commentators suggest that intention be defined to include foresight of virtual certainty (8). Clarkson and Keating, however, believe that the 'line of demarcation' should be set at foresight of certainty ie where the consequence in question is a condition precedent to achieving the primary objective. They argue that not only are there good philosophical and linguistic reasons for restricting intention to primary and secondary *objectives* but also the difference between foresight of virtual certainty and high probability is so slight that the distinction between intention and recklessness would be blurred if intention were extended beyond foresight of certainty.

This approach would mean that if the defendant in the bomb in the plane case contemplated even a remote possibility that the passengers and the crew would survive he could not be said to have intended their death.

Clarkson and Keating refer with approval to the United States Model Penal Code which recognises a level of fault lying between intention and recklessness applying to the individual who foresees a consequence as practically certain. They contend that the virtue of such an approach is that, in addition to restricting intention to its ordinary meaning, it permits more precise discrimination in terms of blameworthiness (9).

The adoption of this approach, however, would entail redrafting the terms of liability for many offences and there would still be a problem of overlap between the intermediate level of fault and recklessness. It is impossible to define neighbouring concepts with such precision that there is no blurring at the borders between them. Whilst permitting greater discrimination in terms of the blameworthiness of defendants, an increase in the number of levels of fault would, in fact, create more problems with borderline cases.

The Law Commission has proposed that a person acts intentionally with respect to a result if (i) it was his purpose to cause it or (ii) he is aware that it would occur in the ordinary course of events if he were to succeed in his purpose of causing some other result (10).

Although the second part of the proposal avoids use of the expression 'knowledge of virtual certainty' it would appear to cover the 'bomb in the plane case' as well as the situation where one event is a condition precedent to another.

The adoption of this proposal would meet the criticisms of the existing law regarding intention. It keeps intention within fairly narrow limits. The overlap with 'recklessness' is minimised. And, although perhaps it extends intention beyond its ordinary meaning, it is expressed in fairly simple language. Thus, juries should be capable of understanding it with little difficulty.

The recent history of the attempt to define intention teaches us that it is not possible to devise a definition that will give equal weight to each of the matters mentioned at the beginning of this essay. The Law Commission proposal gives greater weight to the relevant issues of penal philosophy than it does to semantics. It is submitted that this is the correct approach. It is not always the case that the 'ordinary' meanings of 'ordinary' words reflect the principles and objectives of the criminal law and, thus, pedantic objections of a purely semantic type are best ignored (11). The Law Commission's proposal, whilst perhaps not a definition which would satisfy the compiler of a dictionary, gives proper emphasis to matters of penal policy and thus, it is submitted, should be adopted as a suitable definition of intention (12).

Notes

1 It also corresponds to the meaning given in the Shorter Oxford English Dictionary.
2 See for example the speech of Lord Hailsham in *Hyam v DPP* (1975) 2 All ER 41, p 51-52.
3 Duff *Intention, Recklessness and Probable Consequences* (1980) Crim LR 404.
4 See for example Ashworth *Principles of Criminal Law* (1991)   p 149.
5 It is rather strange that the House of Lords in *Moloney* should express approval of the decision of the Court of Criminal Appeal in *Steane* (1947). D had been charged with 'doing acts likely to assist the enemy with intent to assist the enemy' contrary to Defence Regulations of 1939. As a result of threats to himself and his family he had agreed to take part in propaganda broadcasts for the Nazi Government of Germany during the second world war. Lord Goddard held that as D's motive was a desire to save his wife and children he had not intended to assist the enemy. The decision is surely wrong. It confuses motive with intent. Steane intended to assist the enemy as the lesser of two evils. His acquittal should have been based on the defence of duress and not on the absence of intent.
6 In *Walker & Hayles* (1990) the Court of Appeal held that whilst a direction in terms of high probability is not a misdirection, it is preferable to direct the jury in terms of foresight of virtual certainty.

7   *Criminal Law* (1992) 7th ed p 54. In *Purcell* (1986) the Court of
    Appeal stated that the jury should decide the issue by
    reference to their understanding of the ordinary meaning of
    the word. Commentators, perhaps not surprisingly, are not in
    agreement as to how the jury will deal with this issue. On the
    one hand, Buxton believes that the jury will approach the
    question of intention in terms of the accused's purpose, while
    Professor Card, on the other, believes that they will almost
    invariably equate foresight of virtual certainty with intention.
    1988 Crim LR 484; Card, Cross and Jones (1992) 12th ed p 64.

8   See, for example, Williams *Textbook of Criminal Law* 1983 2nd
    ed pp 84-85; Smith and Hogan Criminal Law p 55.

9   *Criminal Law: Text and Materials* 1990 2nd ed pp 174 -175.

10 Law Commission Report No 122 (1992).

11 'The Law in action compiles its own dictionary' per Edmund-
    Davies LJ in *Caldwell* (1981).

12 Lord Lane in the debate on the Report of the House of Lords
    Select Committee on Murder (1989) agreed that *Nedrick*
    was 'not as clear as it should have been' and that intention
    should be defined in terms corresponding to the Law
    Commission's proposal.

Question 3

'The *Caldwell* test fails to make a distinction which should be
made between the person who knowingly takes a risk and the
person who gives no thought to whether there is a risk or not.
And, on the other hand it makes a distinction which has no moral
basis.' - Smith and Hogan 1992.

   Discuss.

Answer plan

The quotation is critical of the *Caldwell* test of recklessness and
therefore the discussion should explain the grounds of criticism.

   It is not sufficient to give an account of the *Caldwell* formula
nor is it necessary to mention every case in which the *Caldwell* test
has been applied or discussed. The main features of the *Caldwell*
test relevant to this question can be demonstrated by reference to
a small number of cases.

The first part of the quotation refers to the view of many critics that there is a significant distinction between the advertent and the inadvertent wrongdoer - a distinction which it is alleged Lord Diplock in *Caldwell* failed to observe. The implication of the quotation is that the inadvertent wrongdoer should not incur criminal liability or, at least, not to the same extent as the advertent wrongdoer.

The second part of the quotation refers to the apparent arbitrariness of the *Caldwell* loophole.

- the *Caldwell* definition of 'recklessness'
- the justifications for the punishment of the advertently reckless wrongdoer
- the arguments for and against the punishment of the inadvertently reckless wrongdoer
- the failure of the *Caldwell* test to recognise differences in degree of blameworthiness of the advertently and inadvertently reckless wrongdoer
- the justification for the exemption from liability in cases of the *Caldwell* 'loophole'

Answer

In *Caldwell* (1982) the House of Lords ruled upon the precise meaning of the term recklessness in s 1 of the Criminal Damage Act 1971.

Lord Diplock stated that a person is reckless with respect to whether any property would be destroyed or damaged - 'if (1) he does an act which in fact creates an obvious risk that property would be destroyed or damaged and (2) when he does the act he either (a) has not given any thought to the possibility of there being such a risk or (b) has recognised that there was some risk involved and has nonetheless gone on to do it'.

In *Lawrence* (1982) in a judgment concerning reckless driving handed down on the same day as *Caldwell*, Lord Diplock said that the risk must be 'obvious and *serious*'. Dealing with the same offence, the House of Lords in *Reid* (1992) explained that a risk is 'serious' if a reasonable person would consider it not to be negligible. It was also stated that where (2)b - the advertent limb - is relied upon, there is no need to prove that the risk was an obvious one; awareness of *some* risk of the particular consequence required will suffice.

Prior to these decisions it was apparently settled law that the test of recklessness required the prosecution to prove that the accused consciously ran the risk in question. For example, in the case of *Stephenson* (1979) D lit a fire in the hollow of a haystack. The stack caught fire and was destroyed. D claimed that he had not foreseen the damage. Psychiatric evidence was given that D suffered from schizophrenia. This disorder could have deprived Stephenson of the normal capacity to weigh and foresee risks.

The Court of Appeal held that the fact that the risk of damage would have been obvious to any normal person was not sufficient to give rise to criminal liability. The court held that the prosecution were obliged to prove that the defendant himself appreciated the existence of the risk. Recklessness was limited to advertent risk taking.

The *Caldwell* formula - (in 2(a) above) - extends the concept to include inadvertence. Lord Diplock believed that to restrict recklessness to consciously disregarding a recognised risk would impose an unnaturally narrow meaning on the word. In addition, he believed that, as consciously taking a risk was not necessarily more blameworthy than failing to give any thought to the possibility of risk, to restrict recklessness to advertent risk taking was undesirable as a matter of policy.

However, in a case decided two years later, the harshness of the *Caldwell* test was highlighted. In *Elliott v C* (1983) the Divisional Court held that with crimes for which *Caldwell* recklessness will suffice it is not only unnecessary for the prosecution to prove that the accused was aware of the risk in question it is also unnecessary to prove that the accused would have or could have been aware of the risk had he stopped to think about it.

The case concerned a 14 year old backward schoolgirl convicted of unlawfully destroying by fire a garden shed and its contents (contrary to s 1(1) of the Criminal Damage Act 1971). She was acquitted by the magistrates who found as a fact that she was unaware that her behaviour carried with it a risk of damage to the shed and contents and would not have appreciated the danger even if she had stopped to think about it. The Divisional Court allowed the prosecutor's appeal, holding that, an 'obvious' risk is one which would have been obvious to an ordinary reasonable person who gave thought to the matter, whether or not it would have been obvious to the accused if he had given thought to the matter (see also *Stephen Malcolm R* (1984).

The quotation from Professors Smith and Hogan above expresses the view shared by a number of critics that the extended definition of recklessness categorises as equivalent, levels of fault that, contrary to the opinion of Lord Diplock, are morally quite distinct. They argue that the justifications for imposing criminal liability on the conscious risk taker do not apply to the inadvertently reckless individual. It is to those arguments that we shall now turn.

The traditional justification for imposing criminal liability on the basis of 'advertent' recklessness is that a person who pursues a course of conduct aware of the risks of harm displays that he is willing to take a deliberate chance with the person or property of another. As Professor Hall points out, the subjectively reckless individual has *deliberately* chosen to increase the risk of a defined harm occurring (1).

And, although a person who takes a risk in causing harm is regarded, in general, as less blameworthy than the person who sets out *intentionally* to cause harm there is unanimity among commentators that the individual who willingly and consciously takes a risk with respect to another's protected interests *deserves* to be punished.

The commentators are divided however with respect to whether criminal liability should be *restricted* to the advertent wrongdoer. Those who maintain that advertence ought to be a *necessary* condition of liability argue that the standard justifications and objectives of punishment are implicitly based on a concept of 'subjective' fault.

They argue that the retributive theory, for example, is based on the notion that punishment should be administered if, but only if, the accused deserves it, and that an accused deserves punishment *only* where he has chosen to gain an unfair advantage by breaking the primary rules of social life.

The deterrent theory, it is said, also presupposes the existence of a 'guilty mind'. Punishment is threatened to discourage the potential wrongdoer from causing harm or taking risks with respect to the person or property of another. According to this theory, the interests recognised by the criminal law are protected by discouraging potential offenders from deliberately acting in a way that will violate those interests. Similarly, where an individual has deliberately chosen to risk causing harm, the theory of individual deterrence justifies punishing him to discourage him from making similar choices and taking similar risks in the future (2).

Is there any justification for imposing criminal liability on the basis of 'inadvertent' recklessness?

Opponents of objective tests of liability contend that a person who has failed to perceive a risk has not deliberately chosen to break the law and hence does not deserve to be punished. Further, it is argued, there is no room for the deterrence justification as one cannot be discouraged from taking risks of which one is unaware.

Duff, however, has argued that the person who fails to consider an obvious risk may be as culpable as the person who consciously runs a risk. He suggests that the person who is unaware of an obvious risk may manifest not merely stupidity but an attitude and values which reflect a lack of concern for the interests of others (3). Similarly Fletcher (1971) argues that, as the inadvertent wrongdoer could have done otherwise, as he failed to utilise his faculties to estimate and avoid risks inherent in his proposed conduct, his actions are correctly described as voluntary (4). And Professor Hart (1968) argues that if the capacities of the defendant are taken into account there is no injustice in punishing the 'objectively reckless' wrongdoer (5).

From a utilitarian standpoint the threat of punishment for inadvertence is said to promote adherence to a particular standard of care by encouraging reflection. A potential actor is encouraged to consider the possible consequences of his conduct. And, if a person causes harm, having failed to consider an obvious risk, then punishment may serve the purpose of encouraging him to reflect on the potential consequences of his actions in the future.

Of course these arguments do not justify the punishment of an individual like the defendant in the *Elliott* case.

Nor do they justify treating the inadvertently reckless as *equivalent* to the conscious risk taker as the *Caldwell* test does.

Criminal law recognises *degrees* of blameworthiness. Thus, even if we accept that the inadvertent wrongdoer is culpable and that there is some utility in punishing him, ought he not to be distinguished in terms of formal liability from the conscious risk taker?

Professor Kenny argues that the advertent risk taker is not only more wicked than the inadvertent wrongdoer he is also, in general, more dangerous, and that, from a utilitarian standpoint, the threat of a more severe punishment is necessary to discourage a person from pursuing a course of conduct which he knows carries a risk of harm than is necessary for the less dangerous inadvertent actor (6).

Brady doubts whether utilitarian arguments *alone* justify distinctions drawn in terms of levels of fault or blameworthiness. He argues that there is a significant *moral* distinction between the person who consciously runs a risk and the individual who fails to consider a risk. The former is *more* culpable because he has 'manifest a trait' which demonstrates a *greater* degree of indifference to the interests of others. For this reason, we are justified in punishing him more severely (7).

The decision in *Caldwell* fails to recognise this distinction at the substantive level. It may be the case, of course, that differences in blameworthiness are reflected at the *sentencing* stage.

In many cases, however, it will not be clear whether the guilty defendant was objectively or subjectively reckless. A defendant may plead guilty to a charge of 'reckless damage' without the court knowing the morally relevant information of whether he was 'objectively' or 'subjectively' reckless. Greater precision in the substantive law results in more specific categorisation of the guilty prior to sentencing (8).

For these reasons, it is submitted that if criminal liability is to be imposed on the inadvertently reckless a specific offence should be targeted at them and should reflect the lower degree of blameworthiness with an appropriately lower maximum penalty.

The second part of the quotation refers to the fact that if the defendant considered a risk but, for whatever reason, concluded there was none, he is not reckless. This so called loophole or lacuna in the *Caldwell* test was acknowledged, obiter, by the Court of Appeal in *Reid* (1990).

Professors Smith and Hogan argue that the distinction between somebody who considers a risk but negligently dismisses it and the person who negligently fails to think about a risk is unsound (9).

It might be argued, however, that the individual who has thought about the risk but dismissed it has not displayed that same degree of indifference or disregard as either the conscious risk taker or the inadvertently reckless individual. And, from a utilitarian standpoint, it may be argued that if the purpose of the test is twofold - to discourage conscious risk taking and to encourage reflection - then the loophole exemption is a valid one (10).

In conclusion, it has been argued by a number of commentators that the intended meaning given to recklessness by Lord Diplock in *Caldwell* fails to acknowledge an important distinction in terms of the degree of fault of the advertently and inadvertently reckless actor. It not only results in the attribution of responsibility to a defendant like the young girl in *Elliott's* case but it also treats her as morally equivalent to the conscious risk taker (11).

Notes

1 Columbia Law Review 1963
2 See the extract of *Is Criminal Negligence a Defensible Basis for Penal Liability* Fine & Cohen (1967) in Clarkson and Keating (1990) 2nd ed p 208.
3 *Recklessness* (1980) Criminal Law Review 282.
4 See the extract from *The Theory of Criminal Negligence: A comparative analysis* (1971) in Clarkson and Keating p 210.
5 See extract from *Punishment and Responsibility* (1968) in Clarkson and Keating p 203.
  Although the decision of the Divisional Court in *Elliott v C* was not referred to in *Reid*, three of their Lordships made reference to the situation where a failure to advert to a risk is a consequence of a lack of capacity:
  Lord Keith said that a driver may be regarded as not having driven recklessly where his capacity to appreciate risks was adversely affected by some condition not involving fault on his part. It is not at all clear that when he made this statement Lord Keith had circumstances like those in *Elliott v C* in mind (1992 All ER 673 at 675c-d).

Lord Goff made a similar statement in his speech but he restricted himself to cases where the lack of capacity is caused by the sudden onset of an illness or shock which impairs D's capacity to consider the possibility of risk (at p 690 j).

Lord Ackner rejected - as far as reckless driving was concerned - the appellant's submission that recklessness would be lacking if the ignorance of the relevant risk was attributable to incapacity due, for example, to age or mental deficiency of the defendant. It would appear that his Lordship might have been prepared to accept the submission if the case had concerned an offence under the Criminal Damage Act 1971 (at p 683 e-h).

6   See extract from *Freewill and Responsibility* (1978) in Clarkson and Keating p 212.

7   See extract from *Recklessness, Negligence, Indifference and Awareness* (1980) in Clarkson and Keating p 213.

8   In *Hoof* (1980) the Court of Appeal stated that where D is charged under ss 1(2) and 1(3) of the Criminal Damage Act 1971 there should be two counts:

   (i)   arson with *intent* to endanger life and

   (ii) arson being *reckless* as to whether life would be endangered
         This is to ensure that, for the purposes of sentencing, the court is aware of the jury's verdict with respect to the degree of D's blameworthiness.

         However, as the law currently stands no distinction can be drawn *within* category (ii) between those who are inadvertently reckless and those who are subjectively reckless. They are treated as legal equivalents although they are not moral equivalents - see also *Hardie* (1984).

9   *Criminal Law* (1992) 7th ed p 68.

10 In *Reid* Lord Browne-Wilkinson appeared to suggest that the loophole applies in situations where 'despite D being aware of the risk and deciding to take it, he does so because of a reasonable misunderstanding' (at p 696 f).

    There are two objections to this:

   (i)   if D takes a risk of which he is aware he is reckless. As explained above the lacuna in *Caldwell* applies where D has considered whether there is a risk and concluded there is *none*.

   (ii) there is no justification for narrowing the lacuna to the situation where D *reasonably* concludes there is no risk. As Lord Goff pointed out both limbs of the *Caldwell* test of recklessness are tests of *mens rea* and that a bona fide mistaken belief that there was no risk will excuse. The reasonableness of the mistake is merely evidence that it was genuinely held (at p 690 f-h).

11 The Draft Criminal Code Bill, if enacted, would restrict recklessness to where D is aware of a risk that a circumstance exists or will exist, or that a result will occur and it is, in the circumstances known to D, unreasonable to take the risk.

Question 4

When will the courts impose liability on a 'strict' basis? Are they consistent in their approach?

Answer plan

A fairly straightforward question. It requires a discussion of the approach of the courts to the task of interpreting statutory offences where it is not clear whether Parliament intended the offence to be one requiring proof of *mens rea*.

The following points need to be discussed:

- the meaning of strict liability.
- the presumption of *mens rea*
- intrinsic/extrinsic aids to interpretation

Answer

By a crime of strict liability is meant an offence for which a person may be convicted without proof of intention, recklessness or even negligence. The prosecution are only obliged to prove the commission of the *actus reus* and the absence of any recognised defence. For example, in one of the earliest cases to impose strict liability, *Woodrow* (1846), the accused was convicted of the offence of 'having in his possession adulterated tobacco', despite his lack of knowledge that the tobacco was adulterated.

Most crimes of strict liability are the creation of statute. It is a question of statutory interpretation whether a particular offence requires *mens rea* or not. Once a particular provision has been interpreted judicially then that interpretation is binding on subsequent courts in accordance with the ordinary principles of precedent.

Certain words or expressions clearly indicate that proof of a particular form of *mens rea* is necessary. For example, if the offence is defined in terms of 'knowingly' doing some act there is no room for the court to conclude that the crime is one of strict liability (see *Westminster City Council v Croyalgrange Ltd* (1986) and cf *Brooks v Mason* (1902)).

Where the relevant provision does not expressly include a *mens rea* term then the court must decide whether to imply a *mens rea* requirement or to categorise the offence as one of strict liability. Therefore the absence of a *mens rea* term does not automatically result in the crime being defined as one of strict liability.

Indeed, it has often been stated that there is a presumption against imposing criminal liability without fault. That means that whenever a section is silent as to *mens rea* there is a presumption that, in order to give effect to the will of Parliament, the court should imply words of *mens rea* in to the provision. This is a corollary to the principle that where a penal provision is capable of two interpretations the interpretation more favourable to the accused must be adopted (see for example *Sweet v Parsley* (1970)).

The presumption, it is said, is only to be displaced where there is clear indication that the intention of Parliament was to dispense with *mens rea*. And, in one of the earliest cases to deal with the issue, *Sherras v de Rutzen* (1895), Wright J stated that to give effect to the intention of Parliament it is important, first of all, to consider the actual words used in the statute and, secondly, the subject matter of the provision.

This accords with the normal principle of interpretation that the court should look only to extrinsic factors when the intention of Parliament is not clear from the words of the statute.

The words of the statute

Dealing with the first of these issues, the court may look to the wording of the provision in its overall context. Words and terms used in other provisions of the same statute may provide a clue as to the intention of Parliament. For example, in *Pharmaceutical Society of Great Britain v Storkwein* (1986) the House of Lords decided that s 58(2)a of the Medicines Act 1968 was one of strict liability. They were influenced by the fact that, whereas s 58(2)a was silent with respect to fault, there were express requirements of *mens rea* for other provisions of the same statute.

In *Cheshire County Council Trading Standards Dept ex p Alan Helliwell & Sons (Bolton) Ltd* (1991) D was charged with an offence contrary to the Transit of Animals (Road and Rail) Order 1975 of permitting unfit animals to be carried so as to be likely to cause them unnecessary suffering (Art 11(1)). The court held that the offence was one of strict liability. They were partly influenced by the fact that another provision of the order, concerning the transportation of pregnant animals, expressly imposed a requirement of knowledge.

On the other hand, in *Sweet v Parsley*, Lord Reid stated that the fact that other sections of the statute expressly require *mens rea* is not itself sufficient to justify a decision that a section which is silent as to *mens rea* creates an absolute offence. And, in *Sherras v de Rutzen* (1895) the Divisional Court held that a provision of the Licensing Act 1872 should be interpreted to impose a requirement of *mens rea* even though it contained no *mens rea* term and despite the fact that another sub-section used the word 'knowingly' (cf *Cundy v Le Cocq* (1881)).

Although there is some consistency in the interpretation of particular verbal structures it is not of a sufficiently high degree to allow one to predict with absolute certainty whether an offence requires *mens rea* in the full sense. For example, the expression 'permitting' or 'suffering' something to be done features in a number of statutes. Although, normally this will be interpreted to impose a requirement of *mens rea*, the Divisional Court in *Lomas v Peek* (1947) and, more recently, in *Cheshire County Council Trading Standards Department* (above) held otherwise. In the latter case the court held that the word 'permitted' implied only a limited element of *mens rea* confined to the permission of the carriage of the animal. It was not necessary to prove that D was even negligent with respect to whether the animal was unfit.

In recent years the word 'wilfully' has been interpreted as requiring *mens rea* (see *Sheppard* (1981)). However, even here there has been no consistency (see *Maidstone Borough Council v Mortimer* (1980)).

Extrinsic factors

It is often stated that if the subject matter of the provision relates to 'acts which are not criminal in any real sense' the presumption against no fault liability may be displaced (*Sherras v de Rutzen* per Wright J).

The same principle was expressed in a positive form by Lord Scarman in *Gammon v Attorney-General of Hong Kong* (1985) where he stated that the presumption in favour of the implication of a fault requirement is particularly strong where the offence is 'truly criminal' in character.

In *Sweet v Parsley* the House of Lords implied a requirement of *mens rea* into the offence of 'being concerned in the management of premises used for the purpose of smoking cannabis' contrary to s 5(1)(b) of the Dangerous Drugs Act 1965. The House was influenced by the fact that the offence was regarded as serious attracting 'social obloquy' (see also *Alphacell v Woodward* (1972)).

However, in *Gammon v Attorney-General of Hong Kong*, the Privy Council were prepared to impose strict liability in the case of an offence punishable with a fine of $250,000 and imprisonment for three years. Similarly, in *Hussain* (1981) the Court of Appeal held that s 1 of the Firearms Act 1968, which prohibits the unlawful possession of a firearm, should be interpreted strictly even although it carried a maximum penalty of three years imprisonment.

In *Howells* (1977), which concerned s 58 of the same Act, the Court of Appeal stated that the danger to the community resulting from the possession of lethal firearms is so obviously great that an absolute prohibition against their possession must have been the intention of Parliament. This implies that the more serious the offence the stronger the argument that Parliament intended strict liability!

A further factor that may influence the court in favour of imposing strict liability is where the provision is perceived to be concerned with an issue of public safety and particularly where the dangerous activity is performed predominantly by corporate undertakings (see, for example, *Gammon Ltd v Attorney-General of Hong Kong*).

In *Sweet v Parsley* Lord Diplock stated that where the subject matter of a statute is the regulation of a particular activity involving potential danger to public health or safety the court may impose liability on a strict basis to enforce an obligation to take whatever measures may be necessary to prevent the prohibited act without reference to considerations of cost or business practicability.

However, the presumption of *mens rea* remains unless it can be shown that the objects of the legislation will be better promoted by strict liability (*Gammon Ltd* above and see also *Lim Chin Aik v R* (1963)).

Indeed, most offences of strict liability are contained in legislation concerned with the sale of food and drugs, the operation of licensed premises, industrial activity, (for example, pollution) etc and other hazardous activities which individuals may voluntarily engage in, eg driving a car.

The courts often express a willingness to impose strict liability out of a protectionist concern for the welfare of 'ordinary' citizens exposed to the hazardous activities of others. In *Alphacell v Woodward*, for example, it was said that the imposition of strict liability might encourage businesses to comply with important social welfare regulations.

In response to the argument that it is 'unfair' to use the weight of the criminal law in this way and that principles of justice prohibit the imposition of criminal liability where the defendant has not chosen to break the law, the proponents of strict liability point out those principles are not appropriate when we are dealing with questions of corporate liability. A corporate enterprise, when deciding whether to engage in the activities in question, is in a position to consider and weigh the potential costs of any unintentional infringement of the law.

Professor Smith suggests that one of the factors influencing the Divisional Court in the *Cheshire County Council* case was the difficulty of proving *mens rea* of one of the controlling officers of the respondent company. By dispensing with a requirement of *mens rea*, liability could be imposed on the company, thereby encouraging the officers to take positive steps to prevent an offence being committed in the future (1).

Conclusion

There is no single test that the courts will apply in deciding whether an offence is one of strict liability. The courts are influenced by a number of intrinsic and extrinsic factors. Although there is a great deal of inconsistency, the modern cases concerning strict liability have tended to look principally to the subject matter of the offence when in doubt as to Parliament's intentions. And, although there have been a number of cases where the presumption of no liability without fault has been reaffirmed, it would appear that it is most likely to be rebutted where the subject matter of the offence relates to a serious social danger or a matter of social concern and adherence to the law is perceived to be more likely to be achieved by the imposition of strict liability.

Note

1   Criminal Law Review 1991 p 221.

Question 5

(a) When might an omission to act give rise to criminal liability?

(b) Gorge was employed as a life guard at a beach. He returned from his lunch. He noticed that one of the swimmers, Flop, appeared to be distressed and was screaming and shouting. She was swimming in a stretch of water that was renowned for its dangerous currents. Gorge was about to take steps to rescue Flop. However, as Flop was becoming increasingly more tired she stopped screaming. Gorge thought that as Flop had stopped screaming she was not in any danger. He returned to the life station. Flop drowned.

   Discuss Gorge's criminal liability.

   Would your answer differ if he had returned from lunch in a state of drunkenness?

Answer plan

A two part question comprising an essay and a related problem. It is quite acceptable to make reference back to points made in answering the essay section when tackling the problem.

The principal issues are:

(a)
- issues of construction concerning liability for omissions
- the situations recognised as giving rise to a duty to act

(b)
- a duty arising from contract
- reckless manslaughter and the *Caldwell* 'loophole'
- drunkenness and crimes of basic intent

Answer

(a) Generally, criminal law is concerned with prohibiting certain forms of conduct or behaviour. There are, however, a number of situations in which criminal liability may be imposed on the basis of a failure to act.

Firstly, there are a number of offences defined specifically in terms of an omission to act. For example, it is an offence contrary to s 170 of the Road Traffic Act 1988 for a driver involved in a motor accident in which personal injury or damage was caused, to fail to stop and give his name and address to anyone reasonably requiring it. And, by ss 6(4) and 7(6) of the same statute a person who, without reasonable excuse, fails to provide a specimen of breath, blood or urine required for analysis in connection with offences involving impaired driving commits an offence.

Where an offence is not expressly defined in terms of a failure to do something, the question whether liability can be imposed for an omission is, firstly, a matter of construction. Where the verb used to define an offence implies active conduct alone then no liability should attach for an omission. Indeed there are many offences where it is probably impossible to commit them by omission eg burglary, robbery and taking a conveyance.

In *Ahmad* (1986) the Court of Appeal held that the expression 'does acts' in a provision of the Protection from Eviction Act 1977 did not encompass omissions.

The courts, however, have not followed this approach consistently. In *Speck* (1977) a girl of eight put her hand on D's penis. The man allowed her hand to remain there for five minutes.

His appeal against conviction 'for an act of gross indecency' was dismissed by the Court of Appeal. It was held that D's inactivity amounted, in effect, to an invitation to the girl to continue. This interpretation of the provision is, it is submitted, a distortion of the ordinary meaning of the words of the section and is at odds with the general approach of the courts towards omissions liability for similar offences against the person. In *Fagan v Metropolitan Police Commissioner* (1969), for example, the Divisional Court held that an assault could not be committed by omission (1).

The Criminal Law Revision Committee recommended that there should be no liability for criminal damage by omission (but see *Miller* (below)).

Secondly, policy considerations play a part in determining whether liability will be imposed for omissions. For example, although the *actus reus* for murder and manslaughter is framed in active terms - 'to kill' or 'to cause the death of a human being'- it is clear that both may be committed by omission.

(See *Gibbins & Proctor* (1918) for a rare case of murder by omission. The defendants killed the child of one of them by withholding food. As the parties' failure to look after the child was accompanied by 'malice aforethought' they were guilty of murder. Most commonly in cases of 'neglect' of this sort it will be difficult to prove an intent adequate for murder and the person will normally be indicted for manslaughter 'by recklessness').

English law, however, imposes liability for omissions only where it can be said that the defendant was under a duty to act. Furthermore, there is no general obligation to act for the benefit of others. In English law the duty to act to save or preserve the life of another arises only in a number of stereotyped situations.

(i) Where v is dependent on D

The recognition of a duty to act for the helpless and infirm arose from the Poor Law obligations and were initially based exclusively on status. The courts imposed a legal duty on those who occupied certain defined positions. Responsibility was based on the dependent relationship (economic or physical) between the parties. Thus, for example, it has been held that parents owe a duty towards their children (2).

In *Nicholls* (1874) (the defendant was the grandmother of the victim) it was held that a person who elects to care for another who is helpless and infirm is obliged to carry out that responsibility. If he fails to do so, with the result that the person dies, he may be convicted of murder or manslaughter according to his *mens rea*.

In *Stone & Dobinson* (1977) the Court of Appeal held that a duty to care for another may arise impliedly from a voluntary undertaking to look after a dependent person.

In *Pittwood* (1902) it was held that a duty may arise from contract. In that case a railway gate keeper failed to comply with his contractual duty to close a gate at a level crossing. As a consequence, a person crossing the tracks was killed. Wright J held that the defendant could not rely on the doctrine of privity of contract to deny the existence of a duty to users of the crossing; the general obligation arose from the fact that others were dependent on the proper performance of the contract. Likewise a duty may arise by virtue of the 'office' that a person holds (see *Curtis* (1885); *Dytham* (1979)).

(ii) Where D creates a dangerous situation

There is a particular situation in which a failure to act may give rise to liability even though the offence is not one which generally can be committed by omission.

The situation was defined by the House of Lords in *Miller* (1983). It was said that if a defendant failed to take measures to counteract a danger that he himself has created then his failure can be regarded as amounting to the commission of the *actus reus* of an appropriate offence. One is under a duty (Lord Diplock preferred the word 'responsibility') to take steps that lie within one's power to rectify the danger created. If one fails to discharge the duty then one may be convicted of an offence if the failure to act was accompanied by the appropriate *mens rea*.

The case concerned criminal damage but it is clear that Lord Diplock intended the principle to apply to all result crimes.

(b) Manslaughter

Provided that Flop's life could have been saved had Gorge taken reasonable steps to rescue her, then her death may be attributed to Gorge's failure to act. As explained above a duty to act may arise from a contractual obligation (*Pittwood*).

Whether he is guilty of an offence of unlawful homicide depends on his *mens rea* at the relevant time.

There is no suggestion that he had the *mens rea* for murder.

In *Seymour* (1983) it was held that for reckless manslaughter the prosecution must prove that (1) D's conduct carried a serious risk of causing physical injury to another and (2) that D either (a) failed to give any thought to the possibility of there being any such risk where the risk would have been obvious to a reasonable person or (b) he recognised that there was some risk involved but nevertheless went on to take it (*Seymour* (1983); *USA v Jennings* (1983)).

In this case it would appear that Gorge was not reckless. He apparently considered the risk and concluded there was none. It seems that he falls within the so-called 'lacuna' in this test of recklessness (3).

And if, as a number of decisions suggest, there no longer exists a category of manslaughter by gross negligence, Gorge is not guilty of an offence (*Kong Cheuk Kwan* (1985); *Seymour*; *Stanley & Others* (1990)) (4).

Alternative facts

If Gorge had considered the risk of injury but because he was drunk concluded there was none he is guilty of manslaughter if the existence of the risk would have been obvious to him had he been sober. A lack of *mens rea* resulting from voluntary intoxication is no defence to crimes of 'basic intent' like manslaughter (*DPP v Majewski* (1977); *Lipman* (1970); *Caldwell* (1982)).

Notes

1   In *Fagan* - the 'car on the policeman's foot case' - the Divisional Court, somewhat artificially, found that the defendant, by remaining in the car, was performing a continuing act. In *DPP v K* the principle that an assault cannot be committed by omission was apparently overlooked. The conviction of the defendant for assault occasioning actual bodily harm contrary to s 47 may perhaps be justified on the

basis of the *Miller* principle. By putting acid in the dryer K had created a dangerous situation which he had failed to rectify. In *Kaitamaki* (1984) it was held that if a man penetrates a woman with consent or believing that she has consented he may be convicted of rape if he continues the intercourse if and when the woman revokes the consent and/or he appreciates that the woman does not consent.

2   If the parent of a child purposely denies it food with the intention of killing it but they are stopped before it dies it is not clear whether they can be convicted of an attempt. Section 1(1) of the Criminal Attempts Act 1861 provides that a person commits the offence of attempt if, 'with intent to commit an offence ... he does any *act* which is more than merely preparatory to the commission of the offence. Professors Smith and Hogan doubt whether this would be interpreted to include an omission. *Criminal Law* (1992) 7th ed p 313.

3   In *West London Coroner ex p Gray* (1987) the Divisional Court held, in a case concerning manslaughter by omission, that the jury must be satisfied that there was an obvious and serious risk to the *health and welfare* of the deceased and that D was either indifferent to the risk or deliberately chose to run the risk without doing anything about it. This decision is out of line with the authorities; it sets the *mens rea* requirement for the serious offence of manslaughter at a very low level, and, it is submitted, ought not to be followed.

4   Cf *Ball* (1990) in which the Court of Appeal stated, obiter, that this type of manslaughter still existed. It appears that *Seymour* was not cited.

Question 6

(a) Julian and Dick decided to have a picnic in Farmer Giles field. Julian decided to build a fire next to a haystack. When Dick asked him whether it would be safe, Julian explained that the wind was blowing from a direction that would keep the flames away from the haystack. Julian made the fire and began to prepare the food. After a few minutes the wind changed direction blowing the flames towards the haystack. Part of the haystack started to smoulder. Dick suggested that they should pour the contents of their bottle of wine to douse the fire. Julian disagreed and told Dick to help him quickly pick up their belongings and move to a neighbouring field. This they did. The haystack was destroyed.

(b) Anne was taking a walk by a lake. She noticed a young boy in the lake. He was having difficulty swimming and called for help. Anne swam out to him and dragged him back to the edge of the lake. His breathing had stopped. Anne did not give mouth to mouth resuscitation as she was afraid of catching disease. She ran to a nearby public telephone and called an ambulance. When the ambulance arrived the boy was already dead.

Discuss the criminal liability of the parties.

Answer plan

A relatively straightforward question in which both parts relate to the question of liability for omissions. The first part raises the issue in the context of criminal damage where D fails to take steps to counteract a dangerous situation for which he was 'responsible'. The problem can be seen as one relating to the issue of coincidence of *actus reus* and *mens rea*. The second part concerns liability for omissions in the context of unlawful homicide.

Principal issues are:

(a)

* the rule in *Miller* (1983)
* the meaning and application of 'recklessness' for the purposes of offence of criminal damage

(b)

* the voluntary assumption of a duty to act for the benefit of another

Answer

(a) Julian may be liable for the offence of criminal damage contrary to s 1(1) of the Criminal Damage Act 1971. This provides that a person who without lawful excuse destroys or damages any property belonging to another intending to destroy or damage any such property or being reckless as to whether any such property would be destroyed or damaged shall be guilty of an offence.

By virtue of s 1(3) where, as in this case, the unlawful destruction or damage of property is by fire the offence is charged as arson. By s 4 arson is punishable with a term of imprisonment for life.

Julian has committed the *actus reus* of the offence. He has destroyed the haystack belonging to Farmer Giles. The prosecution must prove that he was at least reckless in respect of the damage.

A person is reckless in this context if his conduct (1) created a (serious) risk of causing damage to the property of another and (2) he either (a) gave no thought to possibility of there being any such risk where the risk was in fact obvious or (b) he recognised that there was some risk of damage but nevertheless went on to take it (*Caldwell* (1981)).

A risk is serious if a reasonable person would not have treated it as negligible (*Reid* (1992)). The obviousness of a risk relates to whether the reasonable prudent person would have been aware of the risk irrespective of whether D was or could have been aware of the risk (see *Elliott v C* (1983); *Stephen Malcolm R* (1984)).

In this case it would appear from the facts that Julian thought the construction of the fire near the haystack was safe. He did not consider there to be a risk of damage. Nor had he failed to give any thought to the question of whether there was a risk. He had considered the possibility of there being a risk and discounted it.

His state of mind falls within what is known as the '*Caldwell* loophole' (1).

However, he may be guilty of arson for his later failure to take steps to extinguish the fire that he had caused.

In *Miller* (1984) the House of Lords pointed out that, as criminal damage is a result crime, the *actus reus* may continue over some considerable period of time. If D does an act which he believes initially to be harmless, but he later becomes aware that that act has set in train events that present an obvious risk that property belonging to another will be damaged, then he is under a duty to try to prevent or reduce the damage by taking such steps as are reasonable and without danger or difficulty to himself.

The defendant's state of mind throughout the entire period from immediately before the property caught fire to the completion of the damage is relevant to the issue of liability.

Julian could have used the wine to extinguish the fire and, therefore, as he failed to take what, it is submitted, would amount to reasonable action to prevent further damage, he is guilty of arson.

Dick has committed no offence. He is clearly not liable as a principal offender nor can he be regarded as an accomplice to the offence perpetrated by Julian. Although he assisted Julian to remove their belongings and to get away from the scene Dick neither assisted nor encouraged Julian to commit criminal damage.

(b) Anne's liability for unlawful homicide will depend firstly upon showing that her failure to provide resuscitation was a factual cause or sine qua non of the boy's death. If medical evidence revealed that he was already dead when she pulled him on to the bank or if, for some other reason, attempted resuscitation would have been pointless then the death would not be attributable to Anne's inaction (see eg *White* (1910)).

If her failure was a sine qua non of the boy's death it must also be shown that it was a *legal* cause of his death.

In English law there is generally no liability for omissions. Thus, it is often said that D incurs no criminal liability if he stands and watches a stranger drown even where he could have acted to save the stranger without risk to himself. The death of the stranger in these circumstances is not regarded in law as a consequence of D's inaction. A failure to act which as a matter of fact causes the death of another will give rise to liability only where the defendant was under a duty to act.

In *Stone & Dobinson* (1977) the Court of Appeal held that where one undertakes a duty to care for another incapable of looking after themselves then a failure to discharge this duty may result in criminal liability. The Court of Appeal agreed with the trial judge that the proper approach is to leave the question of whether there has been a voluntary assumption of a duty to the jury.

The evidence in that case showed that the deceased, Fanny, had lodged with Stone and Dobinson for three years; that the defendants had looked after her for many weeks and had been aware of her deteriorating condition for a similar period during which they had taken ineffectual steps to help her.

In Anne's case, although the period of involvement was much shorter, it is submitted that there is sufficient evidence of an assumption of duty to warrant consideration by the jury. The boy's welfare was dependent on the continued provision of care by Anne.

If the jury do conclude that Anne was under a duty to act that is not the end of the matter. It must be determined whether or not she failed to discharge that duty. The duty is not an absolute one. Although there is no clear authority on the issue it is submitted that the defendant must take *reasonable* steps to discharge the duty.

In *Stone & Dobinson* it was said that the appellants could have discharged their duty by summoning outside help. Whether Anne's decision to call the ambulance service constituted reasonable steps in this case is, presumably, a question to be decided by the jury.

If the jury conclude that Anne failed to take reasonable steps to discharge a duty voluntarily assumed - that she had caused the death of the boy by her refusal to provide oral resuscitation - the question whether she is guilty of murder or manslaughter or neither depends upon her *mens rea*.

She neither intended to kill nor cause serious injury. She intended to save the boy's life. It would not be appropriate in this case to draw an inference of intention from foresight. Thus, she lacked the *mens rea* for murder (*Nedrick* (1986)).

If, however, as the facts imply, Anne was aware that her inaction was attended by a risk of harm to the boy then she had the *mens rea* for manslaughter (indeed, a failure to advert to an obvious and serious risk of harm will suffice, *Seymour* (1983)) (2).

Thus, the crucial issues in this case are whether Anne was under a duty to care for the boy, and, if so, whether she took reasonable steps to discharge that duty. Provided both these questions are answered affirmatively Anne may be convicted of manslaughter - an offence which, by virtue of s 5 of the Offences Against the Person Act 1861, carries a maximum penalty of life imprisonment.

Notes

1   Where the prosecution are relying upon limb 2(b) above it is apparently not necessary to prove that D believed the risk to be serious. It is enough that he was aware of 'some' risk. Whether a risk is 'serious' or not is an objective question (see *Reid* (1992)). This, if Julian was aware of even a very

small risk that the property might be damaged then he would not fall within the so-called 'loophole'. Consciously taking even a 'negligible' risk with the property of another is apparently reckless (*Chief Constable of Avon and Somerset Constabulary v Shimmen* (1986)).

2 It is submitted that although the *Lawrence* formula refers to 'an *act* which *creates* an obvious and serious risk etc' it applies also in the case of an omission to act. In *Kong Cheuk Kwan* Lord Roskill stated that Lord Diplock in *Lawrence* was 'not concerned to deal with cases where the conduct complained of was of a defendants reaction or *lack* of reaction to such a risk created by another person'. This might be taken to suggest that the *Lawrence/Seymour* test of recklessness does not apply in cases of manslaughter by omission. But in that case the Privy Council was not concerned with a situation where D was under a duty to act. In addition, their Lordships approved the statement of the Court of Appeal in *Seymour* to the effect that the *Lawrence* direction was comprehensive; it would seem that there is no room to base liability for manslaughter by omission on 'gross negligence'.

Question 7

'All punishment in itself is evil. It ought only to be admitted in so far as it promises to exclude some greater evil.' (Bentham).

'It is only as deserved or undeserved that a sentence can be just or unjust' (Lewis).

Assess critically both of the above statements. With which of the above statements do you agree?

Answer plan

It is fairly common for examiners in criminal law to include a question concerning the aims, objectives and justifications of punishment. The question above requires a critical assessment of the utilitarian thesis (Bentham) and the retributive thesis (Lewis). You are also asked to express a preference for one. Read the quotations carefully. Do they express alternative views or do they actually relate to quite separate issues?

Answer

The first quotation expresses the reductive or utilitarian view that punishment is justified to the extent that it is administered with the objective of reducing the overall level of 'evil' or 'harm' in society. The argument runs that punishment normally takes the form of penalties, eg deprivation of liberty, financial penalties etc, which would in themselves constitute 'evils' were they not justified by reference to the objective of an overall reduction in the balance of social 'evil'.

Thus, reductive theories are primarily concerned with the preventive consequences of punishment. Legitimacy of punishment stems from the attempt to reduce further crime.

The objective may be to deter the *individual* wrongdoer from repeating the offence. (Most sentencers probably have this objective in mind - at least partly - when they impose punishment on convicted criminals.) In addition, the sentencer might attempt to influence the behaviour of potential wrongdoers. This is known as the general deterrence objective. The imposition of punishment is justified according to the utilitarian hypothesis if the reduction in criminal behaviour is greater than the pain inflicted on the individual offender.

Deterrence theories are based on the idea that we human beings are rational creatures motivated by self-interest and that we weigh up the consequences of our actions before acting. It is hoped that when faced with the choice of breaking or observing the law the threat of punishment will persuade us to choose the latter course.

Empirical research based on reconviction rates is often pessimistic regarding the effectiveness of punishment as an individual deterrent. It is more difficult to measure the effectiveness of punishment as a general deterrent. How can one know the number of occasions when potential wrongdoers have decided against breaking the law because they feared detection and punishment?

It is often argued that deterrent effects of punishment are likely to be greater for planned crimes rather than for impulsive or opportunist crimes. In addition, where detection rates are low the potential criminal might feel that his interests are best served by breaking the law (1).

Reductivists contend that punishment also serves an educative purpose. It is suggested that members of any society learn, almost without thinking, to avoid behaviour that they know attracts penalties. Punishment, it is said, expresses general disapproval of the behaviour, reinforces certain standards and, (as human beings are motivated to avoid pain and to gain social approval), results in learned inhibitions against violating those standards.

It is sometimes argued that the educative effects of punishment are of even greater value than deterrent effects because obedience resulting from the absorption of values will not be adversely affected by the perception that the chances of detection are low (2).

There are enormous difficulties, however, in assessing empirically the educative effects of punishment. How could one reliably determine that law abiding behaviour was a result of subconsciously absorbed values rather than, say, a conscious fear of detection and punishment? For many people the consequences of conviction may be so unpleasant that even a relatively low risk of detection would discourage them from breaking the law. Indeed, the inverse relationship between the likelihood of detection, on the one hand, and willingness to break the law, on the other, implies that, for many members of the community at least, educative effects are weak.

Rehabilitation, as an objective of punishment, is also reductive. It is based upon the premise that criminal behaviour is maladjusted. The development of the behavioural sciences like psychology and sociology in the nineteenth century challenged the view that criminality would respond positively to deprivation. Indeed, as the causes of human behaviour were examined, antisocial behaviour was perceived as a response to privations and adopted only where the drive to behave in a prosocial way had been blocked for some reason or another. The individual may have chosen his criminal career because there were, or there appeared to be, no other opportunities available. The criminal may simply not realise that his interests would be better served by adopting a law abiding course of conduct. He may require retraining so that he can satisfy his economic and social needs in socially approved ways. It may be necessary for him to learn the effect of his criminal acts on his victims.

The rehabilitative ideal stimulated reform of punishment and, in particular, reform of the prisons. Research concerning the effectiveness of rehabilitation, however, has not been encouraging (3).

In addition to criticisms regarding the effectiveness of deterrent and rehabilitative sentencing there are a number of 'principled' objections to reductive justifications.

The major objection is that the reductive approach would justify the imposition of a disproportionately severe sentence in certain cases. An individual offender might receive a greater punishment than he 'deserves' because, for example, there is a perceived epidemic of the type of crime he has committed. Similarly, the rehabilitative ideal might justify the imposition of a severe penalty even for a trivial infraction if that was felt necessary to 'cure' him of his criminal attitudes.

This 'retributivist' objection, expressed in the second of the quotations, above, is based, partly, on the Kantian view that respect for individual autonomy requires that a person should never be treated solely as a means whereby certain social ends are achieved. Thus, we ought to punish criminals because they deserve it and the punishment should be proportionate to the seriousness of the offence. Advocates of this approach point out that it ensures uniformity in sentencing practice and does not result in the criminal being used unfairly to achieve some further social purpose.

But what does it mean to say that an offender 'deserves' to be punished?

Desert theory is often based upon the notion that the offender has gained an 'unfair advantage' by breaking the law. The equilibrium with other law abiding members of society must be restored by punishment. Alternatively, it is argued that the offender has broken the 'social contract' which binds him and his fellow citizens to observing the law.

However, critics of this approach ask: 'in what sense can a theory of real obligations be based upon the fiction of a social contract?' In addition, the concept of 'desert' is said to be too vague a basis for sentencing (4).

Professor Hart, among others, has argued that, although just desert should be the guiding principle when determining whether a given individual should be punished and calculating the appropriate level of punishment that individual should suffer, it cannot provide the justification for the institution of punishment as a whole. The 'general justifying aim' of punishment is to reduce or at least contain the level of criminality in society. According to this 'hybrid' theory 'desert' is a necessary but not a sufficient condition of punishment in any individual case; the principle of 'just desert' operates as a limitation on the utilitarian objectives discussed above. It means for example that no punishment may be imposed on a person, even for laudable utilitarian purposes, unless he has voluntarily committed a clear breach of the criminal law. Thus, for example, even although the punishment of a friend or relative of an offender might result in greater obedience by deterring potential offenders, it cannot be justified as neither the friend nor the relative has broken the law. There is, it is argued, no positive obligation to punish on the basis of 'desert' but on the other hand, there is an obligation *not* to punish if punishment is not deserved.

Hyman Gross points out that there is no inherent incompatibility between punishment administered with the objective of reducing the level of crime in society yet limited, out of respect for individual autonomy, to those deserving it. Indeed, individual autonomy - which includes the freedom to plan one's life according to one's own preferences - can only flourish in a legally ordered society and thus, respect for the moral distinctness of persons informs both the general justifying aim and the principles of distribution of punishment (5).

On the other hand, it has been argued that there is no need to turn to abstract notions of 'desert' to explain why victimisation is unacceptable: limiting rules on the application of punishment to those who have broken the law are a feature of reductivism. The deterrent effect of the law depends partly at least on the legal institutions being respected. Victimisation of an innocent person would be counter-productive as it would weaken that respect. In addition, by punishing only those who are guilty, the general population are reminded what conduct amounts to an offence and should, therefore, be avoided. Furthermore, if it were known that an innocent person might be punished instead of the guilty person, the deterrent effect of the law would be weakened.

The point has been made, however, that it is conceivable that unjust victimisation could be an effective deterrent if, for example, the general public were fooled into believing that the convicted person was guilty and, therefore, it follows that reductivist objectives cannot be a sufficient justification of punishment (6).

In conclusion the dominant theory of punishment reflects both of the views expressed in the quotations above. Punishment is justified if two conditions are satisfied - it is deserved and it is aimed at reducing criminal conduct in the future (7).

Notes

1 See, for example, Ashworth Sentencing and Criminal Justice 1992 p 60.
2 See Clarkson and Keating (1990) 2nd ed pp 20 - 24.
3 See Ashworth Ibid p 63.
4 See Nicola Lacey *State Punishment: Political Principles and Community Values* (1988) pp 24 -26; extract in Clarkson and Keating p 10.
5 See *A Theory of Criminal Justice* (1979) pp 382-385; extract in Clarkson and Keating p 48.
6 Clarkson and Keating p 50.
7 The Criminal Justice Act 1991 s 1 states that a sentence shall be proportionate to the seriousness of the offence. The rehabilitation of the offender is mentioned as a legitimate objective in certain circumstances but is limited by reference to desert (see ss 6 and 8). The only justification for imposing a penalty in excess of that which is proportionate to the offence committed is 'to protect the public from serious harm from this offender' (see ss 1 and 2). Section 2(2)(a), whilst permitting a sentencing judge to take deterrence into account, prohibits adding an exemplary element to the sentence. The prevalence of a particular type of offence is, however, a factor which the sentencer may take into account when assessing the seriousness of an offence (*Cunningham* (1992)).

Fatal and Non-fatal Offences against the Person

Introduction

The questions in this chapter concern offences against the person from common assault at one end of the spectrum to murder at the other. Offences of this type are graded partly in terms of the harm caused but also by reference to the *mens rea* of the accused. The harm caused will define the range of offences that ought to be considered, ie if D kills V then liability for murder, manslaughter and/or causing death by dangerous driving should be considered.

Similarly, if serious bodily harm is the result of D's actions then liability for the offences under ss 18, 20 and 23 of the Offences Against the Person Act 1861 should be examined. Consequently, it is *normally* wise, when attempting to resolve a problem involving the offences against the person, to analyse issues relating to the *actus reus* prior to considering issues relating to the *mens rea*.

It should be noted that most examiners set questions where the facts are 'open' with respect to D's *mens rea*. That is, the *mens rea* is normally not disclosed in the facts of the problem. The reason for this is to provide you with the opportunity of displaying your knowledge of the different conditions of liability for a number of offences. For example, if the facts of a question revealed that 'D killed V, intending to cause grievous bodily harm', then it is clear that, in the absence of a defence, *there is only one conclusion* - D is guilty of murder. If, on the other hand, the facts report, in effect, that 'D killed V', without specifying his *mens rea*, the answer involves an explanation of the possible *alternative* conclusions (which, of course, will depend upon D's *mens rea*). The second question provides an opportunity to explain the *mens rea* requirements of murder *and* manslaughter. Where there are 'gaps' in the facts it is not your responsibility to fill them - answers should be expressed in the alternative.

Similarly, if - as is commonly the case - the facts are 'open' with respect to the severity of the bodily harm caused or whether a particular defence is available, express alternative answers.

Checklist

The questions in this chapter concern, principally, the following offences:

* Homicide
    - murder
    - manslaughter
    - causing death by dangerous driving, contrary to s 1 of the Road Traffic Act 1988 as substituted by s 1 of the Road Traffic Act 1992
* Non-fatal offences against the person
    - common assault
    - battery
    - aggravated assaults under the Offences Against the Person Act 1861, ie wounding with intent contrary to s 18; malicious wounding contrary to s 20; assault occasioning actual bodily harm contrary to s 47
    - offences of poisoning contrary to ss 23 and 24 of the 1861 Act
    - sexual offences, ie rape contrary to s 1(1) of the Sexual Offences Act 1956; procuring sexual intercourse by false pretences contrary to s 3(1); indecent assault contrary to ss 14 and 15

In addition, the following defences are dealt with in this chapter:

* Provocation
* Diminished responsibility
* Consent

Note

1   It is important that you have mastered some of the issues dealt with in detail in the previous chapter - in particular, the definitions of 'intention' and 'recklessness'.
2   As 'mixed problems' are popular with some examiners a couple of questions raise issues of liability for property offences.

Question 8

'Infecting another when one knows one has AIDS is an offence.'
   Discuss.

Answer plan

The answer to this question requires an analysis of a number of offences. Fatal and non-fatal offences against the person are considered.

   Principal issues:
* consent, *Clarence* (1888) and aggravated assaults contrary to ss 47 and 20 of the Offences Against the Person Act 1861
* offences contrary to ss 23 and 24 of the 1861 Act
* murder and the 'year and a day' rule
* problems of proof

Answer

Acquired immune deficiency syndrome (AIDS) is a syndrome discovered in the late 1970s/early 1980s which results in reduced immunity to infection. It is contracted from infected blood and other bodily fluids including semen. The disease is transmitted by way of sexual intercourse or other intimate sexual contact or by way of transfusions of contaminated blood or as a result of using contaminated hypodermic needles.

There is as yet no cure for AIDS and mortality is high.

The development of AIDS involves a number of separate stages. Firstly, within three months of initial infection the individual will have HIV antibodies in his system. After a period of, on average, five to six years, the individual may develop 'full blown Aids'. In some cases the incubation period between initial infection and the development of the AIDS syndrome has been as much as ten years. The long period involved between actual infection by the virus and detection thereof makes it extremely difficult to confidently identify the source of the infection.

Thus, in most typical cases, the prosecution would find it practically impossible to prove beyond reasonable doubt that the defendant infected the victim. However, to allow analysis of the legal issues involved in prosecuting those that infect others with the AIDS virus it will be assumed in this essay that difficulties in identifying the source of the infection are surmountable.

There is no offence specifically targeted against the person who infects another with AIDS and therefore it is necessary to consider a number of general offences against the person from assaults to murder.

Aggravated assaults

There are three offences under the Offences Against the Person Act 1861 of relevance here: occasioning actual bodily harm under s 47; maliciously inflicting grievous bodily harm under s 20; causing grievous bodily harm with intent contrary to s 18.

The first issue is whether infection with AIDS constitutes a 'harm' for the purposes of the 1861 statute.

'Actual bodily harm' was defined in *Miller* (1954) to include 'any hurt or injury which interferes with the health or comfort of the victim including injury to the state of the victims mind'. Thus it is arguable that the shock and anxiety caused on discovering that one is infected with the virus would amount to actual bodily harm.

'Grievous bodily harm' means 'serious bodily harm' (*DPP v Smith* (1961); *Saunders* (1985)). It is submitted that a life threatening viral infection is a serious bodily harm even although there may be a considerable delay between infection and the onset of illness.

However, there are a number of difficulties with imposing liability under each of these sections.

Firstly, under s 47 it is necessary to prove an assault or a battery. In *Clarence* (1888) the defendant, knowing that he had venereal disease, had sexual intercourse with his wife. The Court for Crown Cases Reserved held that there had been no assault because the wife had consented to the sexual intercourse. The defendant's failure to reveal his condition did not amount to a fraud of the type that might vitiate her consent. The court also held that there could be no liability under s 20 as the commission of an assault was a prerequisite of that offence too.

Since the decision of the House of Lords in *Wilson* (1984) it is no longer necessary to prove an assault for s 20. It is, however, necessary to prove that D did something which directly resulted in *force* being applied to V.

Thus it would appear that there can be no liability for either offence where infection is a result of consensual sexual intercourse. It is submitted, however, that consenting to intercourse which carries the risk of death is so different from 'normal' intercourse that it would be ludicrous to suggest that the victim consented to the act. *Clarence* should not be followed. And, indeed, modern cases suggest that consent is no defence where actual bodily harm is intended or caused (see eg *Attorney-General's Reference No 6 of 1980* (1981)), or likely to be caused (*Boyea* (1992)) unless it can be justified by public interest. This rule applies where the victim was aware of the risk. It would be strange were it not also to apply where the victim is unaware of the risk. Indeed, it may be argued that there is greater justification for imposing liability in the latter case than the former.

The *mens rea* for s 47 is intention or recklessness with respect to the application of unlawful force. 'Recklessness' in this context bears a 'subjective' meaning (*Spratt* (1991)). In *Savage; Parmenter* (1991) it was held that it is not necessary to prove that D either intended or was reckless with respect to occasioning actual bodily harm. It is sufficient to prove that the harm was a consequence of the intended or reckless assault.

It has been suggested above, however, that, in cases where there was apparent consent, proof of a battery requires the prosecution to demonstrate that the consent was vitiated by showing that it was intended to cause or was likely to cause harm. It would seem to follow, therefore, as a matter of logic, that to prove the *mens rea for battery* in such cases the prosecution should be required to prove that D was aware that, or was reckless, his behaviour was likely to cause harm. If he did not know that, how could it be said that he intended to commit a *battery*? A person who applies force to the body of another believing that they consent does not have the *mens rea* for a battery. In cases of vitiated consent the occasioning of actual bodily harm is, in effect, an essential ingredient of the battery.

In *Boyea* (1992), however, a case involving the question of consent and indecent assault, the Court of Appeal held that D commits a battery if the act consented to is likely to cause harm even though D does not realise that. This decision, surely, is wrong.

As far as s 20 is concerned the prosecution must prove that D was aware that his conduct carried a risk of causing some harm, albeit not serious harm (*Savage; Parmenter*). This requirement should not be difficult to satisfy in the case of a defendant who had unprotected sexual intercourse with another, provided that it can be established that he was aware he was infected.

If the infected person had sexual intercourse forcibly without consent, and thereby transmitted the virus there is little doubt that he could be convicted of the offences mentioned above. As the maximum penalty for rape, however, is greater (life imprisonment s 37, Sched 2 Sexual Offences Act 1956) than that for either the offence under ss 47 or 20 (five years in both cases) there would be no point in prosecuting for either of these latter offences. Similarly, if the virus was transmitted by non-consensual anal intercourse, it would be more prudent to bring a prosecution for buggery contrary to s 12(1) of the Sexual Offences Act 1956, as in those circumstances the maximum penalty would be greater than that available for a conviction under either ss 47 or 20 of the 1861 Act (1).

The major obstacle to a conviction for the offence under s 18 of the Offences Against the Person Act 1861 is the relatively high *mens rea* requirement for that crime. The prosecution are required to prove that the defendant intended to cause gbh (*Belfon* (1976)). And, although the Court of Appeal held in *Bryson* (1985) that the jury may infer intention from foresight of virtual certainty the acquisition and development of the syndrome is so uncertain that prosecutors will have difficulty in a typical case of proving the necessary intent (2).

Administering a noxious thing

By virtue of s 23 of the 1861 Act it is an offence to maliciously administer a noxious thing to any person so as to endanger the life of such person or to inflict upon him any gbh. The maximum punishment is ten years imprisonment.

By virtue of s 24 it is an offence to maliciously administer a noxious thing with intent to injure aggrieve or annoy such person. The maximum punishment is five years imprisonment.

It may seem rather artificial to suggest that infecting another with disease amounts to the 'administration of a noxious thing'. In *Clarence* (above), however, it was said that infection is a kind of poisoning - the application of an 'animal' poison.

AIDS is clearly life endangering and it would appear from *Cato* (1976) that the prosecution merely have to prove that the defendant intentionally or recklessly administered the 'noxious' thing. 'Recklessness' in this context bears a 'subjective meaning (*Cunningham* (1957)). Although the Court of Appeal in *Cato* held that there is no need to prove that the defendant foresaw the risk that the noxious thing would endanger life there are likely to be very few cases where someone who recklessly transmitted the virus was unaware that it was life endangering.

Homicide

Even if it could be established that an infected person transmitted the virus intending to kill or cause grievous bodily harm he could be convicted of murder only if death of the chosen victim or victims occurred within a year and a day of the injury by which death is alleged to occur ie within a year and a day of the original infection (*Dyson* (1908)). This rule also applies to manslaughter and therefore as the disease normally progresses quite slowly, it will be extremely unlikely that a prosecution for either murder or manslaughter will be possible (3).

If, however, the prosecution could prove that the defendant intended to kill he could be convicted of attempted murder contrary to s 1 of the Criminal Attempts Act 1981 (4).

Conclusion

In conclusion, it is submitted that there are difficulties in bringing a prosecution under the general law against a person who has infected another with AIDS. Apart from a few offences the principal difficulty lies not with the substantive law but with issues of proof. In most cases the prosecution will find it impossible to satisfy the jury beyond reasonable doubt that the source of the infection was the defendant. In addition, the fact that transmission takes place as a result of sexual activity will make it equally difficult to prove, in many cases, that the defendant had the requisite *mens rea*.

There have been calls from some quarters for legislation specifically targeted at the AIDS carrier who infects another with the virus. It is difficult to see how this might improve the chances of conviction without the fault requirement for a new offence being set at an unacceptably low level.

Notes

1 The penalties for buggery are complex. There are four offences with different penalties depending on a combination of the following factors: whether or not there was consent; the ages of the parties; and the gender of the victim. Anal intercourse with a man over the age of 16 who did not consent carries a maximum penalty of ten years (Sexual Offences Act 1967 s 3; *Courtie* (1984)).

2 In a case in 1988 tried in Indiana, USA, the jury were apparently satisfied that a defendant had intended to infect others with the AIDS virus. He bit and scratched three individuals who had stopped him committing suicide. He was convicted of attempted murder - see Jerold Taitz, *Legal Liability for Transmitting AIDS*, Medico-Legal Journal 57/4 1989.

3 The Criminal Law Revision Committee in its Fourteenth Report: Offences Against the Person recommended that the year and a day rule be retained. It was felt that it would be wrong for a person to be in an indefinite state of risk for prosecution for an offence of homicide. Cmnd 7844 1981 paras 39 and 40.

4 For reasons discussed above, proving an intention to kill will ordinarily be very difficult.

   In *Walker & Hayles* (1990) the judge instructed the jury that they could infer the necessary intention from foresight of a very high degree of probability of death. (The Court of Appeal whilst not considering that to be a misdirection expressed their preference for a direction in terms of 'virtual certainty').

   If D infects V intending that V die some time in the future but believing that V would probably live for more than a year and a day it is submitted that D lacks the *mens rea* for attempted murder.

Question 9

Colin disliked Matthew, a player for a local football team. He threw a stone at Matthews car as he was being driven past. The stone hit the windscreen and smashed it. The view of George the driver was obscured and he lost control of the car. The car mounted the pavement and crashed into a bus queue, seriously injuring three children. Sandra, their mother, saw the car collide with her children and suffered a heart attack from which she died. George was slightly bruised as a result of the collision and Matthew suffered nervous shock.

Consider Colin's criminal liability.

Answer plan

This problem requires discussion and application of a range of offences from common assault and battery to murder. Appropriate headings are used to separate discussion of each of the groups of offences.

Principal issues:

- the ingredients of assault and battery
- the ingredients of the aggravated assaults - ss 47, 20 and 18 of the Offences Against the Person Act 1861
- the doctrine of transferred malice
- the principle that 'one must take one's victim as one finds them'
- the *mens rea* requirements of murder and manslaughter
- liability for criminal damage

Answer

Non-fatal offences against the person

Assault and battery

Assault and battery are two distinct offences (*DPP v Little* (1991)). The *actus reus* of assault consists of causing another to apprehend the application of immediate and unlawful force (*Venna* (1976)). Thus the prosecution must prove that Colin caused either Matthew or George or both to anticipate that they would be struck.

The *mens rea* requirement for assault is that the accused intended to cause the victim to apprehend the application of immediate and unlawful force or was reckless with respect to that (*Venna*).

The 'recklessness' required in this context is known as '*Cunningham*'-type recklessness. That is, the prosecution must prove that Colin, if he did not intend to cause apprehension of force, was at least aware of the risk that his actions might cause Matthew or George to apprehend force (*Spratt* (1991) overruling *DPP v K* (1990)).

A battery comprises the intentional or reckless infliction of unlawful personal violence by the accused upon another person. Again, *Cunningham*-type recklessness is required (*Spratt*).

Section 39 of the Criminal Justice Act 1988 provides that common assault and battery are summary offences whose maximum penalty is a term of imprisonment not exceeding six months.

Aggravated assaults

More importantly, Colin may be guilty of one of the aggravated assaults in respect of the injuries sustained by George, Matthew and the children.

For these offences it is necessary to prove that the injuries were caused by the actions of the defendant. It is for the judge to direct the jury with reference to the relevant principles of law relating to causation, and then to leave it to the jury to decide, in the light of those principles, whether or not the necessary causal link has been established (*Pagett* (1983)).

In the present case the jury would be directed to consider whether George's 'instinctive' reaction was reasonable foreseeable ie within the range of responses that one might reasonably expect from a person in George's situation, in which case the resulting injuries would be attributed to Colin (*Williams & Davis* (1992)).

(It shall be assumed for the purposes of further analysis that George's reaction was reasonably foreseeable)

With respect to George, who has suffered slight bruising, and Matthew who has suffered severe shock, Colin may have committed the offence of 'assault occasioning actual bodily harm' contrary to s 47 of the Offences Against the Person Act 1861.

For this offence the prosecution are required to prove that the defendant committed an intentional or reckless assault or battery (as above) and that the assault or battery caused actual bodily harm. It is unnecessary to prove any *mens rea* with respect to the harm caused (*Savage* (1991) confirming *Roberts* (1971) and overruling *Spratt* on this point).

In *Miller* (1954) Lynskey J stated that actual bodily harm includes any hurt or injury which interferes with the health or comfort of the prosecutor and held that this included a hysterical or nervous condition. Thus it is submitted that both George and Matthew have suffered actual bodily harm as a result of Colin's assault.

As the children have suffered 'serious' injuries it is proposed to consider Colin's liability for maliciously inflicting grievous bodily harm under s 20 of the OPA 1861 or causing grievous bodily harm with intent contrary to s 18 of the same Act.

(Grievous bodily harm was defined by the House of Lords in *DPP v Smith* (1961) as 'serious harm' (see also *Saunders* (1985).)

It was believed that the word 'inflict' in s 20 imposed a requirement of an act amounting to an assault (eg *Clarence* (1888)). More recently it was decided in *Wilson* (1984) that there can be an 'infliction' of grievous bodily harm without proof of an assault. The House of Lords referred with approval to the judgment of the Supreme Court of Victoria in *Salisbury* (1976) which concerned the Victorian equivalent of s 20. In that case it was held that grievous bodily harm was inflicted *either* where D directly and violently inflicted it by assaulting V *or* where D something which though not in itself a direct application of force directly resulted in force being applied to the body of V such that he suffered grievous bodily harm (1).

It would seem, therefore, that Colin has inflicted serious harm on the children.

The *mens rea* requirement for s 20 is (subjective) recklessness with respect to some harm, albeit not serious harm. Thus, if Colin was aware that throwing the stone at the car carried the risk that some person might suffer harm, he is guilty of the offence under s 20 (*Savage; Parmenter*).

The maximum penalty for an offence under s 20 is a term of imprisonment not exceeding five years.

If Colin intended to cause grievous bodily harm then he may be convicted of the more serious offence of causing grievous bodily harm with intent contrary to s 18 of the 1861 Act.

By virtue of the doctrine of transferred malice, Colin may be convicted of the offence under s 18 with respect to the injuries sustained by the three children if he intended to cause serious injuries to George or Matthew (see *Latimer* (1886)) (2). And, the jury *may* infer that gbh was intended, even if it was not Colin's purpose, if he knew that gbh was a virtually certain consequence of his actions (*Bryson* (1985)).

Homicide

Can Colin be convicted of the manslaughter of Sandra?

The assault committed against George or Matthew would amount to an unlawful and dangerous act for the purposes of constructive manslaughter (see eg *Larkin* (1943)), and by virtue of the doctrine of transferred malice it may provide the basis of liability for Sandra's death (2).

(The requirement of dangerousness is satisfied by proving that all sober and reasonable people would inevitably recognise that D's act subjected another person to the risk of harm, albeit not serious harm. It is not necessary to prove that D was aware of the risk of harm (*Church* (1966); *Goodfellow* (1986); *Newbury* (1977).)

Professor Williams, however, argues that the doctrine of transferred malice should not be applied where an injury intended for V1 causes fright and consequent injury to V2. He suggests that 'the law of constructive manslaughter and transferred intention should not be pushed so far as to say that if D assaults V1 he becomes guilty of the manslaughter of V2, a mere spectator who, remarkably, dies of fright or shock in witnessing what happens to V1'.

Even were the court to reject this argument, the prosecution must prove that Colin's acts were the cause of Sandra's death. Surely her death was too remote to be attributable to Colin. Only in the unlikely event that the jury conclude that the death was a reasonably foreseeable consequence of Colin's acts might he be convicted of manslaughter (3).

The *maximum* punishment for manslaughter is a term of imprisonment for life (s 5 of the Offences Against the Person Act 1861).

Criminal damage

Colin may be convicted of the offence of criminal damage contrary to s 1(1) of the Criminal Damage Act 1971 for smashing the windscreen. The maximum penalty for this offence is a term of imprisonment not exceeding ten years (4). The prosecution must prove that he either intended to damage property belonging to another or was reckless with respect to property being damaged. The meaning of intention is discussed above.

A person is reckless whether any property would be damaged if his conduct creates a serious risk of damage and he either fails to give any thought to the risk where it was obvious to a reasonable person or he was aware there was some risk and nonetheless took it (*Caldwell* (1982)).

By virtue of s 1(2) of the Act a person who intentionally or recklessly destroys or damages property belonging to another 'intending by the destruction or damage to endanger the life of another or being reckless whether the life of another would be thereby endangered' is guilty of the more serious offence of 'aggravated' or 'dangerous' damage. The maximum penalty for this offence is life imprisonment.

In *Steer* (1988) it was held that it is not sufficient to prove that D was reckless with respect to damaging property and that he was reckless with respect to endangering life. It must be shown that D was reckless as to whether life would be endangered *by the destruction or damage* of the property.

Thus if, for example, the prosecution prove that Colin failed to consider an obvious risk that the smashing of the windscreen would endanger the life of another, the necessary *mens rea* will be satisfied.

Notes

1   Lord Ackner in *Savage* stated that there would be an infliction of gbh where D frightens V who suffers serious injury as a result of taking evasive action or where D interferes with the brakes of a car causing the driver to suffer serious harm in an accident.

2   The doctrine of transferred malice states that if D aims to strike V1 but 'accidentally' misses with the result that V2 is struck, then D will be guilty for the injuries sustained by V2 *to the same extent* as he would have been had those same injuries been sustained by V1.

3   There is one possible further requirement - that the act was 'directed at another' (*Dalby* (1982); and see *Ball* (1990)). It is not clear whether this raises issues independent of the requirement that D's act caused the death (*Goodfellow* (1986)). However, even if there is such a requirement it was held in *Mitchell* (1983) that it is not necessary to prove that the act was directed at the person who was actually killed.

4   If the value of the property damaged is less than £2000 the maximum penalty is three months imprisonment and/or a fine of £2500 (Magistrates Court Act 1980 s 22(1) and (2)).

Question 10

Jack had been burgled and his wife viciously attacked. As he was nervous of a further attack he kept a baseball bat by the side of his bed. One night he woke up as he heard footsteps from a neighbouring room. He picked up the baseball bat and went to confront the apparent intruder. He saw a young man about to enter his daughter's bedroom.

In fact, the young man was Carruthers, the new boyfriend of Jack's daughter, Cynthia. Cynthia had invited Carruthers to spend the night with her. Jack had met Carruthers only once and in the dark of the hallway he did not recognised him.

Jack struck Carruthers over the head with the baseball bat. Carruthers slumped, unconscious, to the floor.

Jack made a cursory examination of the body. He now recognised the youth. Jack was horrified at what he had done. Believing that Carruthers was dead, Jack decided to dispose of the body.

He weighted the body and threw it in a nearby lake.

Medical evidence has revealed that Carruthers died from drowning and thus was still alive when thrown in the lake.

Discuss Jack's criminal liability.

Answer plan

This question raises a number of quite separate issues in the context of unlawful homicide.

In particular the answer involves analysis and application of the following:

- the '*habo Meli* principle
- 'private' and 'public' defence and the treatment of mistaken beliefs in this context
- 'reckless' manslaughter and the meaning of an 'obvious' risk
- the *Caldwell* 'loophole'

Answer

Homicide

The *mens rea* for murder or 'malice aforethought' is satisfied on proof of an intention to kill or cause grievous bodily harm (*Moloney* (1985)).

('Grievous bodily harm' means 'serious bodily harm' (*DPP v Smith* (1961); *Saunders* (1985).)

The facts of the problem state that Jack intended to cause Carruthers serious harm and therefore we may conclude that, at the moment he delivered the blow, he had the 'malice aforethought' for murder.

But, in this case the blow struck by Jack although accompanied by 'malice aforethought' did not result in death. And, the concealment of the body, although the immediate cause of death was not accompanied by 'malice aforethought'. As he believed Carruthers was dead, Jack clearly had no intention to kill or cause gbh when he disposed of the body. There is a well established principle of English law that the *actus reus* and *mens rea* of an offence must coincide temporally. The relevant *mens rea* must be present at the time of the act constituting the *actus reus* (*Fowler v Padget* (1798)).

It has been held, however, that if the immediate cause of death is part of what might be regarded as one 'series of acts' or one 'transaction' then liability for murder may be imposed if the defendant acted with malice aforethought at some point during that 'series' or 'transaction' (*Thabo Meli* (1954); *Church* (1966)).

In *Le Brun* (1992) the Court of Appeal held that if a person unlawfully assaults another and, believing he has delivered a fatal blow, attempts to conceal or otherwise dispose of the body then he will be guilty of murder if the blow was struck with malice aforethought even if the immediate cause of death stems from the concealment. And thus, in this case, Jack may be charged with murder.

He may, however, be able to take advantage of the 'defences' of public or private defence. These defences are complete defences and apply to all crimes. In *Cousins* (1982) the Court of Appeal held that a person may in appropriate circumstances take advantage of both defences; the principles applicable are the same. By virtue of s 3(1) of the Criminal Law Act 1967 a person may use such force as is reasonable in the circumstances in the prevention of crime. And, at common law, a person may use such force as is reasonable in the defence of his own person or another's. A person who uses force in these circumstances is acting lawfully (*Abraham* (1973)).

Although, as far as these defences are concerned, the prosecution has the burden of proving that the force was used unlawfully, the defendant has the burden of adducing sufficient evidence that he acted in defence (*Abraham*).

In the *Attorney-General for Northern Ireland's Reference No 1 of 1975* (1977) Lord Diplock, expressing the opinion of the House of Lords, pointed out that the question whether the force used was reasonable is a question of fact for the jury and never a point of law for the judge. The jury should reject the defence only if they are satisfied that no reasonable man in the circumstances would have considered exposing the victim to the risk of harm that was foreseeable. All the circumstances should be taken into account including the serious nature of the harm which the force was intended to prevent and whether it could have been prevented without the use of force (*Allen v MPC* (1980)).

The courts have recognised on a number of occasions that detached reflection cannot be expected from the defendant in circumstances of defence. In *Palmer* (1971) for example Lord Morris stated that if, in the opinion of the jury, the defendant responded to an attack in a way that he honestly and instinctively thought was necessary then that is 'potent evidence' that he took reasonable defensive action. And in the *Attorney-General for*

Northern Ireland's Reference No 1 of 1975 Lord Diplock said that the jury should consider the time available for reflection (1). Therefore the defendants own view as to the necessity for and the reasonableness of the force he used is crucial in determining whether he may avail himself of the defence.

In addition, a pre-emptive strike may be justified. It may be the case, however, that what constitutes reasonable force in the case of a pre-emptive strike is somewhat less than would be justified against an actual attack (*Beckford v R* (1987)).

It is in the light of the above principles that the jury should consider whether Jack used reasonable force when he attacked Carruthers.

Furthermore, the question whether the force is reasonable should be assessed by reference to the facts as Jack believed them to be. In *Williams* (1987). D attacked V believing that V was unlawfully attacking a youth. In fact V was acting lawfully. D was charged with assault occasioning actual bodily harm. The Court of Appeal held that, as the *mens rea* for assault is an intent to apply *unlawful* force, a person who applies force which would be reasonable were the circumstances as he believed them to be, lacks the *mens rea*. This principle was applied by the Privy Council in *Beckford v R* (1988).

Thus, if, in the opinion of the jury, the blow struck by Jack was necessary and reasonable in what he perceived to be the defence of his daughter from rape then he should be acquitted of murder. If, on the other hand, the force was excessive then he should be convicted of murder. The English courts have not adopted the principle (which at one time applied in Australia) that, if a person used excessive force in circumstances where lesser force in defence would have justified the homicide, the person was acquitted of murder and convicted of manslaughter (*Howe* (1958)).

However, even if Jack's attack on Carruthers is excused on the grounds of necessary defence it is arguable that he committed 'reckless manslaughter' when he threw the body in to the lake. Clearly, at that time he was not acting in self-defence.

For 'reckless manslaughter' the prosecution must prove that the defendant did an act which was attended by a 'serious' risk of some physical injury to another and which caused the death of that other (*Seymour* (1983); *Kong Cheuk Kwan* (1985)).

In addition, it must be proved that the defendant either gave no thought to the possibility of there being such a risk in circumstances where the risk would have been obvious to a reasonable prudent bystander or he was aware of some risk of physical injury but nevertheless took that risk (see *Caldwell* (1981)).

We may dismiss the latter alternative as Jack believed Carruthers to be dead.

Thus the issue is whether there was an obvious and serious risk of harm to which Jack gave no thought.

Would the reasonable man have been aware of a serious risk of injury to Carruthers in this case? The answer to this question depends on whether the reasonable man is to be attributed with Jack's mistaken belief that Carruthers was already dead. It is submitted that 'he' is not.

In *Ball* (1990) the defendant fired a gun at two youths mistakenly believing that it was loaded with blanks. One of the youths was killed. (D had grabbed a handful of cartridges from a pocket which he knew contained both live and blank ones.) The Court of Appeal held that an act is dangerous for the purpose of *constructive* manslaughter if the reasonable man would inevitably recognise that the act of the defendant subjected the victim to the risk of some harm and the mistaken belief that there was a blank cartridge in the chamber was not to be imputed to the reasonable man. Although the reasonable man in this context would not necessarily be aware that there was a live cartridge in the gun, he would be aware of the *risk* that the cartridge was live and that, consequently, pointing and firing the gun at the youths was a dangerous act.

Although the jury were not directed to consider *reckless* manslaughter the Court of Appeal appeared to take the view that the defendant could have been convicted of manslaughter by that mode. Presumably, therefore, the question whether a risk is an obvious and serious one is also to be answered by reference to a reasonable man who is aware of the entire course of events and who does not share a mistaken belief of the defendant.

That, however, is not the end of the matter. The test of recklessness requires, in addition, proof that D gave no thought to the possibility of there being a risk of harm. A person who considers a risk and concludes there is none is not reckless (2).

In Jack's case, the facts are ambiguous. If Jack had assumed without thinking, that Carruthers was dead then it could be said he was reckless. But, is it possible for an individual to assume that another is dead without, at the same time, considering whether he might be alive? (3).

It is hard to believe that Jack gave no thought whatever to the possibility that Carruthers might still be alive but, in the event that he did not, he may, it is submitted, be convicted of manslaughter.

Notes

1 In *Shannon* (1980) Lord Ormrod agreed with Lord Morris that the jury should be reminded that one cannot expect the defendant in cases of defence to 'weigh things to nicety'.
2 The speech of Lord Browne-Wilkinson in the House of Lords in *Reid* (1992) (All ER 673 at p 696) suggests a narrowing of the 'loophole' to those situations where D dismisses the risk 'on reasonable grounds'. Lord Goff, however, appeared to accept that the reasonableness of a mistaken belief that there was no risk is relevant only to its credibility (at page 690) This surely is correct. If the loophole were to be limited to non negligent mistakes the definition of recklessness and negligence would coincide.
3 The difficulties inherent in proving a negative - in this case proving the absence of reflection on the part of the defendant - are highlighted in this example. This demonstrates one of the major weaknesses of the *Caldwell* test.

Question 11

Explain and discuss the meaning of an 'unlawful act' for the purpose of constructive manslaughter.

Answer plan

A straightforward question concerning the central component of constructive manslaughter. Note that the nature of an unlawful act for the purposes of constructive manslaughter is partly explained negatively, ie by reference to what is *not* an unlawful act. It should be no surprise to discover that the law in this area is not absolutely clear.

The principle issues:

- the definition of an unlawful act
- the question of whether the prosecution are required to prove that D acted with the *mens rea* for the unlawful act
- the meaning of 'dangerousness'

Answer

It was once the law that a person was guilty constructively of murder if he killed in the course of a felony and guilty of manslaughter if he killed in the course of a misdemeanour. The essence of constructive crime is that liability for one offence is based upon the commission of some other offence.

Although the felony murder rule was abolished by the Homicide Act 1957, and the distinction between felonies and misdemeanours was abolished by the Criminal Law Act 1967, this species of manslaughter remains. What previously amounted to constructive murder was incorporated within manslaughter. Therefore, liability for constructive manslaughter is based upon an unlawful and dangerous act which results in death.

It is not every unlawful act, however, that will suffice for constructive manslaughter. A tort is insufficient (*Franklin* (1883)); as is an offence against property (*Franklin Lamb* (1967)).

Furthermore, it was settled by the House of Lords in *Andrews* (1937) that an offence whose basis is negligence is not an unlawful act for the purposes of constructive manslaughter.

And, in *Lowe* (1973) the Court of Appeal held that the commission of the offence under s 1(1) of the Children and Young Persons Act 1933 of wilful neglect of a child did not make the parent liable for constructive manslaughter. Lord Phillimore stated that a criminal omission would not generally give rise to liability for constructive manslaughter.

Whether or not it is necessary for the prosecution to prove that D had the *mens rea* for the unlawful act is, surprisingly, a moot point. In other words, it is unclear whether the prosecution are required to prove that, even if death had not occurred, D could have been convicted of some offence limited by reference to the above criteria.

In *Lamb* (1967) the defendant pointed a revolver at his friend. He neither intended to injure nor alarm his friend. Neither was the friend alarmed. Lamb and his friend thought it was safe to pull the trigger. They did not realise that the gun was primed. Lamb pulled the trigger and the friend was shot dead.

The trial judge took the view that the pointing of the revolver and the pulling of the trigger was something which could, in itself, be unlawful even if there was no attempt to alarm or intent to injure.

This was rejected by the Court of Appeal. The defendant lacked the *mens rea* for a criminal assault or battery and consequently had not committed an unlawful act 'in the criminal sense of the word' (per Sachs LJ). Constructive manslaughter could not be established without proving that element of intent without which there could be no assault.

Similarly, in *Jennings* (1990) the Court of Appeal held that possession of a knife in a public place was not an unlawful act unless the prosecution could prove that the defendant possessed it with intent to cause injury - ie the intent necessary for the offence of possession of an offensive weapon contrary to s 1(1) of the Prevention of Crime Act 1953.

These cases support the principle that there can be no 'unlawful act' unless the defendant has committed the *actus reus* of an identified offence with the requisite *mens rea* for that offence.

However, the decision of the House of Lords in *Newbury* (1976) casts doubt on this principle. Two 15 year old boys pushed part of a paving stone from the parapet of a railway bridge on to the path of an oncoming train. The stone went through the glass window of the driving cab and struck and killed the guard. The boys claimed that they did not intend to injury anybody.

The defendant was convicted. On appeal, the House of Lords upheld the conviction.

It is unclear from the decision what the exact nature of the unlawful act was. Lord Salmon, with whose speech the other Law Lords concurred, stated that, as manslaughter was a crime of 'basic intent', the only *mens rea* that needed to be proved was 'an intention to do the acts which constitute the crime'. Lord Edmund-Davies said that for manslaughter it is sufficient to prove the 'intentional' commission of the unlawful act.

And, in the later case of *Goodfellow* (1986) the Court of Appeal held that for constructive manslaughter the act must be intentional and unlawful.

These statements are ambiguous.

They could mean (and the general tenor of the speeches in *Newbury* supports this interpretation) that all that is required for constructive manslaughter is that the accused actions are performed deliberately, ie voluntarily.

Although Lamb lacked the *mens rea* for an assault, his actions were performed *deliberately* in the sense that he pulled the trigger of the gun consciously. The gun did not go off 'by accident'. He was not an automaton. This, perhaps, is the reason that Lord Salmon in *Newbury* thought that Lamb was 'lucky' to have his conviction quashed on appeal.

The other possible (but less natural) interpretation of the opinion of the House in *Newbury* is that the statement that the unlawful act must be performed intentionally was not meant to be understood as a complete account of the mental element of manslaughter and that since an act is unlawful for the purposes of the criminal law only if performed with the appropriate *mens rea*, manslaughter is not committed constructively unless D acted with that *mens rea*.

The jury may have decided that the defendants in *Newbury* were at least reckless with respect to frightening or applying force to the crew and passengers.

(One of the difficulties with the case is that the direction to the jury is not reported nor commented upon by the House.)

Lord Salmon stated that there was no basis upon which counsel for the defendant could contend that the appellant's act was unlawful. Without specifying the unlawful act it is difficult to assess this statement.

In *Cato* (1976) we are left in doubt as to the precise nature of the unlawful act. D caused the death of his friend, V, having injected him with heroin. V had consented to the administration of heroin. The Court of Appeal stated that the offence under s 23 of the Offences Against the Person Act 1861 would suffice as an unlawful act. The court added, however, that, even if it had not been possible to rely on the s 23 offence, there would have been the unlawful act of 'injecting the friend with heroin which the accused had unlawfully taken into his possession'.

This is puzzling. There is neither a statutory nor a common law offence of administering heroin. *Cato* suggests that the unlawful act need not be an offence!

The approach of the House of Lords in *Newbury* and that of the Court of Appeal in *Cato* is harsh. As we have seen, the decisions imply that a person may be convicted of the serious offence of manslaughter without proof of *mens rea*. It is submitted that the approach of the Court of Appeal in *Jennings* is preferable (1).

Finally, and here, fortunately, the law is clear, the unlawful act must be 'dangerous'.

In *Church* (1966), Lord Edmund-Davies, delivering the judgment of the Court of Appeal, explained the meaning of 'dangerous'. He said that an unlawful act is dangerous if all sober and reasonable people would inevitably recognise that the unlawful act subjected the victim to the risk of some harm, albeit not serious harm (2).

This was endorsed by the House of Lords in *Newbury* (above). In addition, the House approved of the decision of the Court of Appeal in *Lipman* (1970) to the effect that the test of 'dangerousness' is framed in objective terms. For constructive manslaughter it is quite unnecessary for the prosecution to prove that *the defendant* knew that his conduct carried the risk of harm.

But, as the earlier discussion reveals, it would seem that the House did not appreciate that the requirement that the act is dangerous is additional to, and not a replacement for, the requirement that the unlawful act is performed with full *mens rea*.

Notes

1   The decision of the Court of Appeal in *O'Driscoll* (1977) supports the view that there is no unlawful act without proof of the *mens rea* for the offence in question. The court held that if the unlawful act is an offence of specific intent, there can be no conviction in the absence of that intent and evidence of intoxication is admissible to support a contention that D lacked the intent.

2   In *Dawson* (1985) the Court of Appeal held that 'harm' referred
    to in the test means 'physical harm'. Emotional disturbance
    per se is insufficient. Further, it was decided that the objective
    test should be applied in the context of the circumstances
    known to the accused. If the accused is unaware of a peculiar
    vulnerability of the victim then the 'sober and reasonable
    man' is also taken to lack this knowledge in assessing whether
    the conduct was objectively dangerous.

Question 12

Jason decided to go out for the evening and drove to the local
discotheque. At the discotheque he met Julie. As there were not
many people there, Jason suggested that they go to another club
in a neighbouring town. Whilst driving to the club Jason made
advances towards Julie. When Julie rejected those advances Jason
told her that he had beaten up girls who had refused him in the
past. Julie jumped out of the moving car and suffered serious
injuries. She was taken to hospital where she was informed that
she needed a blood transfusion. As she feared catching AIDS she
refused the transfusion and died.

    Discuss Jason's criminal liability.

Answer plan

This problem is a standard question concerning murder and
manslaughter. It raises issues of causation and is 'open' with
respect to the *mens rea* of Jason. In these circumstances as murder
and manslaughter share a common *actus reus* and differ according
to their respective *mens rea* requirements, it is sensible to analyse,
firstly, the issues of causation and then to proceed to consider the
mens rea issues.

    Principal issues:
*   principles of causation in cases where the victim of an assault
    takes evasive action and where the victim refuses medical
    treatment
*   the *mens rea* requirements for murder and manslaughter

Answer

Unlawful homicide

The first issue to consider in answering this question is whether Julie's death is attributable to Jason's actions - ie whether he has caused the death of Julie.

It is convenient to deal with the issue of causation in two stages: firstly to examine whether Jason's actions were the cause of Julie's injuries and secondly, assuming that they were, to establish whether the injuries were the cause of Julie's death. If Jason's actions were the legal cause of Julie's injuries and the injuries were the legal cause of death then, logically, we may attribute Julie's death to Jason.

(Note: It is for the judge to direct the jury with reference to the relevant principles of law relating to causation, and then to leave it to the jury to decide, in the light of those principles, whether or not the necessary causal link has been established (*Pagett* (1983).)

In *Williams & Davis* (1992) the Court of Appeal held that where, as in the present case, a person leaps from a moving car to avoid some threatened attack the jury should be directed to consider whether that evasive action was within the 'range of responses' that might reasonably be expected from a person in that situation. If the response of the deceased was disproportionate to the threat then it should be regarded as a voluntary act breaking the 'chain of causation'.

It was said that, in applying this test, the jury should consider appropriate characteristics of the victim. Presumably these characteristics include the age and sex of the victim. In addition, the jury should bear in mind that the victim might, in the agony of the moment, act without proper reflection.

To allow further analysis of the problem it shall be assumed that the jury are satisfied, in the light of all the relevant evidence, that Julie's evasive reaction was reasonably foreseeable and proportionate to the threat and therefore that Jason's intimidatory behaviour was the cause of the injuries sustained.

Turning now to the question whether the injuries were the cause of death, we must consider the case of *Blaue* (1975) in which a Jehovah's witness having been stabbed by D, refused a blood transfusion on religious grounds.

The Court of Appeal held that the cause of death was the original stab wound.

Lawton LJ, extending the principle that 'one must take one's victim as one finds them' (ie that a defendant may not point to a particular vulnerability or peculiarity of the victim as the cause of death), stated that, if D attacks another, he may not argue that the religious beliefs of the victim, which prevented treatment, were, in the circumstances, unreasonable; the refusal to have treatment does not break the chain of causation.

In *Blaue* it was the religious convictions of the victim which prevented her from having a blood transfusion. It is not clear whether the principle is of wider application and, in particular, whether it covers a situation like that of the present problem where the victim refuses treatment because of an (irrational) fear of contracting a disease.

If the principle in *Blaue* does apply to the present problem then the injuries are the cause of death and, assuming, as we have above, that those injuries are attributable to Jason, he has committed the *actus reus* of unlawful homicide.

(If the court were to distinguish *Blaue* and to hold that responsibility for the death of Julie were attributable to Jason only if the refusal of the blood transfusion was reasonable foreseeable, (and the jury were to conclude that it was not reasonable foreseeable), then Jason could not be convicted of an offence of homicide. His liability would extend only to the initial injuries sustained as a result of Julie's evasive action in jumping from the car. For a fuller analysis of his liability in those circumstances see the discussion of 'aggravated assaults' (below).)

The next issue to consider is his *mens rea* for it is his intent at the time of the intimidatory behaviour which will determine whether he is to be convicted of murder or manslaughter.

The *mens rea* for murder is satisfied on proof that he either intended to kill or cause grievous bodily harm (*Moloney* (1985)).

'Grievous bodily harm' means 'serious bodily harm' (*DPP v Smith* (1961); *Saunders* (1985)).

If his aim or purpose was to cause death or gbh then he intended death or gbh. If it was not his aim or purpose but the jury are satisfied that he was aware that either death or gbh was virtually certain to result from intimidating Julie then the jury *may* infer that he intended death or gbh (*Hancock & Shankland* (1986); *Nedrick* (1986)).

If, however, as the facts imply, he did not intend to kill or cause gbh, his liability for manslaughter should be considered.

There are two 'modes' of committing (involuntary) manslaughter: 'constructive' manslaughter and 'reckless' manslaughter.

For constructive manslaughter the prosecution must prove that the defendant intentionally committed an unlawful and dangerous act that resulted in death (*Goodfellow* (1986)).

In this case, it would appear that, when he intimidated Julie, Jason committed an unlawful act ie an assault. (An assault is any act by which the defendant intentionally or recklessly causes the victim to apprehend immediate and unlawful personal violence (*Venna* (1976).)

Although recklessness will suffice, the facts of the problem indicate that Jason *intentionally* assaulted Julie (1).

An unlawful act is 'dangerous' if all sober and reasonable people would inevitably recognise that some harm, albeit not serious harm, was likely to result from the unlawful act (*Church* (1966)). Thus, if the jury are satisfied that it was reasonably foreseeable that Julie might jump from the car and sustain some injury then the requirement of 'dangerousness' is satisfied. It is unnecessary to prove that the defendant was aware that his unlawful act was dangerous (see eg *Lipman* (1970); *Williams & Davis; Newbury* (1977)).

The issue of causation was discussed in detail above.

For reckless manslaughter the prosecution would have to prove that (1) Jason's conduct created a serious risk of causing some physical injury to Julie and (2) either (a) he had failed to give any thought to the possibility of there being such a risk in circumstances where the risk would have been obvious to a reasonable prudent person or (b) having recognised that there was some risk, he nevertheless took it (*Seymour;* see also *Kong Cheuk Kwan* (1985)).

As we have seen, Jason's liability is dependent upon a number of questions of fact and judgment for the jury. Thus it is not possible to provide a conclusive answer to this problem. The facts do, however, imply liability for manslaughter, in which case Jason would face a maximum sentence of imprisonment for life (s 5 of the Offences Against the Person Act 1861).

Aggravated assaults

If the court were to conclude that although the injuries sustained by Julie were attributable to Jason her death was not (see the discussion of *Blaue*, above), then Jason's liability would be limited to one of the non-fatal offences against the person according to the gravity of those injuries and his *mens rea*.

As the question states that Julie suffered 'serious injuries' it is proposed to consider, firstly, those offences involving grievous bodily harm, ie causing grievous bodily harm with intent contrary to s 18 of the Offences Against the Person Act 1861 and maliciously inflicting grievous bodily harm contrary to s 20 of the same Act (see *Saunders*, above).

To establish liability under s 18, the more serious offence, the prosecution would have to prove that Jason intended to cause serious harm. Recklessness will not suffice (*Belfon* (1976)). Intention bears the same meaning for this offence as it does for murder (*Bryson* (1985); *Purcell* (1986)).

If intention cannot be proved then liability under s 20 should be considered.

Section 20 uses the term 'inflict' which in a series of cases was understood to imply a requirement of an assault. In other cases no such requirement was recognised. The matter was resolved by the House of Lords in *Wilson* (1984) where approval was given to the decision of the Supreme Court of Victoria in *Salisbury* (1976). The court held that gbh is 'inflicted' either by assaulting the victim or by doing something intentionally which, though not in itself a direct application of force to the body of the victim, does directly result in force being applied violently to the body of the victim so that he suffers grievous bodily harm. In *Savage* (1991) Lord Ackner stated that gbh is inflicted where, as in the present problem, D frightens V into taking reasonably foreseeable evasive action and V suffers serious injury as a result (and see *Lewis* (1970)).

The *mens rea* requirement for s 20 is (subjective) recklessness with respect to some harm. This imposes on the prosecution the burden of proving that Jason was aware that intimidating Julie might result in her suffering some harm, albeit not serious harm (*Savage; Parmenter,* above; *Rushworth* (1992)).

The maximum punishment for the offence under s 20 is five years imprisonment and under s 18, life imprisonment.

If it is not possible to prove that Jason had the *mens rea* for either of these offences, his liability for the offence under s 47 - assault occasioning actual bodily harm - ought to be considered. For this offence it is sufficient to prove that D assaulted V as a result of which V suffered some harm. It is not necessary to prove that D intended or was reckless as to the occasioning of harm (*Savage* above). (The ingredients of assault and the relevant principles of causation are discussed above.)

Notes

1 'Recklessness' in this context bears a 'subjective' meaning. It would be sufficient for the prosecution to prove that Jason was aware that there was a risk that his actions would cause Julie to apprehend immediate and unlawful personal violence (see *Parmenter* (1991)).

Question 13

(a) How did s 3 of the Homicide Act 1957 modify the defence of provocation?

(b) Fernando, a hot tempered Spanish chef, was told by his wife, Isabel, that she was having an affair with Carlos, the waiter. Fernando, seething with rage, went into the kitchen and, intending serious injury, hit Carlos with his chopper. Carlos slumped to the floor and died immediately.
Discuss Fernando's criminal liability.

How would your answer differ if the facts were amended as follows:

Fernando having attacked Carlos sat down and had a cigarette. He then examined Carlos and noticed that he was still breathing. Fernando decided to leave Carlos to die. Carlos died thirty minutes later.

Answer plan

A two part question consisting of an essay part and a related problem. It is quite acceptable to make reference back to the first part of your answer when tackling the problem - as long as you do so clearly.

The principal issues are:

(a)

- the abolition of the restrictions on the availability of the defence of provocation brought about by s 3 of the Homicide Act 1957
- the effect of s 3 upon the 'reasonable man' test as explained by the House of Lords in *Camplin*

(b)

- application of the above
- application of the *Miller* (1983) principle

Answer

(a) The defence of provocation is a partial defence, applicable only to cases of murder. If successfully pleaded liability is reduced to manslaughter. The defence is of common law origin but was significantly modified by s 3 of the Homicide Act 1957.

Where provocation is pleaded, there are, basically, two issues for the jury to consider. The first is whether the defendant, as a result of some provocation, lost his self-control; the second is whether the reasonable man would have done as the accused did.

With respect to the first issue there must be a sudden and temporary loss of self-control. This has been unaffected by s 3 (*Thornton* (1992)).

However, whereas according to the pre-Act case of *Duffy* (1949) provocation was limited to acts done by the dead man to the accused, there is no longer any such restriction. In *Peter Davies* (1975) it was held that the provocation can come from a source other than the victim. And, in *Pearson* (1992) where two sons, William and Malcolm, killed their violent father the Court of Appeal held that in deciding whether William had lost his self-control the jury were entitled to take into account those words and conduct of the father directed against Malcolm which had come to the notice of William. Provocation was not limited to his own personal experience of his father's activities.

Further, whereas in *Holmes v DPP* (1946) the House of Lords held that, generally, verbal insults alone could not constitute provocation, s 3 provides that 'anything done or said' or a combination of things done and things said may give grounds for the defence. In *Doughty* (1986) where a father had killed his noisy and restless 17 day old son, the Court of Appeal held that the trial judge had erred in refusing to allow the baby's crying immediately prior to the killing to go the jury as evidence of provocation.

Turning to the second issue mentioned above, the position prior to the enactment of the Homicide Act 1957 was that the judge had the power to withdraw the defence from the jury if, in his opinion, the provocation was not sufficient to cause the reasonable man to act as the defendant did. Now the position is that, where there is evidence of provocation, the question whether the reasonable man would have done as the defendant did falls exclusively to the jury for their determination. The judge may withdraw the defence from the jury only where there is no evidence of a sudden and temporary loss of self-control (1).

As a corollary to this, the section prevents the judge from instructing the jury how the reasonable man would behave. According to Lord Diplock in *DPP v Camplin* (1978) he is restricted to suggesting considerations which may assist the jury in determining whether the reasonable man would have done as the accused did.

The section, according to the House of Lords, removes from the judge the power to dictate to the jury the characteristics of the reasonable man. In particular, it prevents the judge from instructing the jury to ignore any unusual characteristics of the accused when assessing whether the reasonable man would have done as the defendant did. And, consequently, s 3 reverses the decision of the House of Lords in *Bedder v DPP* (1954).

In *Bedder*, an impotent youth visited a prostitute and attempted unsuccessfully to have sexual intercourse with her. She taunted him whereupon he killed her. The House of Lords approved the judge's instruction to the jury to ignore the fact that the youth was impotent when considering whether the deceased's conduct amounted to such provocation as would cause a reasonable or ordinary person to do as the defendant did. In effect, the jury were directed to allow the defence only if, in their opinion, the ordinary potent man would have responded in the same way as the accused.

In *Camplin*, the appellant, a boy aged 15, having lost his self-control, killed a man who had buggered him and then laughed at him. At his trial for murder the judge directed the jury that the proper test was the effect of the provocation , not on a reasonable 15 year old boy, but on a reasonable man. The Court of Appeal held that this was a misdirection and distinguished *Bedder* on the grounds that youth was not an unusual characteristic.

However, the House of Lords dismissed the DPP's appeal on the more general ground that *Bedder* had been overruled by s 3. They were influenced by the fact that s 3 recognises that provocation may take a purely verbal form and that, as insults are frequently directed at personal idiosyncracies, it would be absurd to ignore those characteristics when determining whether the reasonable man would have reacted as the defendant did.

The House of Lords in *Bedder* appeared to overlook the function of the reasonable man test which is to restrict the availability of the defence to cases where the loss of self-control of the accused was understandable given such powers of self-restraint as we might reasonably expect of each other.

The reasonable man is an imaginary construct serving a normative function in English law. Consequently, it was an error to treat 'him' as if 'he' were identical to the 'ordinary' or 'average' man. In whatever legal context he appears the reasonable man represents a standard. For the purposes of the defence of provocation he represents a standard of self-control and, consequently, no other 'characteristic' of the reasonable man (other than sobriety) is, in this context, relevant (2). And thus, according to Lord Diplock in *Camplin*, the judge should explain to the jury that the reasonable man is a person with the powers of self-control that might fairly be expected of someone of the age and sex of the accused but in other respects sharing those characteristics of the accused, whether normal or abnormal, that would affect the gravity of the provocation upon him (3).

In *Newell* (1980) the Court of Appeal explained that for a characteristic to be attributed to the reasonable man it must have a sufficient degree of permanence such that it constitutes part of the defendants personality. Temporary transient moods including those induced by intoxication are not characteristics to be attributed to the reasonable man.

Nor should the reasonable man be endowed with characteristics that are not directly connected with the provocative words or conduct. Thus, for example, if the accused is a homosexual hunchback, taunted with respect to his homosexuality and not his deformity only the former characteristic should be attributed to the reasonable man.

Clearly as it would be absurd to attribute characteristics to the reasonable man which would, in the context, make him unreasonable, the reasonable man is not to be endowed with exceptional excitability or pugnacity even if the accused suffers from these traits.

In *Roberts* (1990) it was held that the judge was correct in directing the jury to attribute to the reasonable man the deafness and speech impairment of D and to exclude expert evidence that immaturely prelingually deaf persons often suffer from *exceptional* volatility (4).

It is not necessary for the trial judge to use the *ipsissima verba* of Lord Diplock's suggested direction (*Burke* (1987)). In *Raven* (1982) the accused was 22 years old but had a mental age of 9. The Recorder of London ruled that the jury should be directed to consider the effect of the provocation upon ' a reasonable man who has lived the same type of life as the defendant for 22 years but who has the mental age of the defendant.' This seems a rather generous interpretation of the principle in *Camplin*! The court appears to have regarded the 'mental age' of D as his 'real' age.

Finally, s 3 has abolished what used to be known as the 'proportionate retaliation' rule. At common law, the fatal act committed by the defendant had to be proportionate to the acts of provocation for a successful plea of provocation, (*Mancini v DPP* (1942)). Thus, it used to be said that 'fists might be answered with fists but not with a deadly weapon' (*Duffy*).

Lord Diplock in *Camplin* said that *Mancini* no longer represents the law. The proportionality of the response is merely a factor for the jury to consider when dealing with the more general issue whether the reasonable man would have done as the defendant did.

b) Assuming that Fernando had died immediately

Fernando may be charged with murder. He committed unlawful homicide intending serious injury ie grievous bodily harm (*Saunders* (1985)). It was finally settled by the House of Lords in 1981 that an intention to cause grievous bodily harm is sufficient *mens rea* for murder (*Cunningham* (1982)).

Can he take advantage of the defence of provocation to reduce his liability to manslaughter?

As explained in the answer to part (a) above, the immediate act of provocation may originate from some source other than the deceased; in this case, Isabel. And according to s 3 provocation may take a purely verbal form.

The fact that he reacted spontaneously to his wife's revelations is good evidence that, as required by the defence, he suffered a sudden and temporary loss of self-control (1).

If the jury are left in reasonable doubt as to whether Fernando was in control when he attacked Carlos they must allow the defence if they conclude that 'a reasonable man would have done as he did' (s 3 of the 1957 Act).

With respect to this issue the judge should direct the jury to consider whether a person of the same age as the defendant sharing relevant characteristics but having 'reasonable powers of self-control' would have done as the defendant did (see discussion of *Camplin* above).

Fernando's 'exceptional excitability' may not be attributed to the reasonable man but presumably his marital status may be.

Might Fernando's nationality be taken into account?

Newell decides that the defendant may not rely on the fact that he belongs to an (allegedly) excitable race, or that people of his nationality are accustomed to resort readily to violence but it is not clear whether the jury may take into account the cultural significance of the provocative conduct.

Professor Williams points out that the distinction is a fine one and that it would be 'socially divisive' to make a concession to the defendant on the grounds of culture (5). Moreover, it was decided in *Camplin* that evidence is not admissible as to whether the defendant's behaviour was, in the circumstances, reasonable - the issue is to be decided by the jury 'drawing on their experiences of how ordinary human beings behave in real life'. Thus, it would seem to follow that evidence concerning the significance of adultery to a Spaniard would not be admissible (6).

Alternative facts

The defence applies only if the defendant lacked self-control *at the time he killed V*. If, therefore, the jury are satisfied that Fernando lost his self-control initially but that he had cooled down after having had a cigarette, they should, of course, reject the plea of provocation and return a conviction of murder (7).

Carlos parlous state was brought about by the act of Fernando. It is submitted that, on recovering his self-control Fernando had a responsibility to attempt to remedy the situation. As he failed to discharge that duty his inaction may be regarded as causative of Carlos' death. As the facts indicate that *at that time* he intended to let Carlos die he is guilty of murder.

In *Miller* (1983) Lord Diplock said that if D failed to take measures to counteract a danger that he himself has created then his failure can be regarded as amounting to the commission of the *actus reus* of an appropriate offence. One is under a duty (Lord Diplock preferred the word 'responsibility') to take steps that lie within one's power to rectify the danger created. If one fails to discharge this duty, then one may be convicted of an offence if the failure to act was accompanied by the appropriate *mens rea* for that offence (8).

Notes

1 If there is evidence that D was provoked to lose his self-control the defence must be left to the jury. The probative burden is on the prosecution to satisfy the jury beyond reasonable doubt that either D was not provoked to lose his self-control at the relevant time or that the reasonable man would have not done as D did (*McPherson* (1957)).

2 In the context of '*Caldwell*' recklessness he represents a standard of prudence and foresight.

3 It is not always necessary to direct the jury to take into account the age and sex of D when considering the question of whether the reasonable man would have done as D did (*Ali* (1989)).

4 In *Ahluwalia* (1992) the Court of Appeal suggested that post
   traumatic stress disorder or 'battered woman syndrome' is a
   characteristic which may be attributed to the reasonable person.
   If correct, this would involve a significant departure from the
   principle that only characteristics to which the provocation is
   directed and which do not relate to exceptional volatility may
   be attributed to the reasonable person.
5 *Textbook of Criminal Law* (1983) 2nd ed p 542.
6 Cf *Muddarubba* (1956), an Australian case, in which it was held
   that the jury, in assessing the reasonableness of the defendants
   response, should consider the cultural significance of the act of
   provocation. The case involved aborigines and the use of an
   aboriginal insult. Unlike the English courts, however, the
   Australian court allowed evidence regarding both the cultural
   significance of the insult and how the average member of that
   tribe would react. See Clarkson and Keating *Criminal Law: Text
   and Materials* (1990) 2nd ed 649.
7 Indeed, the judge may withdraw the defence from the jury
   if there is no evidence that Fernando lacked self-control prior
   to the conduct that resulted in the death of Carlos (see
   Thornton (1992)).
8 Lord Diplock was speaking in the context of criminal damage
   but it is clear that the principle was intended to apply to all
   result crimes. Further, although *Miller* involved a situation
   where D, having becoming aware of the fact that he had
   accidentally created a dangerous situation, failed to take steps
   to rectify it, presumably it applies also to a situation like the
   present one, where a *defence* which may have been available to
   D at the time he created the dangerous situation, is not
   available at a later stage at which he fails to take remedial steps.

Question 14

Fred, who was an alcoholic, was drinking heavily in his local pub.
He thought he heard Albert, the barman, make insulting
comments about Fred's girlfriend to another customer, John. In
fact Albert had been talking about his own wife.

Fred, intending serious injury, picked up a heavy ashtray, and
threw it at Albert. The ashtray missed Albert and hit John on the
head. John had an abnormally thin skull and died from the blow.

Discuss Fred's criminal liability.

Answer plan

This question raises the defences of provocation and diminished responsibility. Although the facts state that Fred had been drinking heavily, there is no need to refer to the *Majewski* principle as the facts also state that Fred intended serious injury - ie he acted with malice aforethought.

The particular issues are:

- the 'egg shell skull' principle
- the doctrine of transferred malice
- the defence of provocation where D makes a drunken mistake
- the meaning and application of s 2 of the Homicide Act 1957; the defence of 'diminished responsibility'

Answer

It is proposed to consider Fred's liability for unlawful homicide.

Fred may be charged with the murder of John. He has committed the *actus reus* of that offence ie he has caused the death of a human being. Any argument by Fred to the effect that John's condition, ie his thin skull, was the cause of death will be rejected by the court. There is a principle of English law that ' one must take one's victim as one finds him'. This means that one cannot point to a peculiar vulnerability of the victim as the cause of death (see *Hayward* (1908)). The fact that John had a thin skull rendering him more vulnerable to fatal injury does not affect the attribution of the death to Fred.

Turning now to the *mens rea* for murder it was finally settled by the House of Lords in *Cunningham* (1981) that an intention to cause grievous bodily harm to another amounts to malice aforethought. Grievous bodily harm means 'serious bodily harm' (*Saunders* (1985)).

Thus, as the facts of the present problem clearly state that Fred intended serious bodily harm, he may be charged with the murder of John.

The fact that he intended serious injury to Albert but missed him and hit John is of no legal consequence. The doctrine of transferred malice, as explained in the old case of *Latimer* (1886), states that if D aims a blow at 'V1' (Albert), misses, and accidentally hits 'V2' (John), D is responsible for the injuries sustained by 'V2' *to the same extent as he would have been* had those injuries been sustained by 'V1'. (In *Gross* (1913) the principle was applied in a case involving provocation.)

Fred may be able, however, to take advantage of two alternative defences to the charge of murder.

Firstly, he may argue that, at the relevant time, he was acting under provocation. This is a common-law defence, modified by s 3 of the Homicide Act 1957, which, if successfully pleaded, reduces liability from murder to manslaughter.

For a successful plea the jury must be satisfied that:

(i)   at the relevant time the accused had, as a result of provocation, lost his self-control and

(ii) that the reasonable man in those circumstances would have done as the accused did.

Dealing with the first of the issues above it should be pointed out that, although the accused bears an evidential burden in support of his plea that he was provoked to lose his self-control, the burden of disproving provocation lies with the Crown (*Woolmington v DPP* (1935); *McPherson* (1957)).

In determining whether Fred had lost his self-control the jury should consider all the relevant circumstances, including his alcoholism and any other relevant features of his personality. According to Devlin J in *Duffy* (1949) the jury must be satisfied that Albert suffered a 'sudden and temporary loss of self-control'. (This was endorsed in *Thornton* (1992) and *Ahluwalia* (1992).)

It would appear from the facts of the problem that Fred acted spontaneously to the perceived insults and this may be regarded as good evidence that he suddenly lost his self-control.

The fact that Fred mistakenly believed that his girlfriend was being insulted is no bar to the defence. Firstly, the Homicide Act 1957 provides that provocation may be verbal. And, secondly, in *Letenock* (1917) it was held that, even if the accused acts under a mistaken belief induced by drunkenness that he was being provoked, he should be judged in accordance with the facts as he mistakenly believed them to be.

The jury must be satisfied, however, that the reasonable man would have done as Fred did in the circumstances which Fred supposed to exist. By virtue of s 3, this issue is exclusively for the jury's determination.

According to the House of Lords in *Camplin* (1978) the reasonable man is a person having the power of self-control to be expected of a person of the same age and sex as the accused and sharing such characteristics of the accused as they think would affect the gravity of the provocation to him.

In *Newell* (1980) the Court of Appeal held that the jury should not attribute to the reasonable man characteristics such as unusual volatility nor transitory states such as drunkenness. Neither should they attribute characteristics to the reasonable man which do not bear a direct connection with the provocative words or conduct. In this case they need not attribute Fred's alcoholism to the reasonable man as the perceived insults did not relate to that.

Thus, the jury should consider whether a sober man, having reasonable powers of self-control, would, in the circumstances which Fred drunkenly imagined to exist, have responded to the perceived insults in the way that Fred did.

Should the defence of provocation fail Fred may be able to take advantage of the alternative defence of diminished responsibility. This defence was introduced into English law by s 2 of the Homicide Act 1957. Like provocation it is a partial defence, which, if successfully pleaded, reduces liability from murder to manslaughter (s 2(3) of the Homicide Act 1957).

For a successful plea, Albert bears the burden of proving, (s 2(2)), on the balance of probabilities, (*Dunbar* (1958)), that:

(i)   he was suffering from 'abnormality of mind'

(ii) resulting from a condition of arrested or retarded development of mind or any inherent causes or be induced by disease or injury

(iii) that substantially impaired his responsibility for the killing.

In *Dix* (1981) the Court of Appeal held that the defence must not be left to the jury unless there is medical evidence in support of these three elements.

The first and third elements are issues for the jury who should take into account *all* the evidence but, if the medical evidence is unanimous, and there is nothing in the facts or circumstances which could lead to a contrary conclusion, they are bound to accept it (*Byrne* (1960); *Matheson* (1958); *Kiszko* (1978)).

The second element concerns the aetiology or cause of the abnormality. This issue is to be resolved solely by reference to the medical evidence (*Byrne*).

Thus one may offer only a qualified answer to the question whether the defence is available to Fred.

His alcoholism may have caused him to suffer an abnormality of mind as defined in the case of *Byrne*. In that case the Court held that the expression means a state of mind so different from that of ordinary human beings that the reasonable man would term it abnormal and includes not only abnormalities of perception or cognition but also an abnormality affecting the ability to exercise will-power.

And, in *Tandy* (1989) the Court of Appeal held that an abnormality due to alcoholism would satisfy the second element above if it were of such a degree that either the brain had been injured, resulting in impaired judgment or increased volatility, or, even where the brain had not been so damaged, the accused was unable to resist taking a first drink (see also *Inseal* (1992); *Egan* (1992)).

As far as the third element is concerned the jury would have to be satisfied that the difficulty Fred experienced in controlling himself was substantially greater than would be experienced, in like circumstances, by an ordinary person, (ie not suffering from mental abnormality) (*Lloyd* (1967)).

If the evidence supports the view that Fred was suffering from an abnormality of mind due to a combination of alcoholism and intoxication, the jury must ignore the effect of the intoxication and determine whether the alcoholism alone would have caused him to be suffering from such abnormality of mind as substantially impaired his responsibility (*Gittens* (1984); *Aitkinson* (1985)). In other words, the jury should allow the defence only if satisfied that if Fred had not taken drink:

(a) he would have killed as he in fact did and

(b) he would have been under diminished responsibility when he did so.

If Fred successfully pleads diminished responsibility or provocation he will be convicted of manslaughter and the court will have a discretion as to sentence ranging from absolute discharge to life imprisonment (1) or, if appropriate, a hospital order may be made under s 37(1) of the Mental Health Act 1983. If, on the other hand, neither plea is successful he will be convicted of the murder of John and by virtue of the Murder (Abolition of the Death Penalty) Act 1965 sentenced to imprisonment for life.

Note

1 Offences Against the Person Act 1861 s 5.

Question 15

Jason and Donovan were fifteen year old boys who attended the same school. They disliked each other intensely and were always arguing. On one occasion, Jason challenged Donovan to resolve their differences by having a boxing match in the gymnasium. Donovan accepted the challenge as he knew that he was a much stronger boy and a better boxer. They agreed that Dylan, a schoolmate, should act as referee. Watched and cheered on by their respective friends, the two boys began to fight. In the course of the first round, Jason hit Donovan a number of times below the belt. Dylan did not intervene. Donovan was extremely angry but decided to box with Jason until Jason was tired and then to land a knockout punch. In the sixth round, Donovan hit Jason on the head with all of his strength hoping to cause Jason serious injury. Jason collapsed unconscious on to the canvas. As he could not be revived, Dylan immediately informed Mr Stiletto, the headmaster of the school. Stiletto examined Jason and, concluding that he should be taken to hospital without delay, he put Jason in his car and drove to hospital. In his eagerness to get Jason medical assistance as quickly as possible, Stiletto drove to town far in excess of the speed limit. As he took a sharp bend he lost control of the car. It plunged into the river and, although Stiletto managed to save himself, Jason could not be rescued and was drowned.

Discuss the criminal liability of Donovan, Stiletto and the spectators.

Answer plan

This question involves a range of issues in the context of fatal and non-fatal offences against the person. The liability of each of the parties should be treated separately. Note that Donovan's *mens rea* is specified in the facts of the problem.

The principal issues are:

- the problem of causation;the principles of 'ordinary hazard' and 'reasonable foresight'
- the defence of 'consent' and 'public interest'
- self-defence and offensive conduct
- provocation
- accessorial liability and the requirement of 'encouragement'
- the *mens rea* of accessories
- causing death by dangerous driving
- reckless manslaughter
- duress of circumstances

Answer

Donovan
Homicide

The *actus reus* of murder and manslaughter requires the prosecution to prove that the defendant's actions caused the death of the victim.

In this case, although there can be no doubt that Donovan's attack upon Jason was a factual cause of his death (ie 'but for his attack Jason would not have died') it is not clear that it was a 'legal cause' of death.

Although there is no English authority directly on the point, it is often suggested that if the 'immediate' cause of death was an 'ordinary hazard' then the defendant is not responsible for the death. And thus it is argued, that if the victim of an attack dies in a traffic accident when being conveyed to hospital by ambulance, the attacker is not regarded as having caused the death (see *Bush v Commonwealth* (1880) for an American case concerning this principle) (1).

In Jason's case, however, he failed to escape from the car because he was unconscious and thus the ordinary hazard principle cannot apply. The 'ordinary hazard' principle, it is submitted, ought to be confined to those circumstances where the condition of the victim has not contributed to his death because, as in this case, death is not then a result of an *ordinary* hazard'.

The appropriate principle in a case like the present one is, it is submitted, the 'reasonable foresight' principle. That is, if the immediate cause of death was an event or an act of another subsequent to and independent of the act of the defendant, it will break the 'chain of causation' and relieve the defendant of responsibility for the death if that event or act was not reasonably foreseeable (see eg *Pagett* (1983)). In other words, if what happened is particularly unusual or unlikely then it amounts to a *novus actus interveniens'*.

If the jury conclude that the death was reasonably foreseeable then, as Donovan had an intention to cause serious harm, he may be convicted of murder (*Moloney* (1985), unless he can avail himself of the defence of provocation (discussed below).

(An intention to do grievous bodily harm is sufficient *mens rea* for murder and 'grievous bodily harm' means 'serious bodily harm' (*Cunningham* (1981); *Saunders* (1985).)

If the jury conclude that the death of Jason is *not* attributable to Donovan then his liability for a non-fatal offence must be considered.

Non fatal offences against the person

The injuries suffered by Jason were, apparently, serious and thus, as Donovan intended to cause a serious injury, he may be convicted of the offence of causing gbh with intent contrary to s 18 of the Offences Against the Person Act 1861. The maximum penalty for this offence is a term of imprisonment for life.

Attempted murder

Although an intention to do gbh is sufficient *mens rea* for murder, nothing less than an intention to kill will suffice for attempted murder, contrary to s 1(1) of the Criminal Attempts Act 1981 (*Whybrow* (1951); *Walker & Hayles* (1990)).

The jury *may* infer that Donovan intended to kill *if* it is proved that he foresaw death as a virtually certain (or possibly a very highly probable) consequence of his actions (*Walker & Hayles* applying *Nedrick* (1986)).

Consent

Although consent is a defence to many offences, including assaults, its availability is limited on grounds of public policy.

In *Attorney-General's Reference No 6 of 1980* (1981) the Court of Appeal held that a person's consent cannot excuse where the defendant intended actual bodily harm or was reckless with respect to causing it. The court held that a fight engaged in to settle a quarrel is unlawful and the participants may be convicted of an appropriate offence even though the other party agreed to fight. The court were of the opinion that it was not in the 'public interest' that people should cause or intend to cause each other bodily harm 'for no good reason'. Lord Lane added that games and sports were lawful to the extent that they are justified in 'the public interest'.

Although prize fighting is regarded as being against the public interest (*Coney* (1881)), properly organised boxing matches are, presumably, lawful.

What then of the boxing match between Jason and Donovan?

In this case, it is submitted, that, although the fight between Jason and Donovan bore some surface similarities with a lawful boxing match it was not lawful as being in the public interest. Although there was a 'referee' the fight was unsupervised. It was not a 'properly conducted' boxing match.

Self defence

A person may use such force as is reasonable in the defence of his own person or another's. A person who uses force in these circumstances is acting lawfully (*Abraham* (1973)).

The question whether the force used was reasonable is for the jury (*Attorney-General for Northern Ireland's Reference No 1 of 1975* (1977)).

Although, as far as these defences are concerned, the prosecution has the burden of proving that the force was used unlawfully, the defendant has the burden of adducing sufficient evidence to raise the issue that he acted in defence (*Abraham* (1973)).

The defences are not available, however, to one who uses force *offensively*. In *Palmer v The Queen* (1971) Lord Morris said that only if the force used was necessary for defence and was not employed out of revenge or to settle a score or for purely aggressive reasons might the defence succeed. For this reason, Donovan may not take advantage of the defences (see also *Bird* (1985)).

Provocation

(This defence applies only to a charge of murder.)

In *Mancini v DPP* (1942) it was held that if there is evidence at the time of the killing that D had lost his self-control then the judge must direct the jury to consider the defence of provocation, and this rule applies even if D, for tactical reasons, has not raised the defence. D may have set up the defence of self-defence which would be undermined by an admission of loss of self-control. If the defence of self-defence is rejected by the jury, but there is evidence of a loss of self-control, they must consider the defence of provocation.

The jury should consider, firstly, whether there was, at the time of the killing, a 'sudden and temporary loss of self-control' caused by the alleged provocation. The fact that Donovan waited for five rounds between receiving the blows does not, *as a matter of law*, negative the defence. It is, however, one of the relevant circumstances that the jury are entitled to consider in deciding whether there was, at the time of the fatal act, a loss of control. It was stated in *Ahluwalia* (1992) that the longer the delay and the stronger the evidence of deliberation on the part of D the more likely the jury will reject the defence.

If the jury are satisfied that there was, at the time of the killing, a sudden and temporary loss of self-control, they must decide whether an ordinary person having the power of self-control to be expected of a 15 year old boy would have done as Donovan did (*Camplin* (1978)). If yes, the defence succeeds, and liability is reduced from murder to manslaughter.

(The fact that Donovan had willingly exposed himself to the risk of provocation is no bar to the defence (*Johnson* (1989)).

Dylan and the supporters - accessorial liability

Might Dylan and the cheering friends be guilty as accomplices?

Section 8 of the Accessories and Abettors Act 1861 provides that a person who aids, abets, counsels, or procures the commission of an offence is liable to be tried and punished for that offence as a principal offender (1).

To aid means to provide assistance. To abet means to encourage the offender (*National Coal Board v Gamble* (1959)).

In *Coney* (1882) it was held that proof of presence at a prize fight was no more than evidence of encouragement. Some active steps must be taken by word or conduct with the intention of encouraging the perpetrator. In the present problem, the supporters are described as cheering their friends. This, presumably, would be regarded as amounting to encouragement.

Although the encouragement must have some effect on the mind of the principal it would appear that is not necessary to prove that the encouragement was a sine qua non of the commission of the offence (*Clarkson* (1971)). The spectators may, therefore, be guilty as accomplices, even although Jason and Donovan had planned the fight. It is probably sufficient to prove that Jason and Donovan were aware of the encouragement (see also *Wilcox v Jeffrey* (1951)) (2).

It must be proved in the case of each of the alleged secondary parties that they intended to encourage the commission of the principal offence.

Even if Dylan acted as referee out of good motives (perhaps he wished to see that the fight was conducted fairly) he may be convicted if he intended to assist the commission of an offence (*Gillick v West Norfolk and Wisbech Area Health Authority* (1984)).

For what offences might Dylan and the others be liable as accomplices?

Clearly they will be guilty as accomplices to the batteries committed by Jason and Donovan. Whether they will attract liability for the serious injury perpetrated by Donovan is a moot point.

In *Dunbar* (1988) the Court of Appeal held that, in general, a secondary party attracts no liability for injuries sustained where the principal offender has intentionally exceeded the contemplated offence.

In *Betty* (1963) and *Reid* (1976) on the other hand, it was held that the secondary party in these circumstances would be responsible for the injuries sustained *to the extent of their own mens rea*, in which case Dylan etc may be convicted of the offence of 'malicious wounding ', contrary to s 20 of the Offences Against the Person Act 1861, if it could be proved in each case that they foresaw a risk of some bodily harm (*Savage;Parmenter* (1991)).

Further, if they contemplated, as a real possibility, that Donovan might intentionally cause gbh, then they may be convicted of the offence under s 18 of the 1861 Act (*Chan Wing-siu* (1985); *Hyde Sussex & Collins* (1990); *Hui Chi Ming* (1991)).

Stiletto

Provided Stiletto's actions are considered to be a legal cause of Jason's death he may be guilty of either

(i)   'reckless' manslaughter

or

(ii)   causing death by dangerous driving

or both.

(i) For reckless manslaughter the prosecution would have to prove that Stilettos driving carried with it an 'obvious and serious ' risk of causing Jason some physical injury and that Jason had either failed to give any thought to the possibility of there being any such risk or, having recognised that there was some risk of physical injury, he nevertheless took that risk (*Seymour* (1983))

(ii) Section 1 of the Road Traffic Act 1988 as substituted by s 1 of the Road Traffic Act 1991 provides that a person who causes the death of another by driving a vehicle dangerously commits an offence. Driving is dangerous if it falls far below the standard expected of a careful driver, and it would be obvious to a careful driver that the driving was dangerous (s 2A(1)).

Manslaughter carries a maximum punishment of imprisonment for life (Offences Against the Person Act 1861 s 5).

Causing death by dangerous driving is punishable with a maximum of five years imprisonment (s 1 of the 1991 Act).

The facts of the problem are inconclusive with respect to some of these issues but, even assuming that Stiletto's behaviour does fall within the terms of one or both of these offences, he may be able to take advantage of the defence known as 'duress of circumstances' (3).

This recently recognised defence applies, where:

(a) the accused acted as he did because, as a result of some 'objective danger', he reasonably believed that he had good cause to fear that, if he did not act as he did, death or serious physical injury (whether to himself or another) would result, and

(b) a sober person of reasonable firmness would have done as he did.

(*Martin* (1989); *Willer* (1986); *Conway* (1989); *Bell* (1984))

The defence is available where the defendant acts for the benefit of another (*Conway*).

The question as to whether Stiletto's actions were reasonable is one for the jury (*Martin*).

If successfully pleaded, the defence results in a complete acquittal.

Notes

1 As amended by the Criminal Law Act 1977, Sched 12.
2 See Smith and Hogan, *Criminal Law* (1992) 7th ed p 128.
3 All the cases in which the defence has, thus far, been raised have been concerned with road traffic offences. There is no reason, however, why it should not apply to both of the offences under discussion. The analogous defence of 'duress by threats' is available to all crimes except murder and treason (*Howe* (1987)).

Question 16

Late one night Spit went to Tara's house and for 'a prank' climbed a ladder to the open window of her bedroom intending to scare her. When he looked through the window she appeared to be asleep. He changed his mind about frightening her and decided to make his way home. However, just as he was about to climb down the ladder she said 'is that you Tom? Come in'. She made it very clear that she wished to have sexual intercourse.

(Tom, as Spit knew was Tara's new boyfriend. They were very similar in appearance and had been mistaken for each other in the past.)

Without saying anything Spit entered Tara's bedroom.

Tara and Spit had sexual intercourse. When Spit asked her if she had enjoyed it Tara realised that the man with her was not Tom. She was extremely angry and told him to leave.

(Assume that Spit, Tara and Tom are all over 16 years of age.)

Advise the parties with respect to their criminal liability.

Would your answer differ if Spit was thirteen years old?

Answer plan

This question raises issues concerning the offences of rape, procuring sexual intercourse by false pretences, indecent assault, burglary and attempt. The principal issues concern the effect of different types of mistake by V upon D's liability for each of these offences. In addition, the liability of a boy aged 14 for the various sexual offences is discussed.

Answer

Rape

It is proposed to consider whether Spit has committed the offence of rape.

A man commits rape if he has unlawful sexual intercourse with a woman who, at the time of the intercourse, does not consent to it and he knows that she does not consent or is reckless as to whether she consents (s 1(1) of the Sexual Offences Act 1956; Sexual Offences (Amendment) Act 1976).

The maximum punishment is life imprisonment (s 37 SOA 1956, Sched 2).

The absence of consent on the part of the woman and knowledge or recklessness with respect to that fact are essential ingredients of the offence.

Was the 'apparent' consent that Tara gave vitiated by her mistake as to the identity of her partner?

The law is not clear. In *Clarence* (1888) Stephen J was of the opinion that fraud as to the identity of the actor would vitiate any apparent consent (1).

The 1956 Act incorporates a provision of the Criminal Law Amendment Act 1885 s 4 which amended the common law by providing that a man who induces a married woman to have sexual intercourse with him by impersonating her husband commits rape (s 1(2)). Prior to the passing of the 1885 Act the common law rule expressed in cases such as *Burrow* (1868) was that fraud as to identity did not vitiate consent.

Stephen J appears to have assumed that the provision of the 1885 Act amended the common law generally. It is not clear that is was intended to do so.

The weight of academic opinion, however, is in favour of Stephen J's rule (2) and, it shall be assumed, that it represents the law.

In this case, however, Spit did not appear to practise a fraud. Would Stephen J's rule apply to a situation where D simply 'takes advantage of' the woman's own mistake?

An Australian decision suggests that it might.

In *Papadimitropoulos* (1957) the High Court of Australia held that when the issue is whether apparent consent is vitiated it is the mistake that makes it so. It is not the fraud producing the mistake which is important but the mistake itself.

Were the above view of the law accepted, Spit can be regarded as having committed the *actus reus* of rape. There is no requirement of rape that D used force, and, as it would seem from the facts of the problem that he knew that Tara was mistaken as to his identity and that her apparent consent was not real he would appear to have performed the *actus reus* with the appropriate *mens rea*.

Procuring sexual intercourse by false pretences

Section 3(1) of the 1956 Act provides that it is an offence for a person to procure a woman by false pretences or false representations to have unlawful sexual intercourse.

Spit, however, did not induce the false belief in the mind of Tara. Except in a number of fairly stereotyped situations where a false representation can be implied, silence does not generally amount to a deception or a false pretence in English law. Nor is a person under a duty to correct the self-deception of another (see *MPC v Charles* (1977); *Smith v Hughes* (1871)).

In addition, procurement implies a positive and purposive act on behalf of the defendant which was not present in Spit's case (see *Attorney-General's Reference No 1 of 1975*).

Indecent assault

By s 14 of the 1956 Act, as amended by the Sexual Offences Act 1985 s 4(3), it is an offence punishable with ten years imprisonment for a person to make an indecent assault on a woman.

Consent negatives assault, but if a mistake as to identity vitiates consent (see discussion above) Spit has indecently assaulted Tara.

The fact that the contact was neither hostile nor aggressive does not prevent it amounting to an assault (*Faulkner v Talbot* (1981)).

Burglary

By virtue of s 9(1)(a) of the Theft Act 1968 a person commits burglary if he enters a building as a trespasser intending among other things to rape a woman therein.

The maximum punishment is a term of imprisonment not exceeding fourteen years (s 9(4)).

Trespass is a civil law concept involving presence on property without the consent of the occupier. However, in *Collins* (1973) it was held that, for the purposes of burglary, a person does not enter as a trespasser unless he knows or at least is reckless with respect to the facts or circumstances that would make his entry trespassory.

In that case the consent to enter was given under a mistake as to the identity of the defendant. However, the effect of such a mistake on consent for the purpose of trespass was not discussed by the Court of Appeal. As Collins did not know of the mistake (nor was he reckless in respect of it) it was unnecessary to decide the point (3).

If the court accepts that mistake as to identity does vitiate consent then Spit committed burglary at the moment of entering the room.

If, on the other hand, the correct legal analysis is that a mistake of this type does not vitiate consent, Spit entered lawfully, and this would be the case even were the full facts of the problem to reveal that Tara was living with her parents in the family home. Although the son or daughter of the owner is not, in law, the occupier of the premises, the Court of Appeal in *Collins* appeared to assume that, for the purposes of the criminal law, at least, a son or daughter of the occupier has a general implied permission to invite guests in to the house.

Alternative facts

Attempt

A boy under the age of 14 cannot be guilty of rape. This is because at common law there is an irrebuttable presumption that he has not reached the age of puberty (*Groombridge* (1836)) (4).

It is not clear whether he can be convicted of attempted rape contrary to s 1(1) of the Criminal Attempts Act 1981. There are dicta in the case of *Williams* (1893) to the effect that an under age boy cannot be convicted of attempted rape. In *Waite* (1892), on the other hand, the dicta suggest the opposite conclusion.

Professors Smith and Hogan argue that a boy in those circumstances should be liable to conviction. Their argument is that the presumption does not actually state that it is not an offence for a boy under the age of fourteen to have sexual intercourse without consent; it simply denies that the boy is capable of sexual intercourse. It does not follow that the boy may not *try* to rape even if, (according to the presumption) it is impossible for him to do so. And, of course, a person may be guilty of attempting to commit an offence even if the facts (including presumed facts?) are such that the commission of the offence is impossible (s 1(2) of the 1981 Act) (5).

If this view is correct then it would seem that Spit might also be convicted of burglary contrary to s 9(1)(a). As noted above there is liability under that sub-section if, at the time of entry, he *intends* to rape.

No presumption as to capacity applies to indecent assault and thus a boy who has non consensual sexual intercourse can be convicted of that offence (*Williams* (1893)).

As he is under fourteen Spit is exempt from criminal liability, however, unless it can be proved that he has a 'mischievous discretion' - that is, when he committed the offences he knew that what he was doing was 'gravely wrong, seriously wrong' (*Gorrie* (1919)).

Tara's liability

Indecent assault

Assuming Spit to be thirteen years old, it is proposed to consider Tara's liability for the offence under s 15 of the 1956 Act.

This provides that it is an offence for a person to make an indecent assault on a man (including a boy). Although there can be no assault if the 'victim' consented, a boy under the age of 16 cannot give a valid consent (s 15(2)). However, as an assault requires a 'touching', Tara cannot be convicted if she was completely passive. If she indecently handled Spit by, say, touching his penis then she may be convicted of the s 15 offence (*Faulkner v Talbot* (1981)).

As mentioned above it is unnecessary that any touching was 'hostile' (*Faulkner v Talbot* above ; *M'Cormack* (1969)).

The fact that Tara thought that she was having sexual contact with her boyfriend who was according to the facts of the problem, older than sixteen is, it would seem, no excuse. In *Maughan* (1934) it was held that the statute imposes strict liability with respect to the age of the victim. That is, a mistake as to the boy's age, whether reasonable or not, does not excuse (and see *Laws* (1928)).

This conclusion seems particularly harsh when, as in this case, D made a reasonable mistake as to the identity of the boy, believing him to be some other person above the age of sixteen, and he was aware of her mistake (6).

Notes

1   The Criminal Law Revision Committee recommend in their fifteenth report that it should amount to rape if a man obtains sexual intercourse by impersonation of another man.
2   Professors Smith and Hogan argue that *Burrow* was based upon a narrow view of rape and consent that is no longer accepted by the courts (see *Dee* (1884)) *Criminal Law* (1992) 7th ed p 456.
3   For some civil law purposes mistake as to identity does not vitiate consent. In *Phillips v Brooks*, for example it was held that in the law of contract a mistake of identity does not vitiate consent where the person is present.
4   The Criminal Draft Code Bill clause 87 if enacted would abolish this presumption.
5   *Criminal Law* (1992) 7th ed p 459.
6   Tara may also be guilty of the offence of 'indecency with children' (s 1 of the Indecency with Children Act 1960). This makes it an offence to perform acts of gross indecency with a child under the age of fourteen.

Chapter 3

General Defences

Introduction

There are a number of defences of general application in criminal law. Most of them are dealt with in this chapter. Defences which apply only to particular crimes - eg provocation - appear in the chapter concerning the appropriate offence.

Obviously, the problem type questions in this chapter involve issues of liability for various offences - questions concerning the general defences are necessarily set in the context of a particular crime. Logically, you should deal with the positive ingredients of liability before discussing the availability of appropriate defences.

Although 'automatism' and 'mistake' are not truly defences but rather a lack of the positive requirements of 'voluntariness', on the one hand, and *mens rea*, on the other, they have been dealt with in this chapter because of their relationship to other defences.

Note: the point made regarding 'open' questions in the introduction to the previous chapter applies, with equal force to problem-type questions under this heading. The facts of the problem do not always disclose the state of mind of the defendant. In addition, in the case of many of the defences discussed, a successful plea depends upon the action or response of D being 'reasonable' (eg in self-defence the force used must be reasonable). The question is generally one for the jury. Thus it is often not possible to come to a definite conclusion regarding the availability of a defence on the basis of the limited facts stated in an examination problem.

Checklist

The following issues are covered in this chapter:

- Automatism - the distinction between 'sane' and 'insane' automatism - the *McNaghten Rules* - the meaning of a 'disease of the mind'.
- Mistake - the various types of mistakes and their effect upon liability, including mistakes induced by drunkenness and mistakes of law.

- Compulsion - necessity and duress - the ingredients of the recognised defences - the limitations on the availability of defences of compulsion - duress and murder.
- The effect of drunken mistakes upon liability - the distinction between crimes of 'specific' and 'basic' intent.
- The *Dadson* principle - the availability of defences where D is unaware of the justifying or excusing conditions.
- The distinction between justifications and excuses.

Question 17

'No act is punishable if it is done involuntarily and an involuntary act in this context - some people nowadays prefer to speak of it as 'automatism' - means an act which is done by the muscles without any control by the mind ...' per Lord Denning in *Bratty v Attorney-General for Northern Ireland* (1963).

Discuss.

Answer plan

This question requires a discussion of the legal treatment of involuntary conduct. The general principle, reflected in the quotation, and the exceptions thereto, should be discussed.

The principal issues are:
- the general principle regarding automatism
- automatism caused by a 'disease of the mind'
- automatism caused by the voluntary consumption of alcohol or 'dangerous' drugs
- other cases of self-induced automatism

Answer

Automatism is recognised as a defence to all crimes. It refers to the situation where the accused's actions are involuntary in the sense that they are beyond his control. Typical examples are sleep-walking, acts done in a hypnotic trance, reflex actions, and convulsions.

Automatism may exist even though the condition of the defendant does not involve a *total* loss of control. An 'effective' loss of control resulting from impaired consciousness will suffice (*Charlson* (1955); *Kemp* (1957); *Burgess* (1991)) (1).

The rationale for the defence of automatism is quite clear. The defendant in such a situation is not responsible for the consequences of his 'actions'. The act is, in a sense, not his own. He does not deserve to be punished, nor would punishment serve any rational purpose.

Although automatism has been referred to as a 'defence' the legally accurate analysis is that voluntariness is a basic ingredient of criminal liability. The onus, therefore, is on the the prosecution to prove beyond reasonable doubt that the conduct of the accused was willed.

The prosecution, however, are obliged to prove that the acts of the accused were voluntary only if the accused has adduced evidence (generally of a medical type) that he was an automaton at the relevant time (*Hill v Baxter* (1958); *Bratty* (1963); *Stripp* (1978); *Pullen* (1991)).

Automatism caused by a 'disease of the mind'

It is not always the case, however, that automatism will result in a simple verdict of not guilty.

If the automatism results from a 'disease of the mind' the condition amounts to what in law is known as insanity. In such circumstances the defendant is entitled only to a qualified acquittal ie not guilty by reason of insanity (2).

Where a defendant is found not guilty by reason of insanity the judge must make one of a number of various orders which include a hospital order with or without restrictions on discharge (s 5 of the Criminal Procedure (Insanity) Act 1964, as substituted by the Criminal Procedure (Insanity) Act 1991 Sched 1).

Insanity is, of course, a defence. However, in *Bratty*, it was held, following *Kemp* (1957), that, if the defendant adduces evidence of automatism, the prosecution are permitted to adduce evidence that the condition giving rise to the automatism is a 'disease of the mind' and that the defendant is entitled only to a qualified acquittal.

Psychiatric evidence will, of course, be considered as to the nature of the condition but whether or not the condition is a 'disease of the mind' is a question of law. If the trial judge concludes, on the evidence, that the condition is a disease of the mind he is entitled to refuse to let the defence of sane automatism go to the jury. In these circumstances he must instruct the jury that insanity is the only defence available to the defendant (see eg *Bratty; Sullivan* (1984)).

Any disease which impairs the functioning of the mind may amount to a 'disease'. It matters not whether the cause of the impairment is organic, as in epilepsy, or functional, as in schizophrenia. Nor does it matter whether the impairment is permanent or transient and intermittent provided that it was operative at the time of the alleged offence (*Sullivan*).

In *Bratty*, Lord Denning said that any condition which has 'manifested itself in violence and is prone to recur is a disease of the mind'. This reflects what many regard as the central policy underlying the insanity defence: to allow control of those who, although not responsible for the harm caused, are perceived to be suffering from a condition which makes them 'dangerous' (3).

If, however, the malfunctioning of the mind is caused by an 'external factor' such as a blow to the head, or alcohol or drugs, the condition does not constitute a disease (*Quick* (1973); *Sullivan*). Thus, whereas *hyper*glycaemia, caused when a diabetic fails to take insulin, is regarded as internally caused (by the diabetes itself) and, therefore, a 'disease of the mind', *hypo*glycaemia which is a result of failing to take food after taking insulin or taking too much insulin is regarded as externally caused and amounts to sane automatism (*Hennessy* (1989); *Bingham* (1991)).

Automatism caused by the voluntary consumption of alcohol or drugs

If the automatism is caused by alcohol or drugs then, as these are external factors, the resulting condition is not attributable to a 'disease of the mind' (see *Quick*). However, automatism caused by alcohol or drugs is not a 'defence' to all crimes.

The rule is that , where the accused lacks the *mens rea* for an offence due to the effects of alcohol or other (non prescribed) drugs then the absence of *mens rea* is an 'excuse' only for so-called crimes of 'specific intent', such as murder but not for crimes of 'basic intent', such as manslaughter (*DPP v Majewksi* (1977); *Lipman* (1970)). Thus, if a defendant kills a person whilst in a state of automatism induced by the voluntary consumption of alcohol or non prescribed drugs he will be acquitted of murder and convicted of manslaughter, the prosecution being relieved of the burden of proving the *mens rea* for manslaughter (see eg *Lipman*) (4).

The basis for the distinction between crimes of specific intent and basic intent is not at all clear. It seems, however, that the prevailing opinion is that if intention is required with respect to one or more of the elements of the *actus reus* then it is a crime of specific intent and a crime that may be committed recklessly is a crime of basic intent (see the speech of Lord Elwyn-Jones in *Majewski*).

In addition to murder the following have been acknowledged as crimes of specific intent: wounding or causing grievous bodily harm with intent contrary to s 18 of the Offences Against the Person Act 1861, (*Pordage* (1975)); theft contrary to s 1 of the Theft Act 1968, (*Ruse v Read* (1949)); handling stolen goods, (*Durante* (1972)); and attempts (*Mohan* (1976)).

Offences of basic intent include, in addition to manslaughter: malicious wounding or inflicting grievous bodily harm contrary to s 20 of the Offences Against the Person Act 1861, (*Sullivan* (1981)); assault occasioning actual bodily harm, (*Bolton v Crawley* (1972)); rape, (*Fotheringham* (1988)).

Other cases of self-induced automatism

In *Bailey* (1983) the Court of Appeal held that self-induced automatism other than that due to intoxication from alcohol or drugs will provide a defence to all crimes except where the defendant was 'reckless' - in a general subjective sense - as to the risk of becoming an automaton.

That is, if the accused knew that by doing or failing to do something (for example, in the case of a diabetic, taking too much insulin or not eating after having taken insulin,) there was a risk that he might become aggressive, unpredictable or dangerous with the result that he might cause some harm to others, and he persisted in the action or took no remedial action when he knew it was required then he is regarded as having been responsible for his condition. In these circumstances, despite the fact that he lacked the *mens rea*, the defendant may be convicted of an appropriate offence of basic intent.

This rule was also applied in *Hardie* (1984) where the defendant took a quantity of valium, a sedative drug. The valium was not prescribed to the defendant and the judge treated the case as ordinary one of voluntary intoxication, ruling that as it was self-induced it was no defence to a crime of basic intent. The Court of Appeal quashed the conviction. The court held, distinguishing *Majewski*, that the rule regarding voluntary intoxication does not apply where the drug is not generally recognised as 'dangerous'. That is, if the drug does not normally cause unpredictable behaviour, automatism resulting from its consumption may provide an excuse to all crimes, even those of basic intent. Only if the defendant was reckless in the *Bailey* sense can he be convicted of an offence (of basic intent).

Conclusion

Although automatism will often afford a 'defence' entitling the defendant to a complete acquittal, the causes of the condition must be examined. If the defendant is 'responsible' for the condition then he may be convicted, at least as far as basic intent crimes are concerned. If he is not 'responsible' for the automatism but it is the result of an internal condition that is likely to result in recurrent malfunctioning, the defendant will be classified as legally insane and entitled only to a qualified acquittal.

Notes

1   The decision of the Divisional Court in *Broome v Perkins* (1987) implies that a total loss of control is required. This decision is out of line with the authorities and has been criticised by the Law Commission. The draft Criminal Code Bill, clause 33 defines automatism in terms of an *effective* loss of control.

2   The defence of insanity is defined in the *McNaghten Rules* (1843). It must be proved that, at the time he committed the act, the accused was labouring under such a defect of reason , due to disease of the mind, as either not to know the nature and quality

quality of his act, or, if he did know that, he did not know that
what he was doing was wrong.

3 In *Burgess* (1991) it was stated that the fact that a condition
may not recur does not prevent it being classified as a 'disease
of the mind'.

4 It is submitted that the general tenor of the speeches in *Majewski*
supports the notion that the rule is a substantive one - ie that
where a defendant is charged with an offence of basic intent
and he raises evidence that, due to drink or drugs, he was not in
control of his actions at the relevant time, he can be convicted
on proof that he committed the *actus reus*. Liability is, in effect,
strict. Cf *Woods* (1981) in which it was held that, as far as rape is
concerned, the jury should be instructed to decide whether the
defendant had the requisite *mens rea* but to ignore all evidence
of self-induced intoxication! See also *Aitken* (1992) where it was
said that for the purposes of s 20 of the OPA 1861, D acts
maliciously if he foresees the risk of injury or *would have foreseen
injury but for the drink consumed*.

Question 18

Samson is a diabetic. He is required to take insulin regularly to
control his condition. On one occasion he took insulin as
prescribed but, not having eaten, he became semi-conscious whilst
driving his car. He lost control of the car and it collided with
Jeanette, a pedestrian. Jeanette was taken to hospital suffering
from multiple fractures. Two weeks later, whilst still in hospital,
Jeanette was administered an overdose of a painkilling drug by a
nurse. Jeanette died as a result of the overdose.

Discuss Samson's criminal liability.

Would your answer differ if Samson's loss of control had been
caused by a failure to take his insulin?

Answer plan

This question involves consideration of liability for a number of
offences against the person and the application of the rules
concerning involuntary conduct. The same issues of automatism
are raised with respect to each of the offences. Repetition may be
avoided by reference to principles previously explained.

The principal issues are:
- the question of causation and intervening medical treatment
- automatism - the loss of control
- 'reckless' automatism
- automatism caused by a 'disease of the mind'; the distinction between *hypo* and *hyper*glycaemia

Manslaughter

It is proposed initially to consider Samson's liability for manslaughter.

As far as the *actus reus* of this offence is concerned, the only issue requiring consideration is whether it can be established that Jeanette's death was caused by Samson's actions.

Clearly, his conduct was a *factual* cause of death. That is, *but for* Samson losing control of the car she would not have suffered the injuries which led to her hospitalization and subsequent death. The administration of the overdose was also a factual cause of death. The onus is on the prosecution to prove that Samson's actions were a *legal* cause of death.

In *Smith* (1959) D had seriously injured a man who was later subject to improper medical treatment. The man died. The Court of Appeal stated that if the original injuries are still 'operating and substantial' at the time of death then, despite the fact that some other cause of death is also operating, the injuries are a legal cause of death. If, on the other hand, the original injuries are merely the setting in which another cause operates then the injuries are not the legal cause of death.

The rules were elaborated by the Court of Appeal in *Cheshire* (1991). It was stated that even if negligent treatment of the victim was the immediate cause of the death - the injuries having ceased to be operating and substantial - the responsibility of the defendant will not be excluded if the treatment was itself a direct consequence of the defendant's acts and the contribution of the defendant's acts were still significant at the time of death.

Further, the court stated that a direction in terms of the gross negligence of the doctors would be wrong. The jury should be directed to consider the consequences of the treatment and not the degree of blame attaching to the medical authorities. Only if the medical treatment was a 'potent' cause of death and 'independent' of the defendant's actions would it relieve him of responsibility.

It is not at all clear from the judgment of the Court of Appeal in *Cheshire* what is meant by either 'independent' or 'potent'. The treatment is always 'dependent' on the acts of the defendant in the sense that the acts are a sine qua non of the treatment. Similarly, if the immediate cause of death was the treatment, it is difficult to see how the jury are to determine whether it was a 'potent' cause of death without reference to the blameworthiness of the medical staff involved (1).

Assuming, for the purposes of further analysis, that Samson's 'acts' are regarded as the legal cause of death, his criminal liability will be determined by reference to his *mens rea*.

It would appear that Samson went into a hypoglycaemic episode - a deficiency of blood sugar resulting in an impairment of consciousness.

In these circumstances he may raise the 'defence' of automatism, which, if successfully pleaded, results in a complete acquittal.

Samson will be required to produce medical evidence to support his claim that, at the relevant time, he was an automaton (*Hill v Baxter* (1958)). Provided he does so, the probative burden lies with the prosecution. In other words, if the prosecution wish to contest his claim they must satisfy the jury that Samson did not lack conscious control of his actions (*Bratty* (1963)).

The facts of the problem state that Samson was *semi-conscious*. It is not clear from the authorities as to whether this amounts to automatism. There are authorities which support the view that, even where the defendant suffers a less than total loss of consciousness and has some control over his actions, the defence will be available provided he lacks 'effective' control (see *Kemp* (1957); *Charlson* (1955); *Quick* (1973)).

On the other hand, in *Broome v Perkins* (1987) the Divisional Court held that the defendant, although hypoglycaemic, had some control over his car and thus could be said to be 'driving' it. In that case, however, the defendant drove his car, albeit erratically, for five miles (2)

If Samson did not exhibit a sufficient degree of control, the defence of automatism ought to be available to him.

As the condition in this case was caused by external factors - the insulin and the failure to eat food - it was not due to a 'disease of the mind'. It will constitute sane and not insane automatism (*Quick* (1973)).

If, however, Samson was a 'reckless automaton' then he may be convicted of an appropriate offence of 'basic intent'. That is, he will be guilty of manslaughter if, prior to becoming an automaton, Samson was aware that, by not eating food after taking insulin, there was a risk he might lose conscious control of his actions and that others might be harmed as a result (*Bailey* (1983); *Hardie* (1984)).

(It was decided in *Lipman* (1970) that manslaughter is a crime of basic intent. Murder, on the other hand, is a crime of 'specific intent' (see *Sheehan* (1975)).

The maximum punishment for manslaughter is imprisonment for life (Offences Against the Person Act 1861 s 5).

Non fatal offences against the person

Assuming now that the jury were to conclude that the administration of the drug was an 'independent' and 'potent' cause of death ie a *novus actus interveniens* then clearly Samson could not be convicted of manslaughter. In those circumstances his liability would be limited to the injuries suffered by Jeanette.

It is proposed to consider his liability for the offence of malicious wounding contrary to s 20 of the Offences Against the Person Act 1861.

The *actus reus* of this offence involves the infliction of grievous bodily harm ie 'serious bodily harm' (*Saunders* (1985)). Although the question as to whether the harm caused is grievous is an issue for the jury to determine, it shall be assumed that the 'multiple fractures' suffered by Jeanette were serious.

If, therefore, Samson was a 'reckless automaton', as defined and explained above, he may be convicted of the offence under s 20.

(It was held in *Bratty v Attorney-General for Northern Ireland* (1963) that malicious wounding is a crime of 'basic intent'. In the same case it was held that the offence under s 18, wounding with intent, is a crime of 'specific intent'.)

The maximum punishment for the offence of malicious wounding is a term of imprisonment not exceeding five years.

Dangerous driving and causing death by dangerous driving

Samson may be guilty of the offence of dangerous driving contrary to s 2 of the Road Traffic Act 1988, as substituted by s 1 of the Road Traffic Act 1991; if he is regarded as having caused the death of Jeanette, he may be guilty of causing death by dangerous driving contrary to s 1 of the 1988 Act, as substituted by s 1 of the Road Traffic Act 1991.

Again, even were he an automaton, Samson may be convicted of these offences if it can be shown that he was reckless in becoming an automaton (see discussion above).

The offence under s 2 carries a maximum punishment of two years imprisonment and that under s 1 is punishable with up to five years imprisonment.

Alternative facts - Insanity

The ingredients of the defence of insanity were laid down in the *McNaghten Rules* (1843). These state that insanity consists of a defect of reason due to disease of the mind, such that the defendant either did not know the nature and quality of his act or, alternatively, did not know that what he was doing was wrong.

Consequently, automatism resulting from a condition which, in law, is regarded as a 'disease of the mind' amounts to insanity.

If Samson chose to plead the defence of insanity then, as there is a presumption of sanity, he would have the burden of proving the defence on a balance of probabilities (*McNaghten*).

Although insanity is a defence, a successful plea does not result in a complete acquittal. Where a defendant is found not guilty by reason of insanity the judge must make one of a number of various orders. These include a hospital order, which may be made with or without restrictions on discharge (s 5 of the Criminal Procedure (Insanity) Act 1964, as substituted by the Criminal Procedure (Insanity) Act 1991 Sched 1).

Consequently, Samson may choose not to raise the defence of insanity. If, however, he puts his state of mind in issue by raising automatism, the judge may rule that his condition amounts to insanity (*Sullivan* (1984)). And, unfortunately for Samson, it is well established that hyperglycaemia, which may result when diabetes is not controlled by insulin, is a 'disease of the mind'. In contrast to hypoglycaemia it is perceived as the result of internal factors (*Hennessy* (1989)).

If Samson wishes to avoid an acquittal on the grounds of insanity he has no alternative but to plead guilty to the offences charged.

Notes

1   Professors Smith and Hogan suggest that, in such circumstances, the proper question should be whether the medical treatment was grossly negligent: *Criminal Law* (1992) 7th ed p 342.

See also the Law Commission's draft Code clause 17(2):

'A person does not cause a result where, after he does (an act which makes a more than negligible contribution to its occurrence) ... an act or event occurs -
   (a) which is the immediate and sufficient cause of the result,
   (b) which he did not foresee, and
   (c) which could not in the circumstances reasonably have been foreseen.'

2   Professor Smith argues that *Broome v Perkins* is a very harsh decision which if generally followed would severely limit the 'defence' of automatism: *Criminal Law Review* (1987) p 272.

The decision in *Broome v Perkins* was also criticised by the Law Commission in their commentary on the the the draft Criminal Code which in clause 33 defines automatism as a condition depriving a person of *effective* control.

Question 19

Smart held a party during which he laced Tippsy's lemonade with a drug. Tippsy began to feel strange and so decided to leave the party. He drove part of the way home but then, as he started to have hallucinations, he parked his car, got out, and started to walk the remainder of the journey. As Tippsy approached his house he saw Shifty. Tippsy was convinced that Shifty was about to mug him and so he hit him on the head with his umbrella. In fact Shifty was waiting for his girlfriend and had no intention of 'mugging' Tippsy.

Shifty had an extremely thin skull and died from the blow.

Tippsy collapsed from the effects of the drug and suffered some damage to his kidneys.

Advise Smart and Tippsy about their criminal liability.

Answer plan

This question raises issues concerning a number of offences against the person, including poisoning offences, and an offence contrary to the Road Traffic Act 1988. The legal treatment of a (drunken) mistake relevant to an issue of defence is raised with respect to Tippsy's liability. In general, when answering a question which requires analysis of the criminal liability of more than one individual for a number of different offences it is often sensible to deal with all the issues of liability of relevance to one party before turning to the next. In this case, however, the answer deals with an analysis of Tippsy's liability for Shifty's death followed by an examination of Smart's criminal liability for a number of non fatal offences against the person and finally with an examination of the issues of liability of both parties in respect of a possible driving offence under the Road Traffic Act 1988. The RTA issues were dealt with together at the end of the answer as the question of Smart's liability and Tippsy's liability are interrelated.

The principal issues are:

- the 'egg shell skull principle'
- self-defence and mistake: the rule in *Williams* (1983) and *Beckford* (1988)
- administration of a 'noxious' thing contrary to ss 23 and 24 of the OAPA 1861
- the *mens rea* requirement of s 23
- s 4(1) of the Road Traffic Act 1988: driving while unfit
- liability of one who 'procures' the commission of an offence

Answer

Tippsy - homicide

Tippsy committed the *actus reus* of unlawful homicide. That is, he killed Shifty. The fact that Shifty had a thin skull rendering him more vulnerable to fatal injury does not affect the attribution of the death to Tippsy. There is a principle in English law to the effect that 'one must take one's victim as one finds him'. This means that a defendant whose actions are a cause of death may not point to a peculiar vulnerability of the victim as the legal cause (*Martin* (1832)).

To determine whether Tippsy is guilty of either murder or manslaughter his *mens rea* at the time of striking the blow must be examined.

For murder the prosecution must prove that Tippsy either intended unlawfully to kill or to cause grievous bodily harm (*Moloney* (1985)).

If it was his aim or objective to cause death or gbh then clearly he intended death or gbh. If not, but it is proved that he was aware that either death or gbh was virtually certain to result from the blow to the head, then the jury may infer that he intended death or gbh (*Hancock & Shankland* (1986); *Nedrick* (1986)).

For constructive manslaughter the prosecution must prove that Tippsy intentionally committed an unlawful act which was dangerous and caused the death (*Goodfellow* (1986)).

In this case the battery committed against Shifty would amount to an unlawful act (see eg *Larkin* (1943)).

In addition, it would appear that the act of striking Shifty was 'dangerous'. The requirement is satisfied on proof that all sober and reasonable people would recognise that striking Shifty with the umbrella was likely to subject him to the risk of some harm (*Church* (1966); *Goodfellow* (1986)). It is not necessary to show that there was a risk of serious harm, nor is it necessary to prove that the defendant was aware of any risk of harm (*Lipman* (1970)) (1).

There is some doubt as to the meaning of the requirement that the unlawful act was performed 'intentionally'. In *Newbury* (1976) the House of Lords held that the necessary *mens rea* for constructive manslaughter was an 'intention to do the acts which constitute the crime'. This is ambiguous. It may mean that all that is required is proof that the defendant's actions were voluntary. In the case of *Jennings* (1990), however, the Court of Appeal proceeded on the basis that *mens rea* in the full sense is required, in which case the prosecution would have to prove that Tippsy intended or was reckless with respect to the application of unlawful force (*Spratt* (1991)).

It is not clear from the facts of the problem the degree of harm intended by Tippsy, but, in any case, whether he is charged with murder or manslaughter, it must be proved that he intended *unlawfully* to kill or cause gbh or apply force.

It was decided in *Williams* (1983) and in *Beckford* (1988) that a genuine belief in facts which, if true, would justify self-defence is an excuse to a crime of personal violence because the belief negatives the intent to act unlawfully. If the use of force would have been lawful had Shifty, in fact, been about to attack Tippsy then Tippsy has a 'defence' to murder or manslaughter.

Although in *O'Grady* (1987) it was held that if the mistake was made as a result of *voluntary* intoxication it cannot be relied upon, principle would require that a mistake induced by *involuntary* intoxication should be treated in exactly the same way as a sober mistake ie that the accused be judged according to the circumstances as he believed them to be.

The exclusionary rules regarding voluntary intoxication and offences of basic intent are based on the principle of prior fault. The person who has made a mistake as a result of self-induced intoxication is regarded as being to blame for his condition. The individual who, as a result of involuntary intoxication makes a legally relevant mistake, is not responsible for his condition. It is fair, therefore, that he be allowed to rely on the mistake as a defence (see *Majewski* (1977); *Hardie* (1984); *Kingston* (1993)).

Thus, whether charged with murder or manslaughter, Tippsy should be acquitted unless the prosecution prove that Tippsy did not use such force as was reasonable in the circumstances as he believed them to be (*Abraham* (1973); *Shannon* (1980); *Stripp* (1978)).

It should be noted that force may be used to ward off an attack which the defendant anticipated (*Attorney-General's Reference No 2 of 1983* (1984)).

When it comes to assessing whether the force used by Tippsy was reasonable, the jury should be reminded that a person defending himself cannot be expected to 'weigh to a nicety' the exact measure of defensive action necessary. If Tippsy did what he honestly thought was necessary, then that is 'potent evidence' that the force used was reasonable (*Palmer v The Queen* (1971)).

Smart - Aggravated assaults: ss 18 and 20 of the Offences against the Person Act 1861

Under s 20 of the Act it is an offence to 'unlawfully and maliciously ... inflict grievous bodily harm upon any other person'. Under s 18 it is an offence 'unlawfully and maliciously to ... cause grievous bodily harm to any person by any means whatsoever ... with intent to do grievous bodily harm'.

'Grievous bodily harm' means 'serious bodily harm'. It is a matter for the jury to decide whether the harm caused or inflicted is grievous (*DPP v Smith* (1961); *Saunders* (1985)).

However, even if the effects of the drug on Tippsy are regarded by the jury as amounting to grievous bodily harm, there can be no liability under s 20. This is because gbh is not 'inflicted' for the purposes of s 20 unless force is applied violently to the body of the victim. And there is no application of force where, as in this case, a drug is administered (*Hanson* (1849)).

For s 18 there is no such requirement. The section uses the expression 'cause by any means whatsoever' and thus covers a broader range of circumstances than s 20.

The *mens rea* requirement for s 18 is relatively high. The prosecution must prove that Smart intended to cause gbh. Intention in this context bears the same meaning as it does for murder and the reader is referred to the discussion above (*Purcell* (1986)).

Maliciously administering a noxious thing

By virtue of s 23 it is an offence to maliciously administer a poison or other noxious thing to any person so as to endanger the life of such person or to inflict upon him any gbh. The maximum punishment is a term of imprisonment not exceeding five years.

By virtue of s 24 it is an offence to maliciously administer a poison or other noxious thing with intent to injure, aggrieve or or annoy such person. The maximum punishment is a term of imprisonment not exceeding five years.

In *Harley* (1830) it was held that an offence may be committed where, as in this case, the noxious thing is put in to a drink taken by the victim.

The concept of a 'noxious thing' is wide enough to include anything which is even only slightly harmful or which disturbs either physiological or psychological function, bearing in mind not only the quality and nature of the substance, but also the quantity administered. In *Marcus* (1981) the Court of Appeal held that ordinary sleeping tablets administered in a normal dose without the knowledge of the victim were noxious.

For liability under s 23 the prosecution must prove, as an element of the *actus reus*, that either life was endangered or gbh was inflicted (2).

As far as the *mens rea* is concerned the authorities are not absolutely clear.

In *Cunningham* (1957) it was held that the prosecution must prove that the defendant either intended or foresaw that the 'particular kind of harm' might result and went on to take the risk of it.

In *Cato* (1976) the Court of Appeal interpreted this to mean that, although the prosecution had to prove that the defendant intentionally or recklessly administered the thing knowing at least that there was a risk that it would cause harm (ie that it was 'noxious'), it was not necessary to prove that the defendant foresaw the risk that it would endanger life or cause gbh. The crime is one of 'half *mens rea*'.

It would seem, however, that the Court of Appeal intended that this restricted form of the *mens rea* applies only if the noxious thing is applied *directly* (in *Cato* heroin was injected). And, thus, if as in this case, the noxious thing is *indirectly* administered the prosecution apparently must prove recklessness not only with respect to the administration of the noxious thing but also with respect to the risk of endangering life or causing gbh (3).

For s 24 the *mens rea* requirement is (i) intention or recklessness (*Cunningham*-type defined as above) with respect to the administration of a noxious thing and (ii) an intention to injure, aggrieve or annoy.

If Smart is charged with the offence under s 23 but the prosecution fail to prove he had the necessary *mens rea* he may be convicted of the offence under s 24 assuming, as the facts imply, that he had the *mens rea* for that offence (s 25 of the Offences Against the Person Act 1861).

Road Traffic Act 1988

By virtue of s 4(1) of the RTA 1988 a person who drives a vehicle while unfit through drink or drugs commits an offence. The maximum punishment is six months imprisonment or a £5000 fine or both. And, unless there are special reasons the offender must be disqualified from driving for at least 12 months.

By s 4(5) of the Act a person is taken to be unfit to drive if his ability to drive properly was impaired. Whether a driver's ability was impaired is a question of fact.

Medical evidence may be submitted to demonstrate that Tippsy was unfit before he parked the car and decided to walk.

Although the fact that his drink was laced does not absolve him of liability, it may amount to a special reason allowing the court, within its discretion, to refrain from imposing an order of disqualification (*Pugsley v Hunter* (1973)).

Smart, by virtue of the Accessories and Abettors Act 1861 s 8, may be convicted of 'procuring' the commission of the offence under s 4(1) of the RTA 1988.

In the *Attorney-General's Reference No 1 of 1975* the Court of Appeal held in a case involving similar facts to the present problem that 'to procure means to produce by endeavour'. This implies that it is necessary to prove that the defendant intended to bring about the principal offence.

It seems, however, that recklessness will suffice as far as the circumstances of the offence are concerned (*Carter v Richardson* (1974)). In other words, it must be proved that Smart knew that Tippsy was going to drive and was aware that he was probably unfit as a result of the administered drug (4).

Notes

1 The rule in *Watson* (1989) and *Dawson* (1985) to the effect that a peculiar vulnerability of the victim is not relevant to the issue of dangerousness unless it would have been apparent to a reasonable observer of the incident does not apply in this case. The rule applies only where the act of the accused would not otherwise be dangerous as defined.

2   Although the word 'inflict' is used in the section there clearly
    can be no requirement of a direct application of force, cf s 20
    see *Wilson* (above).
3   See Law Commission No 89 p 15.
4   In *Blakely v DPP* (1991) Lord Bingham understood 'procuring'
    to involve intention or 'the willing acceptance of a
    contemplated result'. This implies that advertent recklessness
    with respect to the central conduct of the *actus reus* will
    suffice. Such an interpretation is far removed from the
    ordinary meaning of 'to procure' and, it is submitted, ought
    not to be followed.

Question 20

Tosh is a fanatical supporter of the England football team. He did
not have a ticket for the match against Malta and so he jumped
over the turnstile. He hid in the crowd and watched the match.
England were beaten 6 - 0. Tosh was thoroughly shocked and
depressed. As he walked home he passed by the office of the
Malta Tourist Board. He jumped through the plate glass window
of the office smashing it. He claims that he was so shocked by the
football result that he felt as though he were 'in another world'
and that he did not know what he was doing.

Discuss Tosh's criminal liability.

Answer plan

This question raises issues concerning the distinction between
sane and insane automatism and, in particular, the legal
categorisation of conditions brought about by 'stress and
disappointment'. In addition, it raises a question of liability for
the offence of making off without payment contrary to s 3 of the
Theft Act 1978.

The principal issues are:

*   the distinction between sane and insane automatism; internal
    and external causes;conditions resulting from the 'ordinary
    stresses and disappointments of life'
*   is there an offence of making off without payment contrary to
    s 3 of the Theft Act 1978 where payment is expected or
    required prior to the provision of the service?

Answer

Criminal damage

Tosh may be charged with the offence of criminal damage contrary to s 1(1) of the Criminal Damage Act 1971.

By s 4 the maximum punishment for this offence is a term of imprisonment not exceeding ten years.

The *actus reus* of the offence consists of damaging or destroying property belonging to another which, clearly, Tosh has done.

As far as the *mens rea* is concerned the prosecution must prove that Tosh either intended to cause damage or was reckless with respect to damaging property.

The House of Lords decided in *Caldwell* (1982) that a person is reckless with respect to property being damaged if (1) he does an act which in fact creates an obvious risk that property would be destroyed or damaged and (2) when he does the act he either has not given any thought to the possibility of there being any such risk or has recognised that there was some risk involved and has nonetheless gone on to do it.

Tosh may contend, however, that at the relevant time he was in a state of automatism, that is, that he had lost control of his actions. If he does wish to raise the 'defence' he is required to produce medical evidence supporting the claim that his actions were not voluntary. Assuming he does so, the probative burden lies with the prosecution. In other words, the prosecution must satisfy the jury that, at the relevant time, Tosh did not lack conscious control of his actions (*Hill v Baxter* (1958); *Bratty* (1963); *Pullen* (1991)).

Automatism is not restricted to cases where there was a total loss of control or consciousness. In *R v T* (1990) a Crown Court held that the defence was available where the accused had committed robbery and assault feeling as though she were 'in a dream'. There was a sufficient loss of control even though there was evidence that she had some memory of what had occurred and that she had had sufficient control to open a penknife with which she stabbed her victim. Medical evidence revealed that she was suffering from the condition known as Post Traumatic Stress Disorder as a result of having been raped three or four days earlier (1).

However, if Tosh knew what he was doing in the sense that his conduct was within his immediate control but he acted without normal self-restraint the defence of automatism is not available to him. There is no general defence of 'irresistible impulse' (*Isitt* (1977)).

Furthermore, if Tosh puts his state of mind in issue by raising automatism then the judge may rule that he has raised the defence of insanity (*Sullivan* (1984)).

The ingredients of the defence of insanity were laid down in the *McNaghten Rules* (1843). These state that to establish a defence on the ground of insanity, it must be proved that, at the time of the committing of the act, the party accused was labouring under such a defect of reason, from disease of the mind, as not to know the nature and quality of the act he was doing; or, if he did know it, that he did not know he was doing what was wrong.

Now, by definition, a person who was in a state of automatism was *labouring under a defect of reason ... as not to know the nature and quality of his act*. The crucial issue, therefore, is whether the defect of reason resulted from a *disease of the mind*. It is this which determines whether the condition amounts to sane or insane automatism.

The significance of the distinction for the defendant is that, whereas sane automatism results in a complete acquittal, a verdict of not guilty by reason of insanity may be followed by an order committing the defendant to a hospital and may contain restrictions concerning the minimum period of time for detention. It may specify that the person may be detained until the Home Secretary orders release (s 5 of the Criminal Procedure (Insanity) Act 1964 as substituted by the Criminal Procedure (Insanity and Unfitness to Plead) Act 1991).

Tosh's condition - if it did result in a real loss of control - would be categorised as an instance of insane automatism. This is because only conditions caused be *external* factors are regarded as amounting to sane automatism and psychological states caused by the 'ordinary stress and disappointments of everyday life' are perceived to be a consequence of the predisposing *internal* factors.

The *legal* cause of Tosh's automatism, if that is what resulted, is his psychological or emotional make up and not the 'ordinary disappointment' of his team's defeat, and, thus, *if* he lacked control at the time he caused the damage, the proper verdict is not guilty by reason of insanity (2).

Making off without payment

Finally, it is proposed to consider whether Tosh committed the offence of making off without payment, contrary to s 3 of the Theft Act 1978.

The offence is committed where D dishonestly makes off after having been supplied goods or having had some 'service done'.

There is no definition of 'service' for the purposes of s 3 but, even if it were interpreted to include the provision of the stadium facilities and the football match, the service was not done until the game was over and thus, as payment is neither required nor expected at the end of a football match, Tosh did not make off, 'knowing that payment ... for a service done was required or expected from him'. Section 3 is worded such that it appears only to apply to situations where payment is expected or required *after* the service has been provided.

Notes

1   The decision of the Divisional Court in *Broome v Perkins* (1987) which implied that a total loss of control is required was criticised by the Law Commission in its commentary to the draft Criminal Code as being out of line with the authorities.

2   In T's case (above) the defendant's confused state was categorised as sane automatism. The immediate cause ie rape was not an 'ordinary' stress. The condition was regarded as having been externally caused.

Question 21

'That there exists a defence of necessity at common law ... is not in doubt. But the scope of the defence is by no means clear.' Goff LJ in *Richards v Leeming* (1986).

Answer plan

A relatively straightforward question. It requires an explanation of the limits of defences of compulsion. Terminology is important and should be clarified at the outset.

The principal issues are:

- the meaning of 'necessity'
- recognised defences of necessity
- concealed defences of necessity

Answer

In criminal law the term 'necessity' is sometimes used in a very general sense referring to all those forms of compulsion which excuse criminal acts. In the case of *Martin* (1989), for example, Simon Brown J regarded duress as a well recognised species of 'necessity'. Similarly, in *DPP for Northern Ireland v Lynch* (1975) Lord Simon of Glaisdale regarded duress as 'a particular application of the doctrine of necessity'.

Occasionally 'necessity' is used in a narrower sense to describe those instances of compulsion where the defendant was compelled through force of circumstance to commit the criminal act. Used in this way, necessity is often compared to and contrasted with duress.

As this essay is concerned with the scope of the defence of necessity it is proposed to take the broader view and to examine, firstly those situations in which compulsion has been recognised as an excuse for acts that would otherwise give rise to criminal liability and then to examine the areas of doubt.

Firstly, it is well recognised that a defendant will be excused where he has committed a crime (other than murder, attempted murder, or treason) because he was threatened by someone that, if he did not do so, he or another person would be killed or would suffer serious violence (see eg *Howe* (1987); *Gotts* (1991); *M'Growther* (1746)).

The scope of this defence - duress - is fairly clear. Although in the past there was some uncertainty as to the types of threat which would suffice for the defence of duress, it now appears to be settled that only threats of death or grievous bodily harm are sufficient (*Hudson & Taylor* (1971); *DPP v Lynch* (1975)).

In what Professor Smith has described as a 'happy accident', the Court of Appeal, in a series of recent decisions, has recognised the existence of a related defence which has been termed 'duress of circumstances' (1).

In *Willer* (1986), D had driven along a pavement to escape from a gang of youths who intended violence towards him and his passengers. The Court of Appeal held that the judge had been wrong in refusing to let the defence of compulsion go to the jury and treated the case as one of duress.

Clearly, the case did not raise the defence of duress of the traditional type discussed above. The youths did not say to Willer 'drive recklessly or else we will beat up you and your passengers.'

It was only two years later that the real nature of the defence was explained by the Court of Appeal in the case of *Conway* (1988). This case also concerned reckless driving. D had been urged by his passenger to drive off quickly to escape two youths running towards the car. D feared, apparently with good reason, that the two youths intended a fatal attack upon his passenger. The Court of Appeal held that it was bound by *Willer* to the effect that duress was available as a defence. However, it was stated that the defence was properly termed 'duress of circumstances' a species of necessity analogous to duress in the traditional sense.

The following year, in *Martin* (1989), D was charged and convicted of driving whilst disqualified. At his trial he put forward a plea of necessity asserting that his wife had threatened to commit suicide if he refused to drive their son to work. The trial judge decided that necessity was not a defence to the crime charged. On appeal, the Court of Appeal held that the defence of duress of circumstances should have been left to the jury.

The Court of Appeal held that the ingredients of this defence were equivalent to those for 'duress by threats'. That is, the defence is available only if D has acted reasonably in order to avoid a threat of death or serious injury.

In *DPP v Bell* (1992) the Divisional Court held that the defence was available where D had driven a motor vehicle with excess alcohol to escape a group of youths who were pursuing him.

The defences of duress thus far discussed are limited in scope. Firstly, they do not apply in cases of murder. Indeed, it is not clear whether, there are any circumstances in which compulsion/

necessity may provide an excuse or justification for the intentional killing of another.

Professor Smith refers to an incident reported at the inquest into the deaths resulting from the Herald of Free Enterprise disaster where one of the passengers pushed a young man off a ladder. He fell, probably, to his death. The petrified young man had been incapable of moving and had been obstructing other passengers' escape (2). The passenger was not prosecuted for murder but had he been would he have been able to take advantage of the defence of necessity?

In *Dudley & Stephens* (1884) the Ds had been adrift in a small boat with very little food and water. After more than two weeks they killed the cabin boy and fed on his body until they were rescued. They were convicted of murder. Dismissing their appeal, Lord Coleridge held that necessity was not a defence to murder.

Professor Smith argues that the behaviour of the passenger on the Herald of Free Enterprise was justified. He distinguishes that situation from the facts of *Dudley & Stephens*. Firstly, he says that whereas in *Dudley & Stephens* the appellants deliberately chose who was to be the victim, this element of choice was absent in the Herald case. Secondly the immobile passenger was endangering the lives of other passengers whereas the cabin boy was not. In Professor Smith's view the jury should be allowed to determine whether the use of deadly force was reasonable in all the circumstances (3).

Canadian criminal law recognises the defence in these circumstances. In *Perka et al v The Queen* (1984) the Supreme Court of Canada held that necessity excuses where in situations of emergency the harm inflicted by the defendant is less than the harm threatened.

A second unresolved issue relates to the *type* of threat which may give grounds for a defence of necessity. It is not clear whether there are any circumstances in which necessity will excuse where the threat is of minor injury or of damage to property.

Lord Simon in *DPP for Northern Ireland v Lynch* stated that threats of damage to property could never amount to duress. Lord Denning in *Southwark London Borough v Williams* (1971) expressed the view that hunger could never excuse theft and neither, in a civil context, could homelessness excuse trespass.

Professor Smith argues, however, that it is open to the courts to develop the defence of necessity to cover situations where the threat is a danger less serious than death or grievous harm and contends that necessity should excuse where the evil caused is less than the evil avoided. He points to s 5(2)(b) of the Criminal Damage Act 1971 which provides that a person who acts 'in order to protect property belonging to himself or another' has a lawful excuse to a charge of intentionally or recklessly damaging property belonging to another, and argues that, if threats of damage to property will excuse an offence of criminal damage there is no good reason, in principle, why similar threats should not excuse other offences, provided the harm inflicted is less than the harm threatened. He suggests, for example, that a person who drives through traffic lights to get to a blazing house intending to tackle the fire should not only be congratulated but, if prosecuted, should be excused (4).

In addition, he explains that there are a number of cases where the courts have, in effect, excused the defendant on the grounds of necessity even although there was no real threat of serious injury. One of the most celebrated is *Bourne* (1939) in which a doctor performed an abortion on a girl. The girl had become pregnant as a result of rape. He was charged with the offence of attempting to procure a miscarriage. MacNaghten J held that an attempt was not unlawful if it was done in good faith for the purpose of preserving the life of the mother and this might include protecting her from becoming a 'physical or mental wreck'. And, in *Newton & Stungo* (1958) Ashworth J directed the jury that an attempt to procure miscarriage would not be unlawful if it was done in good faith to preserve the life or *health* of the woman (5).

There are, in addition, cases of 'concealed necessity' where the courts have in effect allowed the defence of compulsion by manipulating one or other of the constituent elements of criminal liability (6).

In *Adams* (1957) Devlin J held that a doctor was entitled to take measures to relieve the pain and suffering of a patient even if those measures might shorten life. Provided the steps taken are, from a clinical perspective, reasonable, they will not be regarded as a legal cause of death.

In *Gillick v West Norfolk and Wisbech Area Health Authority* (1985), a civil case, the House of Lords held that a doctor who provides a girl under the age of 16 with contraception does not aid and abet unlawful sexual intercourse unless he intends to encourage the commission of the offence. If the doctor provides the advice and treatment because he believes it necessary for the physical mental or emotional health of the girl then he lacks the necessary intent.

This implies a very restricted meaning of intention. In general, where a person is aware that a consequence is a virtually certain result of their actions then the jury may infer that they intended that consequence (*Hancock* (1986)).

As Professor Ashworth points out, the conclusions reached by the courts in *Adams* and in *Gillick's* case could have been arrived at by openly developing the defence of necessity. This, he argues, would have been preferable to distorting orthodox principles of causation and intention (7).

Indeed, the lack of certainty concerning the scope of necessity, referred to by Goff LJ in *Richards v Leeming* above, is, in part at least, a consequence of a lack of courage on the part of the judiciary to grasp the opportunities which have arisen to clarify the scope of the defence. The limits of the defence of necessity will always remain unclear as long as the judiciary rely on expedient solutions to hard cases instead of acknowledging new grounds of justification or excuse or expanding established ones.

That the courts do have the power (and sometimes the courage) to develop and extend defences is clear from the decisions of the Court of Appeal in *Willer* (1986) and *Conway* (1989) (8). And it is apparent from cases such as *Bourne* that the failure to exercise that power is not because of entrenched illiberal attitudes but is a reflection of judicial caution with regard to defences of compulsion. This stems presumably from a fear that the defence, if defined too broadly, might result in the law losing much of its force (see the *Southwark* case above)(9). It is submitted, however, that clearly articulated principles of justification are more likely to result in consistently fair outcomes than piecemeal solutions to hard cases.

Thus, in conclusion, it is submitted that the statement made by Goff LJ is an accurate one. Although the judicial development of duress of circumstances has removed some uncertainty regarding defences of compulsion it is reasonable to suppose that the limits of the defence of necessity have not yet been discovered. If the past history of the development of the defence is anything to go by the process of discovery will be slow and gradual.

Notes

1   *Justification and Excuse in the Criminal Law* (1989) p 84.
2   Ibid p 73.
3   Ibid p 77.
4   Ibid p 89.
5   The 'defences' to abortion are now limited by s 5(2) of the Abortion Act 1967 to those conditions defined in s 1 of the Act.
6   *Smith*, ibid p 64-70.
7   *Principles of Criminal Liability* (1991) p 125.
8   The Law Commission, having initially recommended that there should be no general defence of necessity, were persuaded to include in the draft Criminal Code Bill (1989) a defence equivalent in terms to the defence of duress of circumstances (cl 43) and a general provision recognising the power of the courts to 'determine the existence, extent or application of any rule of the common law' which would provide a defence (cl 4(4)).
9   Sometimes administrative solutions are preferred. In *Dudley & Stephens*, for example, the death sentences passed on D and S were commuted to six months imprisonment. Note that if necessity is not a defence to murder it cannot be taken into account in sentencing because of the mandatory penalty.

Question 22

Alfred was kidnapped by a terrorist organisation, SMERSH. Ugly, an agent for SMERSH contacted Barry , Alfred's brother and informed him that, unless he seriously injured Douglas, an agent for a rival organisation, Alfred would be killed. Ugly told Barry not to contact the police and to show that the threat was serious he sent Barry a toe severed from Alfred's foot.

Barry knew that Douglas was very strong and would be difficult to deal with on his own, so he approached Colin and asked him to assist him in carrying out Ugly's order. Barry lied to

Colin, telling him that SMERSH also held Colin's mother captive. On the strength of this, Colin agreed to help Barry.

They waylaid Douglas on his way home one night. As a result of the attack, Douglas suffered severe injuries.

Discuss the liability of the parties.

How would your answer differ if:

(a) Douglas had died as a result of the attack
(b) Barry had himself been a member of SMERSH three years previously

Answer plan

A fairly intricate question raising a wide range of issues. There are a number of offences to discuss. Although one might not expect the prosecution to charge incitement or conspiracy in these circumstances they have been discussed for the sake of completeness. As the facts are fairly 'open' with respect to a number of issues a number of possible resolutions must be considered.

The principal issues are:

• the ingredients of the defence of duress and its application
• duress of circumstances
• duress and murder
• duress and membership of a criminal organisation
• incitement where the incitee has a defence
• conspiracy where one party may have a defence
• the ingredients of the offence of kidnapping
• threats to kill

Answer

Barry and Colin

As the facts of the problem state that Douglas suffered severe injuries it is proposed to consider Barry and Colin's liability for causing grievous bodily harm with intent, contrary to s 18 of the Offences Against the Person Act 1861. (The maximum punishment for this offence is a term of imprisonment for life.)

The facts of the problem imply the necessary intention to cause grievous bodily harm (*Belfon* (1976)) (1).

It is not clear from the facts of the problem whether both parties beat up Douglas. If they did, they may be charged as joint principals. And they will be liable as joint principals, provided the relevant *mens rea* can be proved, if the injuries suffered were a result of the aggregate effect of their individual contributions to the attack even if it could not be proved that their individual contribution would, on its own, have amounted to gbh (*Macklin & Murphy's* case (1838)).

If Colin did not attack Douglas but, say, held him while Barry struck him, he can be convicted as an accomplice (s 8 of the Accessories and Abettors Act 1861) (2).

Duress

Barry and Colin may, however, be able to take advantage of the defence of duress. The defence operates where D committed the *actus reus* of an offence with the appropriate *mens rea* but was compelled to act as he did because of threats made by another.

According to *Graham* (1982) and *Howe* (1987) the jury should consider:

(i)   whether Barry and/or Colin were, or may have been, impelled to act as they did because, as a result of what they reasonably believed Ugly had said or done, they had good cause to fear that, if they did not so act, Ugly would kill or cause gbh

and

(ii) whether a sober person of reasonable firmness would have responded to whatever Barry and/or Colin reasonably believed Ugly said or did by acting as they did.

It should be noted that those tests are expressed in objective terms (3).

In *Ortiz* (1986) the Court of Appeal assumed that threats to D's wife and child could amount to duress. And, in *Martin*, (1989) a case involving the related defence of duress of circumstances, a threat by the wife of D to commit suicide was regarded as sufficient. Thus, presumably, the threats to Barry's brother and Colin's mother will suffice.

The fact that Colin mistakenly believed that SMERSH had kidnapped his mother is not, in itself, fatal to the defence unless the jury believe that his mistake was not one that the reasonable man would have made. (Evidence concerning steps taken to check the veracity of the story, eg by checking the whereabouts of his mother, might be of some importance as far as this issue is concerned.)

Turning to the second test, the question whether a person of reasonable firmness would have given way to the threat and committed gbh is of course a question of judgment for the jury. In *Graham* it was held that the jury should take into account relevant characteristics of the defendant. By analogy with provocation these presumably include the age of the defendant and any other characteristics which might affect the gravity of the duress.

Should the prosecution contend that the defendants ought to have gone to the police instead of acting upon the threat, then the jury must consider what the likely reactions of a reasonable person would have been, taking into account the relevant characteristics of the defendants, (age etc) the circumstances in which they found themselves, and the risks that they faced (see *Hudson & Taylor* (1971)).

The burden of negativing the defence, once raised, rests on the prosecution (*Gill* (1963); *Bone* (1968)). If the prosecution fail to satisfy the jury that Barry and/or Colin are not entitled to the defence, they should be acquitted - duress is a complete defence.

Alternative facts

(a) If Douglas had died Barry and Colin could be convicted of murder.

An intention to do grievous bodily harm is sufficient *mens rea* for murder (*Moloney* (1985); *Cunningham* (1982)). And, according to the House of Lords in *Howe* (1987) duress is no defence to murder whether as a principal or an accomplice.

(b) It was held in *Sharp* (1987) and in *Shepherd* (1988) that, if a person voluntarily joins a criminal organisation which he knows is willing to use violence to achieve its ends, then he must be taken to have voluntarily exposed himself to the risk of compulsion and, on that basis, the defence of duress is denied to him. And in *Fitzpatrick* (1977) the Court of Criminal Appeal in Northern Ireland held that D could not avail himself of the defence of duress for a robbery carried out whilst a member of the IRA, despite the fact that he had tried, unsuccessfully, to leave the organisation. The court said that D could not rely on the duress to which he had voluntarily exposed himself as an excuse, *either* in respect of the crimes he committed against his will, *or* in respect of his continued, but unwilling, association with those who exercised upon him the duress.

In this case, however, Barry left the organisation three years previously. It cannot realistically be argued that he has submitted himself to illegal compulsion. He had broken his links with the organisation before the offence was contemplated and therefore the defence ought to be available to him.

Incitement

Might Barry be guilty of inciting Colin to commit the offence under s 18 of the 1861 Act?

The essence of incitement is intentionally encouraging another to commit a crime. The offence of incitement may be committed whether or not the crime incited is in fact committed (*Higgins* (1801)). But the act incited must be one, which, if performed by the person incited, would be a crime. Could Barry be convicted of inciting Colin if Colin himself escaped liability because he was compelled to act as he did?

In *Curr* (1968) it was held that a person cannot be convicted of incitement unless the person incited had the appropriate *mens rea* for the offence incited. But duress is a defence independent of the *mens rea* and it was held in *Bourne* (1952) that a person might be convicted as an *abettor*, despite the fact that the 'principal' - a victim of duress - was acquitted. It might be argued, by analogy with that case, that a person may be guilty of incitement, even though the other party would have or does have a defence to liability (4).

Barry could not be convicted of incitement, however, if his intention was that Colin was merely to assist him while he beat up Douglas. There cannot be a conviction for incitement to aid and abet the commission of an offence (*Bochin & Bodin* (1979)).

And with respect to alternative answer (a) if Douglas died Barry could not be convicted of incitement to murder. Like attempt, incitement is defined by reference to the defendant's intention (see *Whybrow* (1951)).

Duress of circumstances

Barry could not rely on duress *by threats* to the charge of incitement. He was not ordered to incite Colin.

He might, however, be entitled to avail himself of the defence known as 'duress of circumstances'. This defence is still in its infancy but it would appear that it applies in situations where objective dangers other than threats of the form 'do this or else ...' compel criminal action.

It is subject to the same limiting conditions as duress by threats (see *Graham* above). Thus, it is available if, from an objective standpoint, the accused acted reasonably and proportionately in order to avoid a threat of death or personal injury (*Martin* (1989)).

It is submitted that the defence should apply to a charge of incitement and that, if the jury conclude that Barry was compelled to recruit Colin because of a reasonably held fear of injury to his brother combined with a reasonably held fear of serious injury from Douglas if he attempted to deal with him alone, he should be acquitted.

Conspiracy

Barry and Colin may be charged with conspiracy to cause gbh contrary to s 1(1) of the Criminal Law Act 1977 (5).

The sub-section provides that a person is guilty of conspiracy if he agrees with another to pursue a course of conduct which, if carried out as intended, will necessarily amount to the commission of an offence by at least one of the parties.

The defence of duress may, of course, be available to both Barry and Colin, in which case there could be no liability for conspiracy. But if, for whatever reason, only one of them, D1, was successful in their plea of duress then the other, D2, is guilty of conspiracy, as long as the plan was that D2 would perpetrate the offence. The agreed course of conduct would, in that case, amount to the commission of an offence by D2 (6).

Note with respect to alternative facts (a) that if Douglas had died, Barry and Colin could not be convicted of conspiracy to murder. The *agreed* course of conduct did not include killing Douglas.

A person convicted of statutory conspiracy to commit an offence for which a maximum of imprisonment for life is provided (eg as in this case, the offence under s 18 of the Offences Against the Person Act 1861), shall be liable to imprisonment for life (s 3(2)(b) of the Criminal Law Act 1977).

SMERSH and Ugly

Kidnapping etc

SMERSH and Ugly may be convicted of kidnapping. The ingredients of the offence consist of (a) the taking or carrying away of one person by another (b) by force or fraud (c) without the consent of the person taken and (d) without lawful excuse.

Provided the above criteria are satisfied those responsible commit an offence punishable with a fine or imprisonment at the discretion of the court (*R v D* (1984)).

(In addition they would be guilty of the less serious offence of false imprisonment. See also the Taking of Hostages Act 1982 which provides that it is an offence punishable with imprisonment for life if anyone detains a person and threatens to injure or kill the person detained in order to compel another to do some act. For this offence proceedings may only be instituted with the approval of the Attorney-General.)

Aggravated assaults

Those responsible for cutting off Alfred's toe can be convicted of the offence under s 18 of the 1861 Act (see discussion above).

In addition Ugly can be convicted of the offence under s 16 of the Act. It is an offence to threaten another that he *or a third party* will be killed. The *mens rea* requirement for the offence (ie an intention to cause the other to fear that it would be carried out) appears to be satisfied in this case.

The maximum penalty for this offence is a term of imprisonment not exceeding ten years.

Notes

1   In this problem the facts clearly imply an intention to cause grievous bodily harm and so the lesser offence under s 20 is not discussed.

2   Section 8 of the Accessories and Abettors Act 1861 provides that 'whosoever shall aid, abet, counsel or procure the commission of any indictable offence ... shall be liable to be tried indicted and punished as a principal offender'.

   If it could not be established whether they both took part in the attack, or who had perpetrated the injuries, they could both be convicted if the prosecution could prove they both participated and that they had the relevant *mens rea*. If it was unclear whether Colin perpetrated the offence or acted as an accomplice he could be indicted for causing the injuries to Douglas (or in the second part with his murder) instead of alleging that he aided and abetted Barry to cause those injuries or kill Douglas (*Swindall* (1846)).

3   Professors Smith and Hogan have argued that the first rule in *Graham* is too strict. They suggest that it should be sufficient that the defendant's response was a reasonable one in the light of the circumstances as the defendant believed them to be *Criminal Law* (1992) 7th ed p 240.

4   Smith and Hogan *Criminal Law* (1992) 7th ed p 266.

5   Although counts of conspiracy and related substantive charges may be brought together the prosecution would be required to satisfy the judge that the count alleging conspiracy was demanded by the interests of justice (Practice Note 1977).

6   Professors Smith and Hogan cogently argue that 'commission of offence' in s 1(1) means commission as a principal in the first degree - *Criminal Law* (1992) 7th ed p 280, and see *Hollinshead* (1985).

Question 23

'Bearing in mind, the theoretical basis of the defence , on the one hand, and, on the other, the general restrictions on its availability, there is no good reason why duress is not accepted as a defence to murder.'

   Discuss.

Answer plan

This question requires a critical analysis of the rule that duress is no defence to murder by reference to the rationale of the defence and the limiting criteria regarding its availability.

The principal issues are:

- the rationale of the defence of duress; the distinction between excuses and justifications
- the objective limiting criteria
- the arguments against allowing duress as a defence to murder
- the difference between excuses and justifications

Answer

The defence of duress operates where the accused has committed the *actus reus* of an offence with the appropriate *mens rea* but was compelled to act as he did because of threats made by another. Where the defence applies, it is a complete defence.

In what circumstances is the defence available?

To amount to duress, the threat must not only be such that the accused's will is overborne, but also only threats of death or serious bodily harm will suffice (*DPP v Lynch* (1975)).

Although there is no clear authority it is probable that a threat to kill or seriously harm a third party will suffice. In *Ortiz* (1986) the Court of Appeal assumed that threats to D's wife and child could amount to duress and in the Australian case of *Hurley & Murray* (1967) the Supreme Court of Victoria held that threats to kill or seriously injure the de facto wife of D amounted to duress.

The Court of Appeal in *Graham* (1982) held that that there are two tests to consider where duress is raised.

Firstly, the jury should consider whether the accused was, or may have been, impelled to act as he did because, as a result of what he reasonably believed 'X' had said or done, he had good cause to fear that if he did not so act 'X' would kill him or cause him serious injury.

If so, the jury should consider whether the prosecution have proved that a sober person of reasonable firmness, sharing the characteristics of the accused, would not have responded to whatever he reasonably believed 'X' said or did by acting as the accused did. As with the defence of provocation, which Lord Lane in *Graham* regarded as analogous, this means that the jury should take into account the defendant's characteristics such as age and sex but not, presumably, his personal level of steadfastness or courage.

What is the rationale for the defence?

The defence when it applies, *excuses* the defendant's conduct. It does not *justify* the commission of the offence. The distinction is an important one. There is an element of approval or indeed encouragement in the case of justifications. Thus, for example, a person who uses force to prevent crime is justified in what he does. An excuse, on the other hand, whilst an acknowledgement that the defendant does not deserve to be punished, does not exist to promote the behaviour in question.

Duress excuses the conduct of the defendant because he was effectively denied a 'fair opportunity' to choose between obeying or disobeying the law (1). Lord Morris in *DPP v Lynch* (1975) explained that the law would be 'censorious and inhumane' were it not to recognise the 'powerful and natural' instinct of self-preservation. The 'victim' of duress is not truly responsible for his actions.

In addition, not only would it be unfair to punish the accused for failing to resist the threat if the person of reasonable steadfastness would have done likewise but, also, there is no rational purpose in punishing the defendant in these circumstances. If the defendant acted as a person of reasonable steadfastness would in the circumstances then it is unrealistic to expect that punishment will influence his future response to a similar threat.

The defence is not available, however, to murder (*Howe*) nor attempted murder (*Gotts* (1992)).

In *Lynch* (1975) the House of Lords, by a majority of three to two, held that duress could be a defence to a person charged as accessory to murder. Two years after *Lynch* the Judicial Committee of the Privy Council, sitting on appeal from Trinidad and Tobago, refused, in *Abbott* (1977) to extend the defence to the perpetrator of murder.

The distinction drawn between accomplices and perpetrators of murder was criticised as illogical and unsatisfactory by leading academics. Professors Smith and Hogan pointed out that it is not always true that the perpetrator is more blameworthy than an accomplice. There may be little or no moral difference between them (2). Professor Williams agreed, and suggested that, for example, there is no moral distinction between the individual who is forced to drive a bomber to a pub and the person who is forced to carry the bomb into the pub (3).

When the matter came before the House of Lords in *Howe* (1987) their Lordships held that there was no valid distinction between the perpetrator of murder and an accomplice to it and overruled the decision in *Lynch* holding that duress was not a defence to murder, irrespective of the degree of participation.

Why should the defence not be available to a person accused of murder?

Lord Hailsham regarded it as neither good law nor good morals nor, perhaps more importantly, good policy to suggest that the ordinary man of reasonable fortitude is not capable of heroism. In his Lordship's opinion, it was not 'just or humane' to withdraw the protection of the criminal law from an innocent victim and in the name of 'a concession to human frailty' to offer protection to the 'coward'.

It is submitted, with respect, that this appears to require unrealistic heroism and, in any case, as explained above, the defence is restricted to powerful threats to which a person of reasonable fortitude would also have yielded. As Lord Morris pointed out in *Lynch*, standards of heroism should not be demanded - in the 'calm of the courtroom' - when they could not have been expected of the reasonably resolute person when the threat was made.

Furthermore, the argument advanced by Lord Hailsham would apply equally to other crimes of violence, for example, wounding with intent - a crime for which his Lordship accepted the defence of duress would, in appropriate circumstances, be available.

Some of the 'policy' reasons for denying the defence in cases of murder were explained by Lord Salmon in *Abbott* (1977). Allowing the defence would invite the danger of providing a 'charter for terrorists, gang leaders and kidnappers'. D, if he were allowed to go free, might be approached again by the terrorist etc and, having gained relevant experience and expertise, commit a further murder.

The Court of Appeal in *Gotts* advanced a further rationale based on policy considerations. That is, if the defence were permitted in cases of murder, gangs of criminals might contrive situations where one of their number was subject to threats of death unless he killed. There was, therefore, a risk of the defence being abused.

Again, however, these arguments are arguments against the defence generally and do not justify the special treatment of murder and attempted murder. In addition, a lack of confidence in the ability of the jury to identify bogus claims of duress is surely no justification for refusing to allow the defence. There is no reason to suppose that the jury would be any less capable of recognising a bogus claim of duress than any other bogus defence. If it is proper to reject duress as a defence to murder simply because the wool may be pulled over the eyes of the jury then it would be proper to reject many other defences. Self-defence, for example, is equally capable of abuse.

Lord Hailsham in *Howe* advanced a further argument. He stated that where the accused faced the choice between the threat of death or serious injury and deliberately taking an innocent life, a reasonable man might reflect that one innocent life is at least as valuable as his own or that of his loved one. In such a case, if the man chooses to kill, he cannot claim that he is choosing the lesser of two evils.

There are two objections to this point.

Firstly, and most importantly, the defence of duress is not based upon the idea that the defendant chose the lesser of two evils. The error lies in regarding duress as a justification. As explained above, duress is a defence because, if D was subject to immediate threats which were so powerful that the reasonable man would have acted in a similar fashion, the law was no longer capable of deterring D and it would, therefore, be unconscionably harsh to punish him. As Lord Edmund-Davies correctly observed in *Lynch*, to allow a defence is not necessarily to approve of the defendant's conduct but simply to recognise that it is not deserving of punishment.

Secondly, to give way to the threat *might* amount to choosing the lesser of two evils, where, for example, the threat is to kill a large number of people, say the defendant's family, unless he kills one individual.

Two additional arguments were put forward to justify the refusal of the defence in cases of murder.

Lords Bridge and Griffiths said that Parliament's failure to enact the recommendation of the Law Commission made ten years previously was an indication that Parliament had rejected the proposal. However, as Professors Smith and Hogan have pointed out, the matter has not been put before Parliament for its consideration (4).

Lords Griffiths and Hailsham felt that the interests of justice would be served in hard cases, especially those involving secondary participation in murder under duress, by leaving issues relating to the culpability and punishment of those involved to administrative discretion. According to Lord Griffith it would, for example, be 'inconceivable' that a woman who was forced to act as a getaway driver for the principal offender would be prosecuted. And, in other cases, the Parole Board might be expected to weigh fairly the relative culpability of the defendant and, where appropriate, advise the Home Secretary that an early release would be justified.

However, leaving the fate of the defendant to discretionary executive action is unacceptable as the outcome is by no means certain and neither early release nor the granting of a royal pardon would remove the stigma of a criminal conviction for what most people regard as the most heinous crime.

The decisions in *Howe* and *Gotts* mean that, when charged with murder or attempted murder, it is no excuse that, in the face of threats, the accused behaved with what a jury would consider to be reasonable fortitude. The law seems to require suicidal heroism (5).

Notes

1   Professor Hart *Punishment and Responsibility* (1968) p 22.
2   *Criminal Law* (1992) 7th ed p 235.
3   *Textbook of Criminal Law* (1983) 2nd ed p 629.
4   *Criminal Law* (1992) 7th ed p 236.

5   A compromise solution would be for duress, in cases of
    murder, to operate as a partial defence, reducing liability,
    when successfully pleaded, to manslaughter. Recognising
    duress as a partial defence to murder would allow the gravity
    of the duress and its effect on the culpability of the accused to
    be taken into account at the sentencing stage rather than to
    convict of murder and leave it to executive discretion to order
    early release.
    This compromise was, however, rejected in *Howe*. Lord
    Griffiths said that it would be 'anomalous' for the defence of
    duress to operate as a form of mitigátion for the crime of
    murder alone.

Question 24

In what circumstances will a mistake relieve a defendant of
criminal liability?

Answer plan

A straightforward question requiring explanation of the legal
effect of various types of mistake.

   The principal issues are:

*   the effect of mistakes negativing *mens rea*
*   the inconsistent treatment of mistakes relevant to a defence
*   mistakes induced by voluntary intoxication
*   mistakes resulting from 'a defect of reason caused by a disease
    of the mind'
*   mistakes of law

Answer

In discussing the effect of mistake upon criminal liability it is
important to appreciate that there are different types of mistake.
The mistake may be such that it negatives the *mens rea* for the
offence charge. Alternatively the mistake may relate to an issue of
relevance to a particular defence. Thirdly, the accused may make a
mistake of law. In addition, the causes of the mistake must be
examined. Mistakes caused by the voluntary consumption of
alcohol or drugs, for example, are subject to special legal treatment.

Mistakes negativing *mens rea*

For most crimes the prosecution must prove not only that D performed the *actus reus* of the offence but that he did so with the appropriate *mens rea*. For example, a person is guilty of murder if he kills a human being, intending to kill or cause grievous bodily harm (*Moloney* (1985)). Thus, if a person, whilst hunting, shoots and kills what he believes to be a bear he cannot be convicted of murder if it transpires he has killed a human being. His mistake as to the identity of his target negatives the appropriate *mens rea*.

In *DPP V Morgan* (1976) the House of Lords held that where the law requires intention, knowledge or recklessness with respect to the *actus reus*, a mistake, *whether reasonable or not*, which negatives the *mens rea* will excuse (1).

The case concerned the offence of rape, the *mens rea* for which is an intention (or recklessness) to have sexual intercourse with a woman without her consent. The trial judge, however, had informed the jury that only a reasonable mistake as to whether the woman was consenting would excuse.

The House of Lords disapproved of the trial judge's direction and held that 'as a matter of inexorable logic' any mistake which negatives the *mens rea* requirement of the offence must result in an acquittal. Since an honest mistake clearly negatives the *mens rea*, the reasonableness or otherwise of that mistake is no more than evidence for or against the view that the mistake was made.

From the above, it should be clear that mistake is not really a 'defence'. The burden of proving *mens rea* lies with the prosecution (*Woolmington v DPP* (1935)). The accused does not even bear an evidential burden in respect of mistakes going to the *mens rea* (*DPP v Morgan* per Lord Hailsham).

In *Kimber* (1983) D was charged with indecent assault contrary to s 14(1) of the Sexual Offences Act 1956. He alleged that he thought the woman was consenting. The Court of Appeal held that the *mens rea* for indecent assault is an intention to apply unlawful personal violence. As violence would not be unlawful if the woman consented to it, D should be acquitted if he mistakenly believed she was consenting. Observing the logic of the House of Lords judgment in *Morgan*, the Court of Appeal in *Kimber* held that the burden lay with the prosecution to prove that D did not believe she was consenting.

Where negligence is the basis of liability, (see for example, s 25 of the Firearms Act 1968), only a reasonable mistake will excuse. This follows because an unreasonable mistake is a negligent mistake which, clearly, cannot excuse a crime based on negligence (and see *Tolson* (1889)).

A crime of strict liability is one for which neither *mens rea* nor negligence need be proved with respect to one or more of the elements in the *actus reus*. It follows that no mistake with reference to that element will excuse, even if it is a reasonable mistake.

For example, in *Cundy v Le Cocq* (1884) the defendant was convicted of selling intoxicating liquor to a drunken person contrary to s 13 of the Licensing Act 1872. The Divisional Court held, as a matter of construction, that the offence was one of strict liability and therefore it was unnecessary to prove that D knew the customer to be drunk. Therefore, logically, it was legally irrelevant that he mistakenly believed that the person served was sober; and this was true even though D's mistake was a reasonable one.

Thus, to understand whether a mistake will excuse it is necessary to examine the *mens rea* requirement of the particular crime with which the accused has been charged.

In *Ellis, Street & Smith* (1987) the defendants were charged with an offence contrary to s 170(2) of the Customs and Excise Management Act 1979, under which there are a number of offences of being knowingly concerned in the fraudulent evasion of a prohibition on the importation of various types of contraband, including controlled drugs and obscene material.

The D's imported drugs, mistakenly believing that they were importing prohibited obscene material. The Court of Appeal held that they had sufficient *mens rea* - knowledge that they were importing a prohibited good - despite their mistake as to the nature of the prohibited goods.

Where *Caldwell* recklessness applies, a person acts recklessly if either he has recognised that there is some risk involved in his actions or he fails to consider the possibility of a risk that would have been obvious to a reasonable man (*Caldwell* (1982)).

If D considered whether there was a risk, but mistakenly concluded there was none, it follows that he was not reckless.

This analysis was accepted, obiter, by the Court of Appeal in *Reid* (1990). In the House of Lords, however, the speech of Lord Browne-Wilkinson suggests that it is only where D, *on reasonable grounds*, dismisses the risk that he is not reckless. Lord Ackner, on the other hand, expressed the view that *Caldwell* recklessness concerned the state of mind of the defendant himself. It is submitted that this is the correct view and that the reasonableness of the defendant's mistake is relevant only to the question whether it was honestly held. This was the view taken by Lord Goff who stated that D is not reckless if he, in good faith, mistakenly concluded that there was no risk (2).

Mistake as to a defence element

There is another type of situation where the accused may have made a relevant mistake and that is where, if the facts had been as he believed them to be, he would have been entitled to a defence. For example, imagine that D intentionally wounded another because he *mistakenly* believed that the other was attacking him. Would D be excused in these circumstances?

In *Albert v Lavin* (1982) the Divisional Court held that a mistaken belief in the necessity for self-defence will only excuse if it was reasonable. The court proceeded on the basis that the *mens rea* for assault was an intent to apply force and drew a distinction between the case where D's mistake relates to a defence element and the situation where the mistake relates to an element of the *actus reus*, as, for example, in *DPP v Morgan*.

The decision in *Albert v Lavin* was disapproved in *Williams* (1984). In this case D was charged with an assault occasioning actual bodily harm to a man who he mistakenly believed was unlawfully assaulting another man.

The Court of Appeal held that the mental element necessary for an assault is the intent to apply *unlawful* force to the victim. Force used in defence of oneself or others or to prevent crime is not unlawful force (s 3 of the Criminal Law Act 1967). Therefore, as D acted to prevent what he mistakenly believed to be an unlawful attack on another he did not *intend* to apply *unlawful* force.

In these circumstances, the reasonableness or unreasonableness of D's mistake is material only to the credibility of the assertion that he made the mistake. If the mistaken belief was in fact held its unreasonableness is irrelevant.

In *Beckford* (1988) the Privy Council endorsed this approach in a case where D, having mistakenly believed that his life was in danger, acted in self-defence.

By treating unlawfulness as a definitional element of the *actus reus* to which the accused must have *mens rea* the distinction drawn in *Albert v Lavin* between cases where a mistake relates to an element in the *actus reus* and a mistake relating to a defence like self-defence disappears.

However this approach has not been adopted with respect to all defences. In *Graham* (1982) the Court of Appeal held that the defence of duress is available only where D *reasonably* believed that he was being subjected to duress. It was stated that, where D has committed the *actus reus* of the offence with the requisite *mens rea*, a mistake relating to a defence must be reasonable. The court did not treat duress as relating to the element of unlawfulness in the *actus reus*.

The approach in *Graham* was subsequently endorsed by the House of Lords in *Howe* (1987) and the Court of Appeal in *Martin* (1989) (duress of circumstances).

With provocation, however, the courts have been prepared to allow the defence where the accused mistakenly believed he was being provoked without requiring that the mistake was a reasonable one (*Letenock* (1917)).

This lack of consistency has been criticised. Professors Smith and Hogan argue that the accused should be judged on the basis of what he actually believed without a requirement of reasonableness. It is argued that the effect of the rule in *Graham* is to convict D on the basis of negligence and not on the basis of subjective fault even where the offence may be one requiring *mens rea* (3).

Mistakes and voluntary intoxication

If a relevant mistake of the defendant was induced by alcohol or drugs voluntarily consumed then the treatment of the mistake varies depending upon whether the mistake negatives the *mens rea* or relates to a defence element.

(a) Intoxicated mistakes which negative the *mens rea*

In this case, although a mistake induced by intoxication will excuse, it will only do so for crimes of 'specific intent' (eg murder) but not crimes of 'basic intent' (eg manslaughter) (*Majewski* (1977)).

(b) Intoxicated mistakes and defences

In *O'Grady* (1987) the Court of Appeal held that in relation to self-defence a mistake of fact which has been induced by voluntary intoxication cannot be relied upon by the defendant even for crimes of specific intent. The court held that the decision in *Williams* (above) was of no application where the mistake was caused by voluntary intoxication. Although obiter, this decision was regarded as binding by the Court of Appeal in *O'Connor* (1991) (4).

In the case of those defences for which only reasonable mistakes will excuse, eg duress, an intoxicated mistake cannot excuse.

There is, however, some authority for the proposition that where a statute provides that a belief shall afford a defence to a particular offence a mistake induced by intoxication may be considered. This is a matter of statutory construction. Thus, for example, in *Jaggard v Dickinson* (1981) the court held that the defendant could rely on the 'lawful excuse' defence in s 5(2) of the Criminal Damage Act 1971 even though she had made a drunken mistake. Section 5(3) of the statute provides that 'it is immaterial whether a belief is justified or not if it is honestly held'. The court was of the opinion that, as a matter of statutory construction, no exception could be made to this rule even where the mistake was caused by voluntary intoxication.

Mistakes resulting from a 'defect of reason caused by disease of the mind'

If the defendant's mistake is a result of a 'defect of reason due to disease of the mind' then if the mistake is such that the defendant either did not know the nature and quality of his act or did not know that he was doing wrong' then, in legal terms, the defendant is not guilty by reason of insanity and entitled only to a qualified acquittal (*McNaghten Rules* 1843 HL).

Mistakes of law

It is no excuse that the defendant mistakenly believed his conduct to be lawful (eg *Esop* 1836). However where a mistake as to law is such that the defendant lacks the *mens rea* for the offence charged then it is, generally an excuse (see for example, s 2(1)a of the Theft Act 1968) (5).

Notes

1 This is true of crimes requiring *Cunningham*-type recklessness. See text for an analysis of the position where *Caldwell*-type recklessness will suffice.
2 [1992] All ER 673. See the speeches of:
Lord Ackner at 681 f-g and 684 c-d;
Lord Browne Wilkinson at 695 f-g and 696 f;
Lord Goff at 690 f-h.
3 *Criminal Law* (1992) 7th ed p 240.
The correspondence between 'unreasonableness' and 'negligence' was actually recognised by Hodgson J in *Albert v Lavin* (1981) 2 All ER 628 at p 633 a, 639 e.
4 This part of the decision of the Court of Appeal in *O'Connor* was also obiter dicta.
5 Where D makes a mistake of law as a result of a defect of reason caused by a disease of the mind then D is legally insane. *Windle* (1952).

Question 25

Jeremy is a well known practical joker. One day he went into the office of a colleague, Robin, and pointed a water pistol at him. He was about to fire it in Robin's face when Robin, irritated by Jeremy's constant joking, threw an ashtray at him causing serious injuries. The water pistol was found to contain ammonia and Jeremy has admitted that he intended to injure Robin.

Discuss the criminal liability of Jeremy and Robin.

Answer plan

This question concerns the availability of self-defence where the defendant is unaware of the justifying circumstances. There is an almost total lack of authority as far as this issue is concerned and consequently, reference is made to the arguments of Professors Smith and Williams. The defence arises in the context of aggravated assaults but note that the question also raises issues of attempt and burglary.

The principal issues are:

- the *Dadson* principle
- liability for attempts
- the ingredients of liability for burglary under s 9 of the Theft Act 1968
- possession of an offensive weapon - the meaning of 'public place'

Answer

Robin

As the facts of the problem state that Jeremy has suffered 'serious injuries', it is proposed to consider Robin's liability for causing grievous bodily harm with intent, contrary to s 18 of the Offences Against the Person Act 1861, and maliciously inflicting grievous bodily harm, contrary to s 20 of the same Act.

('Grievous bodily harm' means 'serious bodily harm' (*DPP v Smith* (1961); *Saunders* (1985).)

To establish liability under s 18, the more serious offence, the prosecution would have to prove that Robin intended to cause serious harm. Recklessness will not suffice (*Belfon* (1976)).

If it was Robin's aim or purpose to cause serious harm then he intended grievous bodily harm. In addition, even if Robin did not desire to cause serious harm, the jury *may* infer that he intended it if they are satisfied that he knew serious harm was a virtually certain result of his actions (*Bryson* (1985); *Purcell* (1986)).

If intention cannot be proved then liability under s 20 should be considered.

The *mens rea* requirement for the offence under s 20 is (advertent) recklessness with respect to some harm. This means that it must be proved that Robin was aware when he threw the ashtray that Jeremy might suffer some harm, albeit not serious harm (*Savage; Parmenter* (1991)).

The maximum punishment for the offence under s 20 is a term of imprisonment not exceeding five years and, under s 18, life imprisonment.

Now, it would appear that, had he acted in response to Jeremy's intended attack upon him, Robin would have been able to avail himself of the defence of self-defence. Robin, however, was not aware of the facts which would have justified or excused his conduct, and thus it is necessary to consider whether a defence is available where the defendant is unaware of the facts which form the basis of that defence.

In the 19th century case of *Dadson* (1850) the defendant was a constable whose duty was to guard a copse from which wood had been stolen. P emerged from the copse carrying stolen wood. Dadson shouted at him to stop. P refused to do so and started to run away. Dadson shot him in the leg.

Dadson was convicted of unlawful wounding with intent to cause grievous bodily harm.

It was not unlawful to wound an escaping felon but stealing wood was not in itself a felony unless the thief had at least two previous convictions. In fact, P had numerous previous convictions for theft. Dadson, however, did not know of the circumstances making P a felon and it was held that, as a consequence, he could not take advantage of the defence.

The case has been criticised.

Professor Williams, for example, argues that Dadson did not *unlawfully* wound P. In his view, the element of unlawfulness which appears in the definition of most offences against the person is a component of the *actus reus* and therefore the lawfulness or otherwise of the defendants behaviour may be assessed without reference to the defendant's beliefs. Thus, he argues, if a person assaults or wounds or indeed kills another in unknown circumstances of justification, the assault or wounding or killing is lawful (1).

Professor Smith, on the other hand, maintains that the word 'unlawfully' in the definition of a crime means simply 'in the absence of a recognised defence' but does not imply anything about the requirements of any particular defence. It is a matter of policy whether any given defence requires knowledge of the relevant circumstances. In *Dadson* the court came to the 'perfectly reasonable conclusion', according to Professor Smith, that the particular defence in that case should not be available unless the defendant was aware of the circumstances justifying his actions (2).

Is self-defence to be subject to the *Dadson* principle?

Professor Smith clearly believes that it should be and has argued that the existing law as expressed in *Williams* (1984) and *Beckford* (1988) supports this conclusion.

Those cases dealt with the situation where D mistakenly believed that he was justified in using force and therefore they were not directly concerned with the matter currently under discussion. However, in both cases the court expressed the opinion that a person may use such defensive force as is reasonable in the circumstances *as he believes them to be*. It would appear to follow that if the defendant does not believe it is necessary to use defensive force - if he does not intend to defend himself - then the defence is not available to him.

If this analysis is correct, Robin would not be able to take advantage of self-defence.

Professor Williams disagrees with such a conclusion. He draws a distinction between 'justifications' and 'excuses'. There is an element of approval or indeed encouragement in the case of the former. For example, a person who uses force to prevent crime is justified in what he does. An 'excuse', on the other hand, whilst an acknowledgement that the defendant does not deserve to be punished, does not exist to promote the conduct in question. Duress, for example, excuses. It does not justify (3).

In Professor Williams view, as justifications are concerned with the promotion of particular consequences, they should be available even if the defendant is unaware of the justifying circumstances.

Self-defence, is a justification and thus, if Professor Williams' analysis is correct then, provided that the force used was, in the circumstances, reasonable, Robin will escape liability for the injuries inflicted on Jeremy (4).

However, even if self-defence is available in this case, Robin might be guilty of an attempt to cause grievous bodily harm contrary to s 1(1) of the Criminal Attempts Act 1981. This is because s 1(2) of the Act provides that a person can be convicted of an attempt to commit an offence even though the facts are such that the offence is impossible to commit. This is reinforced by s 1(3) which provides that the question whether the defendant has the necessary intent for an attempt is to be answered by reference to the facts as he believed them to be (see *Shivpuri* (1987)).

For attempt, the prosecution must prove an intention on the part of the accused as to the consequence defined in the *actus reus*. Thus, for an attempt to commit the offence under s 18, it must be proved that the defendant intended grievous bodily harm (*Millard & Vernon* (1987)).

(Intention in this context bears the same meaning as discussed above (*Walker & Hayles* (1990).)

If Robin intended to cause harm but not serious harm then he may be convicted of an attempt to commit the offence under s 47 of the OPA 1861.

Professor Smith argues that Professor Williams analysis leads to an absurd conclusion ie that the defendant was justified in causing gbh but may be convicted of an attempt unlawfully to cause gbh! (5)

It is submitted that Professor Smith's analysis is preferable to that of Professor Williams' and that, as it is sound in principle to limit defences justifying or excusing the use of force to those occasions where the defendant is aware of the justifying or excusing circumstances, the defence of self-defence ought not to be available to Robin.

Jeremy's liability

Jeremy may be convicted of an attempt to cause grievous bodily harm contrary to s 1(1) of the Criminal Attempts Act 1981.

The facts of the problem indicate that he had the requisite intent. Thus, the only issue is whether he has done 'an act which is more than merely preparatory 'to the commission of the offence (s 1(1)).

Provided there is sufficient evidence of acts capable in law of amounting to an attempt the question whether those acts are more than mere preparation is a question to be left to the jury (s 4(3)).

It is submitted that, in this case, there is clear evidence of an attempt. In *Jones* (1990) the defendant jumped into P's car and pointed a loaded sawn off shotgun at his face. P managed to grab hold off the gun and throw it out of the window. Although the safety catch of the gun was on, and D had to put his finger on the trigger and pull it, the Court of Appeal upheld his conviction for attempted murder.

Burglary

Jeremy may be guilty of an offence contrary to s 9(1)(a) of the Theft Act 1968.

This provides that a person is guilty of burglary if he enters a building, or part of a building, as a trespasser, intending to commit therein one of a number of offences including the infliction of grievous bodily harm (s 9(2)).

A person enters as a trespasser if he enters without the occupier's consent.

The facts of the problem do not state whether Jeremy had permission to enter Robin's office. However, even if he did, presumably the permission granted was limited to particular (lawful) purposes. As Jeremy entered the office intending to cause gbh, he entered in excess of that permission (express or implied) and thus entered as a trespasser (*Jones & Smith* (1976)), and, consequently, as he was aware of the facts that made his entry trespassory, he may be convicted of burglary (*Collins* (1973)).

He also committed burglary contrary to s 9(1)b.

This provides that a person is guilty of burglary if, having entered a building or part of a building as a trespasser, he attempts to inflict grievous bodily harm on any person therein.

For this form of burglary the prosecution have to prove, in addition to the elements of attempt (discussed above), that D entered as a trespasser (see discussion of this point above) and that at the time of the attempt he knew or at least was reckless with respect to the facts that made his entry trespassory (*Collins* above).

As he intended to cause grievous bodily harm when he entered the office, the above criteria are satisfied.

Jeremy may be convicted and sentenced to a term of imprisonment not exceeding fourteen years for each offence of burglary.

Possession of an offensive weapon

Section 1 of the Prevention of Crime Act 1953 provides that, any person who has with him in a public place any offensive weapon is guilty of an offence punishable with up to two years imprisonment.

'Offensive weapon' is defined to include things intended to cause injury and thus the water pistol would qualify (s 1(4) as amended by the Public Order Act 1986 s 40(2) and Sched 2).

The only unclear issue is whether he had the offensive weapon with him *in a public place*.

By s 1(4) this includes any highway and any premises to which the public have access.

The facts do not state whether or not the public have access to their workplace but, even if it is not a public place, the jury are entitled to draw the inference, if the evidence permits, that Jeremy brought the ammonia filled water pistol to work and that he necessarily had it with him on the public highway (*Mehmed* (1963)).

Notes

1   *The Criminal Law, The General Part* (1961) p 22.
2   *Justification and Excuse in the Criminal Law* (1989) p 31.
3   *The Criminal Law, The General Part* (1961) p 25.
4   The question whether the force used was, in the circumstances reasonable, is a matter for the judgment for the jury (*Attorney-General for Northern Ireland's Reference No 1 of 1975* (1977).
5   *Justification and Excuse in the Criminal Law* p 43.

Question 26

Bodie and Doyle, two armed plain clothes policemen, saw who they believed to be Budgie, a dangerous escaped criminal, driving through the town.

In fact, the occupant of the car was Hilton, who bore a remarkable resemblance to Budgie.

Bodie and Doyle stopped the car. As they knew Budgie was a very ruthless man, and that he was often armed, Bodie and Doyle approached the car with their guns drawn.

Hilton made to get his drivers licence from the glove compartment.

Doyle, mistakenly believing that he might be reaching for a weapon, fired at the car. He aimed to miss the driver, but hoped to frighten him.

The bullet smashed the windscreen and struck Hilton's arm.

Hilton, fearing for his life, drove the car at Bodie and Doyle. The car struck Doyle who was seriously injured. It then collided with a lamp-post. Hilton was slightly injured.

Bodie ran to the car and pulled Hilton out. Hilton, fearing attack, punched Bodie. Bodie, still believing him to be Budgie, hit Hilton over the head with his gun intending to incapacitate him. Hilton suffered serious injuries.

Discuss the liability of the parties.

Would your answer differ had Hilton been aware that he resembled Budgie and had realised, as he drove at them, that Bodie and Doyle were plain clothes policemen who had mistakenly thought him to be the dangerous criminal?

Answer plan

A fairly complex question involving issues relating to the lawful use of defensive force. A wide variety of offences under the Offences Against the Person Act 1861 provides the context for the defence. The bases of liability for these offences must be discussed before tackling the defence issues.

The principal issues are :

- sections 47, 20, 18 and 38 of the Offences Against the Person Act 1861; s 51 of the Police Act 1964
- force used in self-defence and in effecting a lawful arrest
- the effect of a mistake upon the above defences
- force used against an attack known in the circumstances to be lawful

Answer

Bodie and Doyle

It is proposed to consider the liability of Bodie and Doyle for a number of aggravated assaults and then to examine whether they are entitled to take advantage of any defences.

By virtue of s 47 of the Offences Against the Person Act 1861 it is an offence to 'assault another occasioning actual bodily harm'.

The *actus reus* of common assault consists of unlawfully causing another to apprehend the application of immediate and unlawful force. The *mens rea* requirement is intention or recklessness (subjectively defined)with respect to the elements of the *actus reus* (*Venna* (1976); *Spratt* (1991)).

In addition to the requirement of a common assault, as defined above, it must be shown for the s 47 offence that the victim suffered actual bodily harm as a result of the assault. Any harm or injury which interferes with the health or comfort of the victim is 'actual bodily harm' (*Miller* (1954)).

There is, however, no requirement that the defendant intended, or was reckless as to the, occasioning of actual bodily harm. The *mens rea* for this offence is the same as for common assault (*Savage*; *Parmenter* (1991); confirming *Roberts* (1971) and overruling *Spratt* on this point).

It is clear from the facts of the problem that Bodie and Doyle intentionally caused Hilton to apprehend the application of force. (Although they thought he was Budgie the offence requires only that *'any person'* is intentionally or recklessly put in fear etc ...)

The question whether bodily harm was occasioned by the assault is one for the jury. In *Williams* (1992) the Court of Appeal stated that where V takes evasive action to escape a threat the chain of causation between the assault and the harm is not broken if the reaction of the victim was within the range of responses which one might reasonably expect from a person in his situation. In applying the test, the jury should bear in mind that the victim, in the agony of the moment, might act without proper reflection.

With respect to the bullet injury sustained by Hilton, if the continuity of the whole skin was broken, ie if the injury amounted to a 'wound', then Doyle may be charged with the offence under s 20 of the 1861 Act (*Moriarty & Brookes* (1834)).

For this offence it must be shown that the defendant was 'malicious'; that is, that he intended or was reckless with respect to some harm resulting. In this context recklessness bears a subjective meaning and thus, the prosecution would have to prove that, although aiming to miss, Doyle foresaw the risk that some harm might result (*Savage; Parmenter* (1991)).

(If the injury does not amount to a 'wound' then Doyle may be charged with the s 47 offence (above) in respect of any actual bodily harm caused.)

However, for assault there is no liability unless the defendant intentionally caused the other to apprehend *unlawful* force and in the case of s 20 a person is only liable if he '*unlawfully* and maliciously ... wounds ... etc'.

Similarly, although Bodie intentionally caused Hilton grievous bodily harm, his liability for the offence under s 18 of the 1861 Act will depend upon whether there was an intentional use of *unlawful* force (1).

By virtue of s 24 of the Police and Criminal Evidence Act 1984, a police constable may arrest, without warrant, anyone whom he, with reasonable cause, suspects to have committed, be in the act of committing, or be about to commit an arrestable offence. And, by virtue of s 3 of the Criminal Law Act 1967, 'a person may use such force as is reasonable in the circumstances in the prevention of crime, or in effecting the lawful arrest of offenders or suspected offenders or of person unlawfully at large. Similarly, the common law defence of 'private defence' allows the use of reasonable force in defence of one's person or that of another.

Thus, if (and it is a question for the jury) the force used by the officers was reasonable, either in self-defence, or to effect the arrest of the suspect, then their use of that force was not unlawful (*Attorney-General for Northern Ireland's Reference No 1 of 1975* (1976).

In this case, the officers have made a mistake with respect to the identity of the driver of the car.

In *Williams* (1983) the Court of Appeal held that the question whether the force used was reasonable is to be answered by reference to the facts as D believed them to be, irrespective of whether any mistaken belief was reasonable (confirmed in *Beckford* (1988)).

Although there is no duty to retreat, a failure to do so is a factor that might be taken into account when assessing the reasonableness of the defendant's actions. It is generally accepted, however, that police officers attempting to effect an arrest may advance, using such defensive measures as are reasonable, as they do so (*McInnes* (1971); *Finch and Jardine* (1983)).

Furthermore, self-defence may be used, as in this case, to ward off an attack which the defendant anticipated. Again, if the defendant mistakenly believes he is in imminent danger, the mistake need not be a reasonable one (*Beckford*).

When it comes to assessing whether the force used by Bodie and Doyle was reasonable, the jury should be reminded that a person defending himself cannot be expected to 'weigh to a nicety' the exact measure of defensive action necessary. Assuming that, in the heat of the moment, Doyle and Bodie did what they honestly thought was necessary, then that is 'potent evidence' that the force used was reasonable (*Palmer v The Queen* (1971)).

In *Finch & Jardine* (1983) the trial judge agreed with the submission of the prosecution that force that is reasonable in self-defence may be excessive if done in order to effect an arrest. And thus Bodie and Doyle might be advised to rely on self-defence.

Hilton

There are a number of offences with which Hilton may be charged.

    (i)   assault with intent to resist arrest contrary to s 38 of the 1861 Act

(ii) assault on a police constable in the execution of his duty contrary to s 51 of the Police Act 1964

(iii) the offence under s 18 of the 1861 Act in respect of the 'serious injuries' caused to Doyle

(It shall be assumed that the attempted arrest was lawful ie that Bodie and Doyle had reasonable grounds for suspicion.)

As far as s 38 is concerned, it must be shown that there was an intent to resist arrest, and, as Hilton did not know they were police officers (nor, presumably, did he believe that they were individuals making a citizen's arrest!) he should, on that basis alone, be acquitted (see *Brightling* (1991)).

A police officer making a lawful arrest is acting in the execution of his duty for the purposes of s 51 (*Waterfield* (1964)). According to *Forbes & Webb* (1865) the only *mens rea* required for this offence is the same as that required for a common assault.

As explained above, however, a defendant may rely upon a mistaken belief in circumstances which, if true, would render the use of force lawful (*Gladstone Williams* above). Thus, assuming the use of force was reasonable, Hilton should, despite his mistake, be acquitted of all the offences on the grounds that he was acting in self-defence.

Alternative facts

Although Hilton knew that the men were police officers who suspected he was a dangerous criminal, he may have mistakenly believed that the arrest was unlawful. This mistake, however, being a mistake of *law*, would not excuse him (*Bentley* (1850)).

Is he entitled, however, to take advantage of self-defence even though he knows the officers are acting in circumstances that make their use of force lawful? May one use force lawfully against a *lawful* attack?

(Clearly, Hilton cannot rely on s 3 of the Criminal Law Act 1967 - force used in the prevention of crime' - if he knows that Bodie and Doyle are acting lawfully.)

In *Browne* (1973) the Court of Appeal in Northern Ireland stated, obiter, that when an officer is using lawful force in effecting the arrest of a suspect, self-defence against him is not lawful. It was said that this was the case, even if, as in the present problem, according to the true facts, the police were acting unjustifiably.

In *Fennell* (1971) on the other hand, Lord Widgery implied that where a person honestly believes that he, or another person, is in imminent danger of injury from an arresting officer he may use reasonable force in defence. This statement was obiter. It is also ambiguous - it is not clear whether it was meant to apply to the situation where the defendant, as in Hilton's case, knows the circumstances making the police behaviour lawful.

Professor Smith argues that the wide dicta in *Browne* should not be followed. He points out that, although an innocent person must submit to arrest, it is unreasonable to expect him him to do nothing in the face of a serious attack. Thus, he suggests, that an otherwise innocent person should not be convicted of an offence for taking reasonable defensive action, even although he knows that the police officer he assaults or injures has reasonable grounds for suspicion and is therefore acting lawfully (2).

It is submitted that this view is preferable to that expressed in *Browne*, and that Hilton should be acquitted if the force used was, in all the circumstances, reasonable.

Notes

1 In *Finch & Jardine* (1983) the trial judge agreed with the submission of the prosecution that force that is reasonable in self-defence may be excessive if done in order to effect an arrest. And thus Bodie and Doyle might be advised to rely on self-defence.
2 *Justification and Excuse in the Criminal Law* (1989) p 26.

Modes of Participation, Inchoate Offences and Vicarious Liability

Introduction

In this chapter will be found questions where the principal issues relate to one or more of the following topics: accessorial liability, attempts, conspiracy, incitement and vicarious liability. (These topics also arise as subsidiary matters in a number of other questions - see, in particular, questions 15, 19, 22, 41 and 42.)

Checklist

- Modes of participation. Liability as an accomplice. Section 8 of the Accessories and Abettors Act 1861, Aiding, abetting, counselling, procuring. Joint unlawful enterprises. The *mens rea* requirement of accessorial liability. In addition, the offence of aiding and abetting a suicide contrary to s 2 of the Suicide Act 1961 is covered in this chapter.
- Attempts. The Criminal Attempts Act 1981. The rationale for the punishment of attempts. The *actus reus* of attempt - an act more than merely preparatory to the commission of the full offence. The *mens rea* for attempts. Attempting the impossible.
- Conspiracy. Statutory conspiracy - the Criminal Law Act 1977. The *mens rea* for conspiracy. Exemptions from liability for conspiracy. Common law conspiracy to defraud. Conspiring to do the impossible.
- Incitement. The ingredients of liability.
- Vicarious liability - the 'delegation' principle and the principle of 'extensive construction'. Corporate liability. The liability of unincorporated associations.

Question 27

Why do we punish attempts? Should they be punished as severely as the full offence?

Answer plan

A straightforward question concerning the policy underlying the punishment of attempts.

The principal issues are:

- the distinction between 'complete' and 'incomplete' attempts
- the justification for the punishment of attempts - 'utilitarian' and 'desert' theories
- arguments for and against the equal punishment of attempts and the full offence

Answer

By virtue of s 1(1) of the Criminal Attempts Act 1981 a person is guilty of an attempt if, with intent to commit an offence triable on indictment, he does an act which is more than merely preparatory to the commission of that offence.

The maximum sentence for an attempt is generally the same as for the complete offence (s 4(5) of the 1981 Act). However, normally, a person convicted of attempt receives a lesser sentence than he would have, had he been successful. A 'discount' of fifty per cent is not uncommon.

As far as the *mens rea* requirement for an attempt is concerned the prosecution must prove that the accused intended the result defined in the *actus reus* of the full offence (s 1(1) of the Act; *Pearman* (1985); *Walker & Hayles* (1989)). It would appear, however, that if recklessness as to circumstances in the *actus reus* will suffice for the full offence, it will also be sufficient for an attempt (*Khan* (1990)).

Before discussing the justifications for the punishment of attempts, a distinction must be drawn between two types of attempt, both of which attract criminal liability.

Firstly, there are those attempts where the person has done all that he believes is necessary to achieve the intended object but fails for some reason. These may be termed 'complete attempts'.

An 'incomplete attempt', on the other hand, occurs where, although he has done an act that is more than merely preparatory, the defendant has not yet taken the step which would amount to the commission of the full offence.

Complete attempts

An example of a complete attempt is where the defendant has planted a bomb, intending to kill, but the bomb fails to explode.

In such a case, the defendant has engaged in conduct with a manifestly blameworthy intent. Clarkson and Keating point out that such a person is as much in need of rehabilitation or restraint or deterrence as if he had been successful. There is a danger that, if unpunished, he might try to commit the offence again (and, perhaps, with some success the next time) (1).

From a utilitarian standpoint, the punishment of an attempt is justified in terms of general deterrence just as it is where the full offence is committed. Others who, perhaps, would be more successful should be discouraged from attempting to commit the crime.

Should the person who is guilty of a 'complete' attempt be punished to the same extent as he would, had he been successful, or does the fact that no 'harm' was caused justify a lower penalty?

Clarkson and Keating argue that the fact that the specific harm intended has not occurred does not mean that no harm at all has been caused by the behaviour of the defendant. As Clarkson and Keating point out, the 'complete attempt' is a threat to the general security of the members of society (1).

Brady argues, however, that the social consequences of criminal activity which results in specific harm eg fear resentment and apprehension are qualitatively different from the situation where general harm results (even if by accident) and that no theory of 'equal harm' could justify the equal treatment of attempts and consummated crimes (2). He suggests that the equal treatment of the failed attempt and the completed offence may, however, be justified on the basis that a person who attempts to cause harm but fails is *equally culpable* to the person who succeeds.

According to this 'subjectivist' view, the influence of morally neutral chance elements is minimised. The failed attempt 'deserves' the same degree of punishment as the successful offender. A person who, due to incompetence, has failed in his attempt may be less of a social danger than a successful criminal, but if failure is a consequence of factors beyond his control, then he should be treated as if he had been successful (3).

Indeed, as the *mens rea* for attempts is based upon an intention to commit the *actus reus*, it is arguable, that in some cases, the degree of culpability of the attempter is greater than that of the person who commits the full offence. For example, whereas a person may be guilty of murder 'merely' on proof of an intention to cause grievous bodily harm, attempted murder requires proof of an intention to kill (*Cunningham* (1982); *Whybrow* (1951)).

Professor Williams, on the other hand, cautions that the equal treatment of attempts and consummated crimes might result in the law losing public support. He argues that, from the crudely retributive perspective adopted by much of the general public, according to which punishment should relate to the harm done, the equal treatment of attempts and consummated crimes might appear harsh (4).

There may be additional 'emotional' reasons justifying a lesser punishment for attempts. Hart, for example, argues that a greater punishment is necessary to deprive the successful offender of the 'illicit satisfactions' and gratification that follows success. And, he argues that the retributive 'instinct' of the victim is stronger and the demand for revenge is greater where harm has actually been caused than in cases where the intended victim has escaped harm (5).

Incomplete attempts

An example of an 'incomplete' attempt is where the defendant has planted a bomb and is apprehended as he is about to detonate it.

The requirement of acts that are more than 'merely preparatory' should ensure that attempts of this sort are not simply 'thought crimes'. The law insists upon some conduct because an individual who has taken steps to achieve the prohibited result has manifest a 'firm resolve' and may be regarded as more disposed to criminal activity than one who merely expresses an intention to commit a crime without acting on that intent (6). In addition, there is a greater degree of psychological commitment to completing the crime concerned as one approaches its actual commission. The person who sets out to commit an offence becomes progressively less likely to change his mind the more steps that he takes (7).

Many of the arguments in favour of punishing complete attempts apply, with equal force, to this type of attempt. In addition, the criminalisation of the incomplete attempt enables and justifies law enforcement officials to intervene before any real harm has been caused.

Does the person who makes an 'incomplete attempt' deserve equal punishment to the person who consummates the crime?

Ashworth argues that arguments in favour of relative leniency may be advanced in the case of incomplete attempts that do not apply to completed attempts. As it is conceivable that the interrupted attempter might have changed his mind and not gone through with his intentions to the point of consummation his 'moral blameworthiness' may be less than that of either the complete attempter or the person who commits the full offence. As liability for an attempt attaches before the commission of the last act there must always be some doubt that the accused had the necessary firm resolve (8). In addition, the less severe punishment of incomplete attempts may provide some incentive to stop at the last moment (9).

In conclusion, therefore, it may be said that although the punishment of attempts is justified, there are utilitarian arguments in favour of relative leniency especially in the case of 'incomplete' attempts.

Notes

1   *Textbook of Criminal Law* (1990) 2nd ed p 434.
2   *Punishing Attempts* (1980) The Monist.
3   *Ashworth Principles of Criminal Liability* (1991) p 399.
    And note s 1(2) of the Act:- a person may be guilty of attempting to commit an offence even though the facts are such that the offence is *impossible*. Does the degree of incompetence of the individual who sets out to achieve an event which fails through impossibility deserve the same punishment as the successful offender or the chance failure? Does the person who attempts to kill by poisoning, but uses a substance which he does not realise is innocuous, present the same danger as the person who administers a poisonous substance, but fails in his attempt to kill due to the intervention of a doctor? They are equally culpable.
4   *Textbook of Criminal Law* (1983) 2nd ed p 405.

5   *Punishment and Responsibility* (1968) p 1314.
6   Morris, Punishment for Thoughts, in *Essays in Legal Philosophy* ed Summers 1968.
7   Ibid p 108.
8   Ibid p 399.
9   If a person gives up after having done an act that is more than merely preparatory then although this does not affect his liability it may affect the level of punishment that the court imposes *(Taylor* (1859)).

Question 28

(a) Cliff, who was drunk, tried unsuccessfully to have sexual intercourse with Paula.
(b) Anson had sexual intercourse with Hilda. He was not sure whether she had consented. In fact, she had consented.
(c) Sam and Dave agree to sell a necklace left to them by their grandmother. They agree to advertise the necklace as being made of pure gold. In fact, as Sam knows, it is gold plated. Dave suspects that it is not pure gold but is not sure.

Consider the criminal liability of Cliff, Anson, Sam and Dave.

Answer plan

The three parts of this question involve issues of attempt and conspiracy. There is a lack of authority regarding some of the issues and it is necessary, therefore, to provide reasoned solutions, making reference, where appropriate, to the opinion of academic commentators.

The principal issues are:

- 'reckless' attempts and intoxication
- 'reckless' attempts and impossibility - s 1(3) of the Criminal Attempts Act 1981
- 'recklessness' and statutory conspiracy - s 1(2) of the Criminal Law Act 1977
- 'recklessness' and common law conspiracy to defraud

Answer

(a) Attempted rape

Cliff may be convicted of attempted rape, contrary to s 1(1) of the Criminal Attempts Act 1981.

This provides that, if with intent to commit an offence, a person does an act which is more than merely preparatory to the commission of the offence, he is guilty of attempting to commit the offence.

By s 1(1) of the Sexual Offences (Amendment) Act 1976, a man commits the *actus reus* of rape if he has unlawful sexual intercourse with a woman who at the time of the intercourse does not consent to it.

We are not told exactly what Cliff did but it shall be assumed that his acts were more than 'merely preparatory'.

Section 4(3) of the 1981 Act provides that where there is evidence that the defendant had done something that was more than 'merely preparatory' the question whether it does or does not amount to an attempt is to be left to the jury (*Jones* (1990)).

As far as the *mens rea* of attempt is concerned, the prosecution must prove that the acts of the defendant were intentional ie he was not an automaton and as far as so-called result crimes are concerned it must be proved that the defendant intended the appropriate result even if proof of recklessness will suffice for the full offence (*Pearman* (1985)).

However, where recklessness as to *circumstances* will suffice for the full offence, it would appear from the decision of the Court of Appeal in *Khan* (1990) that recklessness as to those circumstances will suffice for an attempt to commit the offence. As rape may be committed where the man is reckless with respect to the lack of the woman's consent, so may attempted rape.

The Court of Appeal explained that the attempt related to the physical activity and thus the intent that had to be proved was an intention to have sexual intercourse with a woman, the defendant either being aware that she was not consenting or being reckless with respect to that fact.

For the complete offence of rape, recklessness bears a 'subjective' meaning. The same, presumably, is true for attempted rape. That is, the prosecution must prove that the defendant was aware there was a possibility that the woman was not consenting (*Satnam & Kewal S* (1983); *Breckenridge* (1984)).

The facts of the problem state that Cliff was drunk. It is not clear, however, whether he was so drunk that he lacked the *mens rea* for an attempt. If, despite his intoxicated state, he had the *mens rea*, as defined above, then, of course, he is guilty of attempted rape.

What is the position if, due to his drunkenness, he lacked the *mens rea* for attempted rape?

The House of Lords in *DPP v Majewski* (1977) held that self-induced intoxication negativing *mens rea* is a defence to a crime requiring a 'specific intent' but not to a crime of 'basic intent'.

Although the authorities are not consistent, it is submitted that a crime of basic intent is one for which recklessness is enough to constitute the necessary *mens rea* (*DPP v Majewski* per Lords Elwyn-Jones, Edmund-Davies and Russell).

Rape is a crime of basic intent (*Woods* (1982)) What, then of attempted rape?

There are authorities which suggest that attempts to commit an offence are crimes of specific intent (see eg *Majewski*; *Mohan* (1976)). However, the Court of Appeal decided in *Khan* that the *mens rea* for attempted rape is no different from that for rape - ie recklessness with respect to the woman's consent - and thus, logically, attempted rape must be a crime of basic intent.

It would seem from the speeches of Lord Elwyn-Jones and Lord Simon in *Majewski* that the rule regarding self-induced intoxication is a rule of substantive law which relieves the prosecution from the burden of proving *mens rea* where the accused, as a result of voluntary intoxication, lacked a basic intent.

The Court of Appeal in *Woods*, however, took a different approach as far as the offence of rape is concerned. Section 1(2) of the Sexual Offences (Amendment) Act 1976 provides that where the jury are required to consider whether the defendant had the necessary *mens rea* it should have regard to the reasonableness of the defendants belief and 'any other relevant matters'. The court held that self-induced intoxication was not a legally relevant matter and should be ignored by the jury, but it should consider all the other relevant evidence before deciding whether the defendant had the necessary *mens rea*. That is, where a defendant introduces evidence that he was so intoxicated that he lacked the *mens rea* for rape the jury should be directed to consider whether he was reckless *disregarding the evidence that he was drunk.*

If this approach were followed in the present case the jury would, in effect, be directed to consider whether Cliff would have had the *mens rea* if he had not been drunk!

If convicted of attempted rape, Cliff will face a maximum penalty of life imprisonment (s 4(1) of the Criminal Attempts Act 1981).

(b) Attempted rape

Clearly, Anson cannot be convicted of rape. Although he had the *mens rea* he did not commit the *actus reus* of rape ie he did not have sexual intercourse with a woman without her consent (s 1 of the Sexual Offences (Amendment) Act 1976.

Can he be convicted of attempted rape?

He was reckless with respect to Hilda's consent and as the discussion to part (a) points out there can be liability for attempted rape where the defendant is reckless (*Khan*).

Furthermore, according to s 1(2) of the Criminal Attempts Act 1981 a person may be guilty of attempt even though the facts are such that the commission of the offence is impossible.

Thus, it is submitted that Anson may be convicted of attempted rape although he was merely reckless and the commission of rape was, in the circumstances, impossible.

Professors Smith and Hogan have argued that such a conclusion is neither desirable nor inevitable. They suggest that s 1(3) requires us to assess the defendant's liability by reference to the facts 'as he believed them to be'. The reckless defendant does not believe that the woman is not consenting; he merely believes she *might* not be consenting. Thus, they conclude that the rules relating to impossibility do not apply to the reckless defendant (1).

With respect, it is submitted that their argument is fallacious. Section 1(3) only applies where, otherwise, a person's intention would not be regarded as having amounted to an intent to commit an offence. Anson's intention in this case is to have sexual intercourse with a woman who, as far as he is concerned, may not be consenting. That is sufficient *mens rea* for rape and attempted rape and thus, there is no need to rely upon s 1(3) (2).

(c) Statutory conspiracy

The offence of statutory conspiracy is defined in s 1 of the Criminal Law Act 1977, as amended by the Criminal Attempts Act 1981 s 5.

It provides that a person is guilty of conspiracy if he agrees with any person or persons to pursue a course of conduct which, if carried out as intended, will necessarily amount to the commission of an offence by one or more of the parties to the agreement.

In this case, it is proposed to consider Sam and Dave's liability for conspiracy to obtain property by deception.

It is an offence contrary to s 15(1) of the Theft Act 1968 to dishonestly obtain property belonging to another intending to permanently deprive the other of it.

By virtue of s 15(4) a deception may be made 'deliberately or recklessly'. Thus, had they continued with the representation and induced someone to buy the necklace on the strength of it, both would have been guilty of the s 15 offence.

However, one cannot be guilty of a statutory conspiracy to commit an offence where one is merely reckless as to a relevant circumstance, even if recklessness suffices for the substantive offence.

This is the effect of s 1(2) of the 1977 Act. The sub-section provides that, even when the full offence does not require knowledge of a circumstance, conspiracy requires that the defendant and at least one other party to the agreement know that any relevant circumstance will exist when the conduct constituting the offence is to take place.

Thus, clearly, Dave cannot be convicted of conspiracy. Neither can Sam despite the fact that he *knows* that the necklace is not made of solid gold. There is no conspiracy.

Common law conspiracy to defraud

In *Scott v Metropolitan Police Commissioner* (1975) the House of Lords stated that an agreement by two or more by dishonesty to deprive a person of something which is his constitutes a conspiracy to defraud.

Dishonesty is an issue to be determined in accordance with the *Ghosh* (1982) test. That is, if what the accused did was in accordance with the ordinary standards of reasonable people or he mistakenly believed that it was, then he is not dishonest.

The law is not clear, however, as to whether a reckless deception will suffice for common law conspiracy to defraud.

In *Wai Yu-Tsang* (1991) the House of Lords, whilst stating that they did not wish to become enmeshed in a distinction between intention and recklessness said, obiter, that it is enough that the conspirators have dishonestly agreed to bring about a state of affairs which they realise will *or may* result in the victim being deceived.

Furthermore, as recklessness sufficed for attempt at common law, it would be remarkable were it not sufficient for common law conspiracy (see *Pigg* (1982)).

The maximum punishment for a common law conspiracy to defraud is a term of imprisonment not exceeding ten years (s 12 of the Criminal Justice Act 1987).

Notes

1 *Criminal Law* (1992) 7th ed p 323.
2 As Professors Smith and Hogan acknowledge elsewhere, sub-section (3) 'does nothing'. It simply spells out what is obvious from sub-sections (1) and (2) ie that liability for attempts depends upon the intent of the defendant even if founded upon some mistake or misunderstanding.

Question 29

(a) 'Criminal law regards a person as responsible for his own crimes only ... *Qui peccat per alium peccat per se* is not a maxim of criminal law.' Per Lord Diplock in *Tesco v Nattrass* (1972).

What are the exceptions to this 'rule'?

(b) Matthew gave Chump a gun and ammunition. Although nothing was said, Matthew thought that Chump intended to use it to shoot his neighbour, Funny. Matthew was aware that

Chump and Funny had had a series of disputes. In fact, Chump had bought the gun as he intended to kill himself. His girl friend, Chagrin, had left him. He returned home, put the gun to his head, and pulled the trigger. The gun jammed. He decided to hang himself. He tied a rope to the ceiling and stood on a chair. Just as he was about to jump, Funny peered through the window. He smiled to himself when he realised that Chump was about to commit suicide. Chump, who had not seen Funny, jumped from the chair. The rope broke. Funny was disappointed. Later that evening he gave Chump a leaflet, published by an organisation called JUMP (an unincorporated association), which explained tried and tested methods of suicide. He hoped that this would strengthen Chump's resolve to kill himself. Chump, however, was no longer interested in committing suicide. Chagrin had realised that Chump was the most lovable man in the world and had decided to marry him.

Discuss the liability of Matthew, Funny and JUMP.

Answer plan

The first part of this question concerns the exceptions to the general rule of English law that one person is not liable for the criminal acts of another. These exceptions define vicarious liability and the liability of corporations. The second part relates to the offence of aiding and abetting a suicide contrary to s 2 of the Suicide Act 1962. It also raises the issue of criminal liability of an unincorporated association.

The principal issues are:

(a)

• vicarious liability
• the delegation principle
• the 'extensive construction' principle
• liability of corporations

(b)

• aiding and abetting a suicide
• attempting to aid and abet (s 1(4)(b) of the Criminal Attempts Act 1981)
• criminal liability of an unincorporated association

Answer

(a) Vicarious liability

The general rule in criminal law that a person is not liable for the unauthorised acts of another is subject to two major exceptions. The first is the 'delegation principle'. This applies where a statutory offence imposes liability on a person occupying a particular position, for example, the owner or licensee of premises, who has delegated the management of the premises to another. The owner or licensee will be vicariously liable for the acts of the delegate.

For example, in *Allen v Whitehead* (1930) the licensee of a cafe employed a manager to run the premises. Despite instructions from the licensee not to allow prostitutes to enter, the manager permitted women he knew to be prostitutes to meet on the premises.

The licensee was convicted of 'knowingly suffering prostitutes' to meet on the premises, contrary to s 44 of the Metropolitan Police Act 1839. The licensee was liable on account of the manager's acts and knowledge.

Were it not for the principle allowing vicarious liability in such a case the legislation would be devoid of effect as it, (in common with many other statutory offences applying to licensed premises), creates an offence which applies only to the licensee or keeper and not to the manager. But, even in the case of offences which impose personal liability upon the manager, vicarious liability may, additionally, be imposed on the delegator (see eg *Howker v Robinson* (1972)).

The delegate need not be an employee of the licensee. The licensee will be vicariously responsible for the acts of a partner or co-licensee committed in his absence (*Linnett v MPC* (1946)).

The principles whereby delegation will be found to have taken place are not totally clear. The absence of the licensee is, however, of great importance as this is consistent with delegation of authority.

In *Vane v Yiannopoullos* (1965) a licensee was charged with an offence contrary to s 161(1) of the Licensing Act 1964 of 'knowingly selling or supplying alcohol' contrary to the conditions of his licence. A waitress, contrary to the licensee's instructions, served drinks illegally while he was in the basement of the restaurant.

The House of Lords held that the licensee was not guilty of the offence. Lord Hodson held that the principle imposing vicarious liability applies only where there is a complete delegation of authority which had not occurred in this case. Lord Reid based his decision on the fact that the licensee had not left the premises in the charge of the waitress.

In *Howker v Robinson* (1972) the Divisional Court held that whether or not there has been delegation is a question of fact. In that case a licensee who was serving in the public bar was found to have delegated authority to a barman in the lounge bar. There was complete delegation as far as that part of the premises were concerned.

In *Winson* (1969) Lord Parker pointed out that the delegation principle applies only where the statutory offence requires *mens rea*. In cases of strict liability, the second of the two exceptions to the general principle of personal liability may come into play.

This second exception is based on the construction of certain verbs used in penal statutes. For example, where the *actus reus* of an offence consists of 'selling' goods of some description then, as the legal transaction of sale is made by the owner of the goods, the employer and not the assistant commits the offence (*Coppen v Moore (No 2)* (1898)).

The principle has been held to apply to statutes imposing liability for, among other things, 'supplying goods', (Trade Descriptions Act 1968 s 1), and 'using a motor vehicle' (Motor Vehicles (Construction and Use) Regulations).

Vicarious liability based on this construction principle does not allow for the attribution of the employees *mens rea* to the employer. The principle is limited to offences of strict liability unless it can be proved that the employer has the appropriate *mens rea* (*Winson* (1969)). For this reason, there can generally be no vicarious liability for aiding and abetting an offence nor for an attempt to commit the offence (*Ferguson v Weaving* (1951); *Gardner v Akroyd* (1952)).

The justification for vicarious liability is pragmatic. The offences concerned are of a regulatory nature concerned with the sale and supply of food, drugs and alcohol. Were it not for the principle of delegation a licensee could avoid responsibility for an offence requiring *mens rea* by turning the management over to an employee. The manager himself would escape liability where the offence strikes at the licensee.

Furthermore, by imposing liability on the employer for the acts of an employee, it is hoped that the employer will be encouraged to take steps to prevent the commission of offences by his staff.

This solution, however, involves, in the case of the delegation principle, at least, interpreting statutes in clear contradiction of the words used. A licensee may be convicted of an offence of 'knowingly allowing etc' even although he neither allowed it nor was aware of it, and despite expressly instructing his employee to observe the legislation.

A fairer solution would be to impose liability on the employer for the unauthorised acts of an employee only where the employer was negligent and that, in general, ineffectual legislation should be redrafted rather than applied by imposing a fictitious interpretation on it (1).

There is one final situation in which one person may be responsible for the acts of another and that concerns the liability of corporations. A corporation is, in English law, a legal person distinct from its members or directors.

Corporate liability

In addition to those situations where a company might attract liability, vicariously, for the acts of its employees there is a more direct form of liability which may be imposed on a corporation for the unlawful acts of a controlling officer. In this situation the corporation is regarded as having committed the offence. In *Tesco Supermarkets Ltd v Nattrass* (1972) Lord Reid explained that a corporation, although a separate entity, acts through living individuals. The controlling officer is an embodiment of the company. His acts are the acts of the company and his mind is the mind of the company.

The principle of identification applies to those who constitute the 'directing mind and will' of the company eg directors and others to whom management authority has been delegated. Lords Diplock and Pearson stated that the constitution and organisation of the corporation should be considered.

The corporation is only liable for the acts of a controlling officer who acts *as* the company and not in some other capacity. But subject to that limitation, a corporation may be personally liable for any offence subject to two exceptions: firstly, offences which 'by their very nature' cannot be committed by a corporation eg rape, bigamy etc; secondly, offences which cannot be punished with a fine, eg murder, treason.

In *ICR Haulage Ltd* (1944) the company's conviction for common law conspiracy to defraud was upheld. And in *P&O European Ferries Ltd* (1991) a judge at the Central Criminal Court held that a corporation can be indicted for manslaughter.

It is sometimes argued that fining a corporation is futile or even unjust. The expense is either borne by the shareholders or employees or passed on as a cost to the consumer. On the other hand, the point has been made that the behaviour of the officers of the corporation may be shaped by the subculture of the organisation as a whole and that, in order to influence the behaviour of the group, it may be necessary to punish the corporation. In addition, the potential of bad publicity resulting from a conviction might encourage good practice. In any case, the officers of the company can, as an alternative, be convicted personally as perpetrators or, if the company is convicted as perpetrator, the officers can be convicted as accessories. Further, offences of omission - where there is a duty on the company to perform some act - may not attach to individual officers. If the company could not be convicted the law would be ineffective (2).

(b) Matthew

Section 2 of the Suicide Act 1961 provides that it is an offence to aid or abet counsel or procure the suicide of another or the attempt by another to commit suicide. The maximum punishment is a term of imprisonment not exceeding fourteen years.

The words 'aid and abet etc' have the same meaning for this offence as they do for the general law relating to the liability of accomplices to crime (*Reed* (1982)).

Has Matthew intentionally helped the attempted suicide by Chump?

Supplying a gun is clearly capable of amounting to assistance (*NCB v Gamble* (1959)), but Matthew mistakenly believed that Chump was going to murder Funny.

In *Bainbridge* (1960) the Court of Criminal Appeal held that a person may be liable as an accomplice even if he did not know the particular crime intended. It was enough that he knew the type of crime intended. This decision was referred to with approval in *Maxwell v DPP for Northern Ireland* (1979).

However, although murder and suicide both involve the intentional killing of a human being they are not similar types of crime. This is because, although aiding a suicide is an offence, neither suicide nor attempted suicide is an offence (s 1 of the Suicide Act 1961). Thus, the principle in *Bainbridge* ought not to apply in this case and, therefore, Matthew ought not to be convicted of the offence under s 2.

Nor can Matthew be convicted of *attempting* to aid and abet murder (s 1(4)(b) of the Criminal Attempts Act 1981).

Funny

Funny's deliberate failure to attempt to save Chump's life when he saw him about to hang himself does not amount to aiding and abetting his attempted suicide. It is only where a person has a duty to act, or controls the actions of another, that he can be regarded as assisting through inactivity (*Russell* (1933); *Tuck v Robson* (1970)).

However, when Funny gave Chump the JUMP leaflet, intending unsuccessfully to encourage Chump to commit suicide Funny committed an attempt contrary to s 1(1) of the Criminal Attempts Act 1981.

Section 1(4) of the 1981 Act states that a person may be convicted of attempting to commit any offence which, if it were completed, would be triable on indictment.

Section 1(4)(b) (mentioned above in relation to Matthew's liability) does not apply in this case because 'aiding etc a suicide' is the principal offence and it is triable on indictment.

In *Attorney-General v Able* (1984) it was held that, although the distribution of a book explaining methods of suicide is not in itself an offence, an offence would be committed if the distributor intended that the booklet would encourage or assist someone who was contemplating suicide and that the person was in fact assisted or encouraged by the book.

JUMP

In *Attorney-General v Able*, Woolf J stated that an unincorporated association could not be guilty of an offence. However, unincorporated associations are 'persons' as far as statutory offences passed since 1889 are concerned (Interpretation Act 1889 s 19 and Interpretation Act 1978 Sched 1).

Section 2 of the 1961 Act imposes liability on any 'person' as does s 1 of the Criminal Attempts Act 1981 and, it is submitted, therefore, that there is no reason why JUMP may not be prosecuted for the full offence where someone has, in fact, committed or tried to commit suicide, having been assisted or encouraged by the leaflet, or an attempt to commit that offence if it cannot be proved that anyone has committed or tried to commit suicide.

The prosecution would have to prove, of course, that a 'controlling official' was responsible for the distribution of the leaflet and had the appropriate *mens rea* defined and explained above (3).

Notes

1   See Card, Cross and Jones *Criminal Law* (1992) 12th ed p 558.
2   Ashworth *Principles of Criminal Law* (1991) p 85.
3   Although the question does not raise the issue, members or controlling officials of JUMP may, of course, be personally responsible either as perpetrators or accessories depending on their involvement in the production of the leaflet and their own *mens rea*.

Question 30

Charles was angry at his girlfriend Josephine as she had been unfaithful. Charles asked Andrew, who had recently been discharged from a psychiatric hospital, to rape Josephine. Andrew agreed. He lay in wait for her near her house. He saw a woman approach and, believing her to be Josephine, he attacked and raped her. In fact the woman attacked was not Josephine but her neighbour, Kathy. When arrested, Charles maintained that he did not think that rape was against the law.

Discuss the criminal liability of Andrew and Charles.

Answer plan

This question raises the defence of insanity and issues concerning conspiracy, incitement and accessorial liability where one of the parties is insane.

The principal issues are:

- the defence of insanity and the requirement that D knew the act was wrong
- liability for conspiracy where one of the parties is insane
- accessorial liability where the perpetrator is not guilty by reason of insanity
- incitement where the incitee would escape liability on the grounds of insanity

Answer

Section 1(1) of the Sexual Offences Act 1956 provides that 'it is an offence for a man to rape a woman'. The maximum punishment is life imprisonment (s 37, Sched 2).

Although ignorance of the law is no excuse (eg *Esop* (1836)), Andrew may be able to take advantage of the common law defence of insanity.

The criteria of the defence are set out in what is known as '*the McNaghten Rules*' (1843). These were accepted by the House of Lords in *Sullivan* (1984) as providing the authoritative definition of insanity in English criminal law.

The Rules provide that, to establish a defence on the ground of insanity, it must be proved that, at the time of committing the act, D was 'labouring under such a defect of reason, from disease of the mind, as not to know the nature and quality of the act he was doing or if he did know that, he did not know that what he was doing was wrong.'

A person is presumed sane unless the contrary is proved to the jury's satisfaction on 'a balance of probabilities' (*Bratty v Attorney-General for Northern Ireland* (1963)).

There is no suggestion in this case that Andrew did not know the nature and quality of his act and thus it is proposed to consider the alternative limb - ie that at the time he 'raped' Josephine he was labouring under a defect of reason caused by disease of the mind such that he did not know that what he was doing was wrong.

The facts of the problem are very sketchy with respect to Andrew's psychological state and consequently it is only possible to make a number of general observations regarding the availability of the defence in this case.

Whether Andrew suffers from a condition amounting to a 'disease of the mind' is not a medical question but a question of law (*Kemp* (1957); *Bratty*). Any disease, whether organic or functional, that results in a malfunctioning of the faculties of the mind is a disease of the mind. It matters not whether it is temporary or permanent, curable or incurable (*Kemp*). Lord Denning in *Bratty* said that any condition which has manifest itself in violence and is prone to recur is a 'disease of the mind'.

The requirement that the defendant experienced a defect of reason means that it must be proved that there was a deprivation of cognitive ability (*Clarke* (1972)).

Turning finally to the requirement that the defendant did not know that the act he was doing was wrong, we are told that Andrew maintained that he did not realise rape was a crime. Provided that he can prove this to the jury's satisfaction, it would seem on the strength of obiter statements made by the Court of Criminal Appeal in *Windle* (1952), that the requirement is satisfied even if he believed that it was *morally* wrong to commit an act of rape.

If the defence is successful, Andrew will be found not guilty by reason of insanity (s 1 Criminal Procedure (Insanity) Act 1964) and, by virtue of the Criminal Procedure (Insanity and Unfitness to Plead) Act 1991, the court may make a hospital order with or without a restriction as to discharge, a guardianship order, a supervision and treatment order, or an order of absolute discharge.

Conspiracy

It is now proposed to consider Charles' liability for conspiracy to rape contrary to s 1 of the Criminal Law Act 1977.

The central issue here is whether a person can be guilty of conspiracy where the alleged co-conspirator is insane within the *McNaghten Rules*.

Section 1(1) of the Act provides that a person is guilty of conspiracy if he agrees with another to pursue a course of conduct which, if carried out as intended, will necessarily amount to the commission of an offence by at least one of the parties.

In this case, the agreement was that Andrew should rape Josephine. If he was insane, the agreement was not one which if carried out as intended would necessarily amount to the commission of an offence by Andrew. As explained above, a successful plea of insanity results in an acquittal. And, as it appears to have been accepted that 'commission of an offence' in s 1 means commission of an offence as a principal, and not as a secondary party, the agreement was not one which, if carried out as intended, would amount to the commission of an offence by Charles (see *Hollinshead* (1985); the House of Lords did not consider it necessary to decide the matter).

There is, therefore, no conspiracy between Andrew and Charles.

Secondary liability

The Accessories and Abettors Act 1861 s 8 provides that a person who aids, abets, counsels or procures the commission of an offence is liable to be tried and punished for that offence as a principal offender.

Charles has 'counselled' ie encouraged the commission of the offence (*Calhaem* (1985)). The fact that he asked Andrew to rape Josephine and he, mistakenly, raped Kathy has no effect upon Charles' liability. It would be different if Andrew had *intentionally* deviated from the agreed plan to rape Josephine (see eg *Saunders & Archer* (1573)).

The principal issue concerns whether Charles may be convicted as an accomplice if the alleged principal offender, Andrew, is not guilty by reason of insanity.

The traditional view is that accessorial liability is derived from the liability of the principal and that, unless there was a perpetrator responsible for the offence, there is no basis for the the conviction of the accomplice (*Thornton v Mitchell* (1940)).

In *Bourne* (1952) however, the Court of Appeal held that a person may be guilty as a secondary party even although the 'principal offender' is excused. In that case the principal was excused as she had been the victim of duress. The Court of Appeal stated that, despite the duress, there had been an offence committed to which the other party could be an accessory.

The decision has been criticised by the supporters of the traditional view as being based on the conceptually improper notion of an 'excused offence' (1).

However, in *Cogan* (1976) the Court of Appeal gave some support to the decision in *Bourne* by holding, obiter, that a man may be convicted as an accessory to rape even although the 'perpetrator' is acquitted due to a lack of *mens rea*.

Although there are difficulties with the reasoning of the Court of Appeal in *Bourne* and *Cogan*, it is submitted that the outcome of both cases is correct (1).

Alternatively, there is some authority to suggest that Charles might be convicted as the principal offender acting through the innocent agency of Andrew.

The doctrine of innocent agency states that a person may be regarded as the perpetrator of an offence where he intentionally causes the *actus reus* of an offence to be committed by a person who is himself innocent because of a lack of *mens rea* or lack of capacity (*Anon* (1634)).

Indeed, the main ground for the decision in *Cogan* was that a man might be convicted of rape through an innocent agent.

This reasoning has, however, been criticised. It is generally accepted that the doctrine of innocent agency applies only where it is possible to say that the defendant performed the *actus reus* and that there is no room for its application where, as in the case of rape, the offence is specified in terms implying personal conduct on the part of the offender (see eg *Thornton v Mitchell* (1940)) (2).

Incitement

Charles may be guilty of inciting Andrew to rape (3).

The essence of the offence is intentionally encouraging another to commit a crime. Incitement may be committed whether or not the offence incited is in fact committed (*Higgins* (1801)).

In *Curr* (1968) it was held that a person could not be convicted of incitement to commit an offence unless it could be proved that the persons 'incited' had acted with the requisite *mens rea* for that offence. The case has been criticised. It is argued that it should not be necessary to prove that the individual incited acted with *mens rea*. It should suffice that the accused believed the incitee would so act.

In this problem Andrew, despite his defence of insanity, did apparently rape with *mens rea* and thus the narrow rule in *Curr* presents no obstacle to the conviction of Charles.

However, there is some authority for the view that a person may not be convicted of incitement where the person incited is in law incapable of committing that offence.

In *Whitehouse* (1977), for example, it was held that it was not an offence for a man to incite a girl of fifteen to permit incestuous intercourse as the girl committed no offence by permitting it.

Whitehouse is, however, distinguishable from the present problem on the basis that *Whitehouse* would not have committed the *actus reus* of an offence had she allowed sexual intercourse to take place, whereas Andrew committed the *actus reus* of rape and did so with *mens rea*. There is no good reason why Andrew's lack of personal capacity due to insanity should exempt Charles from liability - whether or not Charles was aware of Andrew's disability. It is submitted, therefore, that Charles is guilty of incitement.

Incitement is a common law offence, the penalty for which depends upon whether the offence incited is triable summarily or on indictment. Incitement to rape, an indictable offence, is itself an offence triable on indictment and Charles if found guilty may receive a sentence of imprisonment at the discretion of the court (*Morris* (1951)).

Notes

1 The principle in the cases would appear to be that if D1 induces D2 to commit the *actus reus* of an offence he may be convicted as an accomplice provided he has the necessary intent even though D2 is not guilty of an offence because, for example, he lacks *mens rea*.

2   See *Williams Textbook of Criminal Law* (1983) 2nd ed p 371.
3   Where the substantive offence has been committed it is not
     normal practice to charge with incitement - the inciter will be
     charged as an accomplice. However, the fact that the crime was
     committed is no defence to a charge of incitement and so Charles
     liability for incitement is discussed in answer to this question.

Question 31

Dougal had been persistently making advances to Susan, Simon's
girlfriend. He had phoned her up on a number of occasions to
invite her out. When Simon found out, he was extremely angry,
and decided to visit Dougal. He asked his brother, Peter, to
accompany him. They decided they would 'warn' Dougal that, if
he did not agree to stop making advances toward Susan, they
would smash up his flat and they agreed that, if Dougal 'gave
them lip', they would give him a severe beating.

They visited Dougal and told him that they wanted him to
stop making advances towards Susan, and that, if he did not agree
to stop visiting her, they would smash up his flat. Dougal
responded by saying that he would not be intimidated and had no
intention of changing his behaviour. He said that Susan preferred
him to Simon and that she would be happier if Simon left her
alone. At this, Simon flew into a rage and pulled out a cosh with
which he struck Dougal on the head, intending to kill him.

Dougal fell to the floor, unconscious.

He was taken to hospital where it was discovered he had
suffered severe brain damage. In addition, a medical examination
revealed that he had a duodenal ulcer. The doctors decided that
because of the brain damage they could not operate on the ulcer.
Two weeks later, while still unconscious, Dougal died when the
ulcer burst.

Discuss the criminal liability of Simon and Peter.

Answer plan

A fairly complicated question raising a variety of issues
including those relating to the effect of provocation upon the
liability of an accessory.

The principal issues are:

- principles of causation where injuries prevent medical treatment
- the defence of provocation: cumulative provocation
- accessorial liability: the effect upon secondary liability where the principal is provoked to kill
- conspiracy and conditional intention

Answer

Simon

It is proposed to consider Simon's liability for murder.

Firstly, the prosecution must prove that Simon's actions were the legal cause of Dougal's death.

In *McKechnie* (1992), a case involving similar facts to the present problem, the Court of Appeal held that it must be proved to the jury's satisfaction that the injuries significantly contributed to Dougal's death and, where they prevent life saving medical treatment, injuries will be regarded as a significant contribution if the prosecution prove that the decision not to operate was reasonable and competent. It is unnecessary for the prosecution to prove that the decision not to operate was the only decision that a competent doctor might arrive at, nor that it was necessarily the correct one.

It shall be assumed, for the purposes of further analysis, that Simon's actions were the legal cause of death. The next issue to consider is his *mens rea* at the time he administered the blow.

The facts state that he intended to kill and thus, he will be convicted of murder unless he can take advantage of the defence of provocation (*Moloney* (1985)).

Provocation is a common law defence modified by s 3 of the Homicide Act 1957, which, if successfully pleaded, reduces liability from murder to manslaughter.

The defence is available where:

(i) at the time of the fatal attack the defendant had, as a result of provocation, lost his self-control and

(ii) the reasonable man in the same circumstances would have done as the defendant did.

(i) With reference to the first of these issues it should be noted that, although the defendant bears an evidential burden in support of his plea that he was provoked to lose his self-control, the burden of disproving provocation lies with the Crown (*Woolmington v DPP* (1935); *McPherson* (1957)).

The jury must be satisfied that Simon suffered a 'sudden and temporary' loss of self-control as a result of provocation (*Duffy* (1949); *Thornton* (1992); *Ahluwalia* (1992)).

In deciding this issue the jury may consider not only things said and done immediately prior to the fatal act (ie in this case Dougal's statement that he would continue his advances towards Simon's girlfriend) but also the effects of earlier provocative behaviour which may have contributed to the loss of control (Dougal's prior advances) (*Pearson* (1992)).

In other words, the jury are entitled to conclude that the comments of Dougal immediately prior to the attack upon him amounted to 'the straw that broke the camel's back' (*Pearson* (1992)). It would appear that Simon acted spontaneously to the perceived insults and this is good evidence that he suddenly lost his self-control.

Although there is no authority on the point it is submitted that if, as a result of provocation, the defendant loses his self-control and kills with malice aforethought, the fact that the defendant had a conditional intention to cause gbh prior to the provocation should be no bar to the defence. The prior intention may not have been carried out. As long as the jury are satisfied that the the murderous attack was a result of a sudden and temporary loss of self-control the causal nexus between the provocation and the fatal attack is satisfied. And, in *Johnson* (1989) the Court of Appeal held that a person may avail himself of the defence of provocation even if the attack was a foreseeable result of his own conduct.

(ii) The second issue mentioned above is exclusively for the jury's determination.

According to the House of Lords in *Camplin* (1978) the reasonable man is a person having the power of self-control to be expected of a person of the same age and sex as the accused and sharing such characteristics of the accused as they think would affect the gravity of the provocation to him.

In this case Simon does not appear to possess any distinguishing characteristics and thus the jury should be invited to consider simply whether the reasonable man in the circumstances would have acted as Simon did in response to Dougal's statements.

If the two tests are satisfied then Simon will be convicted of manslaughter.

Simon may also be convicted of the offence, contrary to s 2 of the Criminal Damage Act 1971, of making threats to destroy or damage property belonging to another. It is unnecessary to prove that Dougal actually feared Simon would damage his property. It is sufficient that Simon *intended* Dougal to fear that his property would be damaged.

The maximum penalty for this offence is ten years imprisonment.

Peter

It is proposed to consider Peter's liability as a secondary party.

Section 8 of the Accessories and Abettors Act 1861, as amended by the Criminal Law Act 1977, provides that a person who aids, abets, counsels or procures the commission of an indictable offence is liable to be tried, indicted and punished as a principal offender.

Now, where, as in this case, two persons embark on a joint unlawful purpose each of the parties is equally liable for the consequences of such acts of the others as are done in the pursuance of that joint enterprise and also for the unforeseen consequences of the others acts done in pursuance of that agreement (*Anderson & Morris* (1966)). And, if an accomplice lends himself to a criminal enterprise on the understanding that grievous bodily harm should, if necessary, be inflicted, he will be guilty of murder if the principal kills in accordance with this agreement (*Hyde, Sussex & Collins* (1990)).

However, in general, if one of the parties goes beyond the scope of the agreement then the other is not liable for that act or its consequences (*Davies v DPP* (1954)). Thus if the parties to a joint enterprise agree to cause gbh to V but one of them, D1, unforeseeably departs from the agreed plan and intentionally kills V then, although D1 will be guilty of murder the other party or parties will not because the act causing death went beyond the agreed plan.

And thus, if the full facts reveal that Simon had *unforeseeably exceeded* the tacit agreement to give Dougal 'a severe beating' Peter would incur no liability for the homicide.

However, in a series of cases it has been held that a secondary party may be guilty of an offence which he foresaw the principal might commit, as a possible incident of the common unlawful enterprise, even if the principal did not at the outset contemplate the commission of the offence (*Chang Wing-Siu* (1985); *Hyde* (1990); *Hui-Chi-Ming* (1992); *Roberts* (1992)). And thus, if Peter had known that Simon carried a cosh and had foreseen that there was a possibility that he might use it with an intention to kill then he may be convicted of murder.

How might a finding that Simon was provoked affect Peter's liability?

In *McKechnie* (1992) the principal killed having been provoked whilst carrying out the joint enterprise. The Court of Appeal held that the provocation was incompatible with a joint enterprise to cause gbh to the deceased. Thus, although the principal was guilty of voluntary manslaughter, the other parties were neither guilty of homicide nor of causing gbh with intent.

Professor Smith suggests that this implies that the loss of self-control brings a prior joint enterprise to an end. But, it is submitted that it is not at all clear that this is what the court intended (1).

The Court of Appeal appeared to take the view that the jury's finding that the principal was provoked ruled out the possibility that there was, *prior to the provocation*, a joint enterprise to cause gbh to which the other defendants could have been parties.

The court added that, if the principal had been labouring under long term provocation and the parties had agreed upon a joint enterprise to do gbh prior to the final act of provocation then, although the principal would be convicted of manslaughter, the other parties would have been guilty of murder.

In *Pearson* (1992) the Court of Appeal, distinguishing *McKechnie*, held that the existence of provocation does not necessarily terminate a joint enterprise. In that case both parties were provoked prior to undertaking the joint enterprise and, although it is not clear from the judgment, it is submitted that the possible basis of the distinction is that in *Pearson* there was evidence that both parties intended to kill or cause gbh from the outset.

Moreover, it was said in *Hui Chi-Ming* that if, for example, two men embark upon a robbery and the principal is carrying a weapon which he intends to use merely to frighten if they met resistance but, through panic at the scene changes his mind and uses it with malice aforethought, then the secondary party will be guilty of murder if he foresaw *at the outset* that the principal might use the weapon with malice aforethought.

It is submitted, therefore, that the question of secondary liability where the principal is provoked to kill depends primarily upon whether the secondary party had the appropriate *mens rea* prior to the provocation. If Peter was aware that Simon carried a cosh and foresaw that he might be provoked to use the weapon with an intent to kill, then he may be convicted of murder although Simon might be guilty only of manslaughter (2).

In addition, Peter may be convicted as an accomplice to the offence, perpetrated by Simon, of making threats contrary to s 2 of the Criminal Damage Act 1971.

Conspiracy

Did Peter and Simon conspire to cause grievous bodily harm?

It is submitted that they did not.

By virtue of s 1(1) of the Criminal Law Act 1977 a person is guilty of statutory conspiracy if he agrees with another that a course of conduct shall be pursued which, if the agreement is carried out as intended, will necessarily amount to the commission of an offence by at least one of the parties to the agreement. As their agreed course of conduct would not *necessarily* involve the infliction of grievous bodily harm they did not conspire to commit that offence (*Reed* 1982 CA) (3).

They are however, guilty of a conspiracy to make threats to damage property belonging to another (4).

Notes

1   See Professor Smith's commentary to *McKechnie* in the *Criminal Law Review* (1992) p 197.
2   Cf Williams, *Textbook of Criminal Law* (1983) 2nd ed p 429.

3   If, however, Professor Smith's analysis of *McKechnie* is correct
    and provocation of one party terminates the joint enterprise
    then Peter will incur no liability for the homicide nor for gbh
    with intent even if he foresaw the possibility that Simon might
    use the weapon with malice aforethought.
4   Where the defendants have been charged with a substantive
    offence, the prosecution may not also proceed with a charge of
    conspiracy to commit it, unless they can satisfy the judge that
    the interests of justice demand it (Practice Note 1977).

Question 32

Husband and wife, Bonnie and Clyde, decided to manufacture a
controlled drug. Clyde approached Darrow and, explaining to
him the plan, asked him to supply certain chemicals. Although he
knew that it was not possible to manufacture the drug from the
process that Bonnie and Clyde intended, Darrow agreed to
supply the chemicals.

Darrow supplied the chemicals.

Clyde went to his basement laboratory with the chemicals
to begin the process of manufacture. He was arrested a short
time later.

Discuss the criminal liability of the parties.

Answer plan

This question raises issues relating to liability for conspiracy and
attempt and liability as an accessory.

The principal issues are:
- whether D can be convicted of conspiracy when he does not
  believe that the agreed plan will succeed
- agreements between spouses
- when is an act 'more than merely preparatory' for the
  purposes of an attempt
- attempting the impossible
- the *mens rea* of an accomplice

Answer

Conspiracy

The offence of statutory conspiracy is defined in s 1 of the Criminal Law Act 1977, as amended by the Criminal Attempts Act 1981 s 5.

It provides that a person is guilty of conspiracy if he agrees with any other person or persons to pursue a course of conduct which, if carried out as intended, will necessarily amount to the commission of an offence by one or more of the parties to the agreement or would do so but for the existence of facts which render the commission of the offence impossible.

The production of a controlled drug is an offence under s 4 of the Misuse of Drugs Act 1971.

By virtue of s 2(2)a of the Criminal Law Act a person cannot be convicted of conspiracy if the only other person with whom he/she agrees is his/her spouse. Bonnie, however, may be convicted of conspiring with Darrow, even although her agreement is with Clyde, if she knows of the existence of Darrow and that he has agreed to play some part in the unlawful object. It is neither necessary that she knows the identity of Darrow nor that she has met him (*Chrastny* (1992)).

The fact that it is impossible to produce the drug does not preclude liability for conspiracy. The decision of the House of Lords in *Nock* (1978) has been overruled by s 1(1)b of the Act.

Further, there is some authority for the proposition that Darrow may be convicted of conspiracy, even although he *knew* that the production of the drug was impossible. In *Anderson* (1986) the defendant had agreed with others to take part in a plan to effect the escape of one of them from prison by providing cutting equipment etc. He said that he did not intend that the escape plan be put into effect and that he believed that it had no chance of succeeding. It was held that this was not a defence. Lord Bridge, in a speech with which the other Lords concurred, said that it was not necessary to prove that the defendant intended that the substantive offence be committed.

The case has been criticised. It has been argued that as s 1(2) requires proof of knowledge of the circumstances necessary for the commission of the offence it would seem to follow that intention as to the consequences is a requirement of liability (1).

Anderson was not cited in *Edwards* (1991) where it was held that the defendant could not be convicted of conspiracy to supply amphetamine, as agreed, unless it could be proved that he intended to carry out the agreement. And in *McPhillips* (1989) the defendant was not guilty of conspiracy to murder as he intended to issue a warning to the authorities explaining the location of a bomb that he and others had planted.

If *Anderson* is not followed then, as a result of the rule regarding spouses, there is no conspiracy to produce a controlled drug in this case (2).

Attempt

Section 1(1) of the Criminal Attempts Act 1981 provides that a person is guilty of attempting to commit an offence if, with intent to commit the offence, he does an act which is more than merely preparatory to the commission of the offence.

The facts of the problem do not state whether Clyde had commenced the process of manufacture but, if he had performed an act which was more than merely preparatory to the process of production he may be convicted of attempt.

The question whether an act is more than merely preparatory is a question of fact for the jury and not a question of law for the judge (s 4(3)). If, however, there is insufficient evidence or it would be unsafe to leave the evidence to the jury the judge can rule that there was no attempt and direct a verdict of not guilty. It is only where he is satisfied that, in law, there is sufficient evidence for a jury to consider that there may have been an attempt that he is obliged to leave the issue to the jury. So, although one cannot say whether as a matter of law something is an attempt, the law may tell us what is *not* an attempt (*Campbell* (1991)).

The Court of Appeal in *Gullefer* (1990) and *Jones* (1990) held that the proper course is to look to the natural meaning of the statutory words.

In *Gullefer* Lord Lane identified 'two lines of authority' prior to the statute. One line endorsed what came to be known as the 'last act' or 'Rubicon' principle where only acts immediately connected with the offence could be attempts. The alternative test was that an attempt was an act done with intent which formed part of a series of acts which, if not interrupted, would amount to the commission of the offence (see eg *Eagleton* (1855); *DPP v Stonehouse*; *Robinson* (1915)).

Lord Lane in *Gullefer* rejected both tests: the former was too restrictive and the latter too vague and possibly too broad. He preferred a 'midway course'. In his Lordship's opinion an attempt begins when it can be said that the defendant embarks on the crime proper. This approach was endorsed in *Jones* and *Campbell*.

Thus only an inconclusive answer can be offered to the question whether Clyde may be convicted of an attempt: ie it is a question of fact for the jury assuming that there is sufficient evidence that he was engaged in the commission of the offence of production of a controlled drug.

It should be noted that even although production of the drug was impossible Clyde can be convicted of an attempt to produce it (Criminal Attempts Act ss 1(2) and (3)).

Accessorial liability

A person can be convicted as an accomplice to an attempt and, therefore, Bonnie will be liable for any help or encouragement which she has given to Clyde, assuming that he has done an act which is 'more than merely preparatory' (*Dunnington* (1984); s 8 of the Accessories and Abettors Act 1861).

With respect to Darrow, the position is less clear.

In *NCB v Gamble* (1959) it was held that, although it must be proved that the accused intended to do acts of assistance, it is not necessary to prove that he intended that the crime be committed. Devlin J said that indifference to the result of the crime does not negative aiding. Similarly in *Lynch v DPP for Northern Ireland* (1975) it was said that, if the accused knowingly assisted another in a criminal purpose, he aided the offence.

These decisions suggest that Darrow is guilty of aiding the commission of the attempt. He knowingly assisted Clyde in his (futile) attempt to produce a controlled drug. But, in this case, Darrow was not merely indifferent as to whether a controlled drug was produced. He knew that it was impossible to produce.

Clyde, if he did acts that were more than merely preparatory, is guilty of an attempt because he intended to commit the full offence. The 'real mischief' is, of course, the production of a controlled drug, but there is no difference, in terms of *culpability*, between an unsuccessful attempt at production and a successful one. The attempt is punished to discourage the offender from trying again, perhaps with more success, in the future.

Darrow, on the other hand, did not intend the full offence to be committed, because he knew that, in the circumstances, it could not be. In terms of Clyde's real purpose, Darrow gave no assistance, nor did he intend to and, therefore, it is submitted that he ought not to be treated as an accomplice.

Being concerned in the management of premises etc

Section 8 of the Misuse of Drugs Act 1971 provides that an occupier of premises commits an offence if he knowingly permits or suffers the production or attempted production of a controlled drug in contravention of s 4(1) of the same Act.

The facts do not reveal Bonnie and Clyde's domestic arrangements but, assuming they are co-occupiers, Bonnie may be convicted of the offence (*Ashdown, Howard & Others* (1974)).

The maximum punishment for this offence is dependent on the drug which Clyde attempted to produce. If a Class A or Class B drug, the maximum is a term of imprisonment not exceeding 14 years; if a Class C drug, the maximum is five years.

Notes

1 The Law Commission disapproved of *Anderson*; draft Criminal Code, Law Com No 177, (1989). And see Smith and Hogan *Criminal Law* (1992) 7th ed 273 where it is suggested that *Anderson* should have been convicted as an accomplice to the conspiracy. That would not be possible in this case as by virtue of s 2(2)(a), there is no conspiracy between Bonnie and Clyde, see Card, Cross and Jones *Criminal Law* (1992) 12th ed p 487.

2 Quaere: Is there a conspiracy to *attempt* to produce a controlled drug in this case?

Section 1 applies to agreements to commit *any* offence. The parties have agreed a course of conduct which, if carried out in accordance with their intentions, will necessarily amount to the commission of an attempt by Clyde.

Clyde and Bonnie intend the attempt to produce the drug, but does Darrow?

As Darrow presumably does not care whether or not Clyde carries out the planned process, he lacks the necessary intent and thus it is submitted there is no conspiracy.

Offences against Property

Introduction

Questions of liability for property offences occupy a considerable part of most examinations in criminal law. There are many such offences and they often overlap. Consequently, most of the questions in this chapter require discussion of the defendant's potential liability for a number of offences. Occasionally, questions raise issues concerning offences against the person.

The principal statute in this area is the Theft Act 1968. In addition, this chapter deals with offences created by the Theft Act 1978 and with the major offences of criminal damage under the Criminal Damage Act 1971.

Checklist

Theft and related offences

One of the major current issues concerns the meaning of an appropriation for the purposes of theft, and, in particular, the question whether there can be an appropriation of property belonging to another if the owner consents to what D does in relation to the property. It is important that you have a good understanding of the decision of the House of Lords in *Gomez* (1992).

Also, as most of the offences in this section are offences of 'dishonesty' it is most important that you are well acquainted with the decision of the Court of Appeal in *Ghosh* (1982) and later cases concerning the meaning of that concept.

Issues of civil law - eg rules concerning the passing of ownership - are of relevance to the law of theft and the basic principles should be learnt.

The following offences are dealt with:
* Theft: s 1 of the Theft Act 1968
* Robbery: s 8 Assault with intent to rob; s 8(2)
* Blackmail: s 21
* Burglary: s 9(1)
* Offences involving deception: ss 15 and 16 of the 1968 Act and ss 1 and 2 of the Theft Act 1978

- Making off without payment: s 3 of the 1978 Act
- Handling stolen goods: s 22. The meaning of 'stolen goods' in s 24
- Aggravated burglary: s 10
- Taking a conveyance: s 12
- Abstracting of electricity: s 13
- False accounting: s 17
- Going equipped: s 25

Offences of damage. The Criminal Damage Act 1971

- 'Simple' damage: s 1(1). The defences of 'lawful excuse' in s 5(2)
- 'Dangerous' damage: s 1(2)
- Arson: s 1(3)
- Threats to destroy or damage property: s 2

Note

A number of the problem questions raise issues dealt with in earlier chapters.

Question 33

'In the context of s 3(1) (of the Theft Act 1968) the concept of appropriation involves not an act expressly or impliedly authorised by the owner but an act by way of adverse interference with or usurpation of those rights.'

Per Lord Roskill in *Morris, Anderton v Burnside* (1984).

Discuss.

Answer plan

This quotation should be familiar to all students of the law relating to theft. It concerns the question whether D can be guilty of theft where, despite a secret lawful intention to steal, D acts with the consent or authority of the owner.

Principal issues involved are:

- the meaning of 'appropriation'
- appropriation and consent/authority

Answer

The case from which the above quotation is taken concerned two appeals against conviction of theft. The appellants had taken goods from the shelf in a self-service supermarket removed the price labels and replaced them with a lower price label. One was arrested after he had passed through the checkout paying the lower price; the other was arrested prior to passing through the checkout.

The Court of Appeal held that the appellants appropriated the goods when they removed them from the shelf and before the labels were switched. This approach would mean that D might be convicted of theft if he had a secret dishonest intention in relation to the goods even though, to all outward appearances, what he was doing was lawful.

The House of Lords preferred a narrower construction. They agreed that both defendants were guilty of theft but held that the appropriation was complete only when they switched the price labels. The combination of switching the labels and removing the items from the shelf amounted to an usurpation or assumption of a right of the owner. It was unnecessary to show an assumption of all the rights.

Lord Roskill in the passage quoted above explained that there is no usurpation if what is done is expressly or impliedly authorised by the owner.

(As the defendants clearly acted without consent or authority the quotation above was obiter. All their Lordships, however, concurred in the statement.)

The House reviewed some of the previous decisions concerning the issue of appropriation and consent.

In *Eddy v Niman* (1981) the Divisional Court held that there was no theft when D, intending to steal goods, took them from a shelf and put them in the basket provided. He had not *done* anything inconsistent with the right s of the shopowner. He was doing what was authorised, ie taking items from the shelf and putting them in the receptacle provided.

On the other hand, in *MacPherson* (1973) D concealed two bottles of whisky in her own shopping bag and not in the wire basket provided. The Court of Appeal held that there had been an appropriation.

Both these cases were expressly approved by Lord Roskill in *Morris*. In his opinion, the appropriation in *MacPherson* was effected by the combination of the acts of removing the goods from the shelf and of concealing them in the shopping bag.

Similarly the authority of the cases of *Meech* (1974) and *Skipp* (1975) was confirmed their Lordships.

In *Meech*, D agreed to cash a cheque for P who had obtained it by fraud. After paying the cheque into his account, but before the funds had cleared, D discovered how P had come by the cheque and decided to keep the proceeds. To provide an explanation of his failure to return the money D staged a robbery with two friends. The issue before the court was to identify when the appropriation took place. Lord Roskill in the Court of Appeal held that the money was not 'misappropriated' (sic) until the fake robbery was acted out. Prior to that point D was acting as authorised.

In *Skipp*, D pretending to be a genuine haulage contractor collected as instructed three loads from different pick-up points in London. He was supposed to deliver them to Leicester but, as he had intended from the outset, he absconded with them. It was held that despite the fact that he had a dishonest intention when he received each of the individual loads he did not appropriate any of them until he deviated from the authorised route. Until then he had not done anything inconsistent with the rights of the owner.

The approach taken in *Morris* has been followed in a number of subsequent cases.

In *Fritschy* (1985) D had been instructed to convey some Krugerrands from England to Switzerland. He took them to Switzerland but then sold them and kept the proceeds. The issue before the court was whether he had committed theft in England. It was held that even although he had formed the intention to steal the Krugerrands when he collected them he could not be regarded as having stolen them in England as there was no evidence of any act by *Fritschy* within the jurisdiction that was not authorised by the owner of the coins.

In *McHugh & Tringham* (1989) the Court of Appeal considered whether a sole director and shareholder of a company who had diverted company assets to private use could be convicted of stealing those assets.

In English law a company is a separate legal person (*Salmon v Salmon* (1897)). The assets are owned by the company and not the shareholders or directors. And, although the company can act only through the directors/shareholders, decisions made by the board are decisions of the company. Thus, as the *company* had authorised the distribution of its assets, there could be no appropriation and consequently no theft.

However, twelve years before the case of *Morris* the House of Lords in *Lawrence* (1972) had taken a quite different approach to the issue of appropriation and consent. The facts of the case were that a Mr Occhi, an Italian student who spoke little English, arrived at Victoria station, London. He approached the appellant, who was a taxi driver, and showed him a piece of paper on which an address on Ladbroke Grove was written. The appellant made out that it was very far and that the fare would be very expensive. Mr Occhi got into the taxi and tendered £1. Lawrence took that but said that it was not enough and took a further £6 from Occhi's open wallet. He then drove Mr Occhi to Ladbroke Grove. The correct fare for the journey was approximately ten shillings. Lawrence appealed against his conviction for theft 'of the approximate sum of £6' arguing that he had not stolen the money as he had taken it with the consent of the Italian. The House of Lords, dismissing his appeal, held that s 1(1) of the Theft Act was not to be construed as though it contained the words 'without the consent of the owner'.

Viscount Dilhorne whilst accepting that *belief* in the owners consent was relevant to the issue of dishonesty appeared to reject the proposition that consent was relevant to the question whether there had been an appropriation.

Despite the apparent contradiction between the decisions the House of Lords in *Morris* did not overrule *Lawrence*. Lord Roskill thought that the taxi driver had appropriated the student's money. Perhaps he believed that the Italian student had only authorised Lawrence to remove the *correct* fare from his wallet (1).

Lawrence was followed in *Philippou* (1989), in which the Court of Appeal held (on facts almost identical to those in *McHugh* (above)) that the sole directors of a company could be convicted of theft of the company assets. The court held that Lord Roskill could not have meant that the authority of the owner precludes an appropriation 'because that would be contrary to what was said in *Lawrence*'!

(*McHugh* was not discussed in *Philippou*.)

And in *Dobson v General Accident, Fire and Life Assurance Corp plc* the Civil Division of the Court of Appeal held that there could be an appropriation even though the owner had consented to what was done. A rogue had 'purchased' a watch and ring from Dobson using a worthless cheque. Clearly the rogue had obtained the jewellery by deception. The issue for the court was whether for the purposes of a claim on his insurance policy he had lost the items through 'theft'.

The Court of Appeal held that the jewellery had been stolen.

Parker LJ in an attempted reconciliation of the case law held that whereas 'mere consent' to the dealing with property would not preclude an appropriation 'express authority' would and that, as Dobson had merely consented to the taking of the jewellery by the rogue, the latter had appropriated it.

Bingham LJ took a different approach. His attempted reconciliation of the cases was based on the interpretation of *Lawrence* mentioned above viz that the Italian student had not consented to the taxi driver taking more than the correct fare. Whilst accepting that this was not a 'wholly satisfactory reconciliation' of the cases he held that Dobson had not 'in truth' consented to the rogue becoming owner of the jewellery without giving a valid cheque.

The Court of Appeal in *Gomez* rejected both of these approaches. It regarded itself as bound by the principle expressed in the quotation from *Morris*. The facts of the case were that D1, an assistant manager of a shop, obtained authority from his manager, P to supply goods to D2 in return for two cheques. D1 knew that the cheques were worthless. The court held that as P had authorised the transaction there was no appropriation of the goods and the defendants convictions for theft were quashed.

Lord Lane concluded that *if* there was a conflict between *Lawrence* and *Morris*, then *Morris* should be followed.

The House of Lords, by a majority, allowed the prosecutors appeal. Lord Keith stated that, although the actual decision in *Morris* was correct, it was unnecessary and erroneous to suggest that an authorised act could never amount to an appropriation and, whilst he rejected the distinction drawn in *Dobson* between consent and authority, he agreed with Lord Parker that *Morris* could not be regarded as having overruled the 'clear decision' in *Lawrence*. In Lord Keith's opinion, *Lawrence* unequivocally decided that an act may be an appropriation notwithstanding that it is done with the owners consent.

Lord Keith referred to the cases of *Skipp* and *Fritschy* (discussed above), and concluded that, as they were both inconsistent with *Lawrence*, they were wrongly decided.

Lord Browne-Wilkinson concurred in the speech of Lord Keith. He thought that the view expressed by Lord Roskill in *Morris* was erroneous as it introduced the mental state of the owner and the accused into the concept of an appropriation. In his opinion, the word 'appropriation' related purely to the act done by the accused. He expressed his support for *Lawrence* and, of the company cases, *McHugh* and *Philippou*, he agreed with the decision in the latter.

Lord Lowry delivered a lengthy dissenting speech. He reviewed the Eighth Report of the *Criminal Law Revision Committee, Theft and Related Offences* (1966) and concluded that the intention of the framers of the Act was to define appropriation by reference to its 'ordinary and natural' meaning which, in Lord Lowry's opinion, is a unilateral act done without the consent or authority of the owner. The decision in *Lawrence* was, he suggested, a misconceived refutation of a misconceived argument; the contention that the words 'without the consent of the owner' should be implied into s 1(1) obscured the fact that the word 'appropriates' itself connotes a lack of consent by the owner.

In Lord Lowry's view, although the House in *Morris* did not overrule *Lawrence*, the decisions in those cases were irreconcilable. He preferred the opinion of Lord Roskill, and referring to the *Practice Statement on Judicial Precedent* (1966) recommended that the House should depart from the decision in *Lawrence*.

With respect to the company cases, Lord Lowry agreed that *Philippou*s was correctly decided, but the Court of Appeal could have reached its conclusion without relying on *Lawrence*. He referred to *Attorney-General's Reference No 2 of 1982* (1984) which explained that the principle of 'identification' by which a corporation attracts criminal liability for the acts of its officers does not apply where the officers themselves are charged with an offence *against* the company (2).

The remaining Lords, Lord Jauncey and Lord Slynn, agreed with the speech of Lord Keith.

Thus, in conclusion, the view expressed by Lord Roskill in *Morris* no longer represents the law. The endorsement of the decision in *Lawrence* by the House of Lords in *Gomez* means that a person who takes another's property dishonestly and with an intention to permanently deprive him of it may be convicted of theft without the necessity of proof of any objective element of unlawfulness. As Professor Williams has pointed out this approach 'comes close to dispensing altogether with the *actus reus* that is supposed to be required for a consummated crime ... It makes theft depend not on anything wrongful that the defendant does but merely on what goes on in his mind' (1).

Notes

1   *Textbook of Criminal Law* (1983) 2nd ed p 761.
2   Lord Browne-Wilkinson, whilst agreeing with this point, nonetheless believed that *Morris* was incorrect.

Question 34

One day, Colin visited his friend Tom. When Colin was about to leave, he discovered that he had lost his car keys. After searching for them, he decided to take the train home, where he kept a spare set. When Colin had gone, Tom found the keys and decided to use Colin's car to go into town.

He drove into town and had lunch at the Snappers restaurant. He left the restaurant without paying for the meal.

He noticed an advertisement in a local newspaper from a minicab firm seeking 'drivers with clean cars and clean licences for immediate work with good pay'. He decided to apply and went to the minicab office. Harry, the owner of the firm, asked Tom whether the car was his. Tom responded that it was. Harry told Tom that he could start work immediately. He was supplied with radio equipment for which he was required to pay a daily fee.

His first customer was Franco, a foreign visitor, who had arrived at the airport and wished to be conveyed to the town centre. Prior to getting in his car, Franco asked Tom what the fare would be. Tom said that it would be 'reasonable'. When they arrived at Franco's destination Tom asked for £180. Franco expressed surprise that it was so expensive. Tom said that it was the proper fare and said that he would call the police if Franco did not pay. Franco felt that he was being overcharged but, having just arrived in England, he was not sufficiently confident to protest. He reluctantly paid the fare.

Tom worked for a few hours and then decided that he had had enough. He returned the radio equipment to the minicab firm.

He drove home.

Colin returned the following morning to collect his car. Tom did not tell him that he had used it.

Discuss Tom's criminal liability.

Answer plan

A fairly typical question about a rogue who commits a variety of property offences - mainly those involving deception. There is a lot to discuss in this type of question but none of the points are very complex. The answer has been structured according to the various 'scenes'. This is a useful technique when the question consists of a number of distinct incidents each involving questions of liability for a number of offences.

The principal issues are:

- the meaning of 'dishonesty'
- obtaining by deception - the requirement of a causal link
- the relationship between theft and obtaining property by deception
- the meaning and application of 'menaces' for the purposes of blackmail

Answer

Colin's car: taking a conveyance; theft of the petrol; abstraction of electricity - s 13

Section 12 of the Theft Act 1968 provides that it is an offence for a person who, without having the consent of the owner or other lawful authority, takes any conveyance for his own or anothers use.

According to s 12(6) there is no offence if the accused believed, at the time of the taking, that the owner would have consented had he known of the circumstances (1).

The test is subjective and, of course, is a matter for the jury. The facts, however, imply that Tom did not believe he would have had Colin's consent and, as there is no requirement of an 'intention to permanently deprive' for s 12, it would appear that he is guilty of the offence.

Tom may also be convicted of theft of the petrol contrary to s 1 of the Theft Act 1968.

And, perhaps, he may be convicted of the 'dishonest use without authority of electricity (in the car battery)' contrary to s 13 of the Act. The jury may conclude, however, that, as there was no intention to cause loss, the use was not 'dishonest' (see the discussion of dishonesty below) (2).

Lunch at Snappers: theft; obtaining by deception; making off without payment

It would appear that Tom has committed the offence of 'making off without payment' contrary to s 3 of the Theft Act 1978.

There is no suggestion in the facts of the problem that he was not dishonest but, as the facts are 'open'- there is no indication given as to the reason he left without paying - it should be pointed that, if there is evidence that Tom was not dishonest, the jury should be directed with respect to the meaning of the term and informed that the issue is a matter of fact for their determination (*Feely* (1973); *McVey* (1988); *Price* (1989)).

For the purposes of s 3, a person who makes off is not dishonest if the jury consider that what he did was not dishonest according to the ordinary standards of reasonable people or he mistakenly believed that it was not dishonest according to those standards (*Ghosh* (1982)).

Whether Tom may be convicted of obtaining the meal by deception contrary to s 15 of the Act will depend upon whether the prosecution can prove, to the jury's satisfaction, that he intended not to pay for the meal prior to consuming it.

When a person orders a meal in a restaurant, he impliedly represents that he intends to pay for it on presentation of the bill and this representation continues until the bill is paid. Thus, if the customer does not intend to pay, he practises a deception (*DPP v Ray* (1974); s 15(4) of the 1968 Act).

If Tom formed the intention not to pay for the meal only after having consumed it then he is not guilty of the s 15 offence. By that stage he would, as a matter of civil law, have obtained ownership and possession of the meal, and thus, it would not be possible to say that he had obtained the meal *by* deception. Put simply, the deception must precede the obtaining (*Collis-Smith* (1971)).

The fact that he left the restaurant without paying is evidence, but no more than that, of his prior dishonest intention when he ordered the meal (see *Aston* (1970)).

The same issues are relevant to the question whether he can be convicted of 'obtaining services (ie the production of the meal etc) by deception contrary to s 1 of the Theft Act 1978.

Can Tom be convicted of stealing the meal contrary to s 1 of the Theft Act 1968?

If Tom formed the dishonest intention not to pay *after* having consumed the meal then, it is submitted, he could not be convicted of stealing it. The ownership in the meal having previously transferred to him, he could not be said to have 'dishonestly appropriated property belonging to another' on leaving the restaurant.

If, however, he had intended not to pay from the outset, he is, according to the decision of the House of Lords in *Gomez* (1992), guilty of theft as well as obtaining by deception.

Prior to *Gomez*, although the law was not clear, the balance of authority supported the conclusion that if a cheat deceived another into selling him something, the victim intending to transfer his entire proprietary interest, the cheat got a voidable title and could not be convicted of theft because he was the owner of the thing (3). In addition, Lord Roskill in *Morris* (1984) stated that a person did not appropriate property unless he did something in relation to it that he was not authorised to do. If the owner had consented to the act there could be no appropriation, even where that consent was obtained by fraud.

On the other hand, the House of Lords in *Lawrence* (1971) appeared to hold that a person could be convicted of theft where they obtained a voidable title to property by a deception practised on the original owner, and in *McHugh* (1977) it was assumed that a person who formed the dishonest intention not to pay for petrol prior to filling his car committed theft when he made off.

Lord Lane, delivering the judgment of the Court of Appeal in *Gomez* (1992), stated that *Morris* decided that it was not theft when D, by deception, induced the owner P to transfer his entire proprietary interest. He added that, if there was a conflict between *Lawrence* and *Morris*, then *Morris* should be followed.

The House of Lords disagreed. Lord Keith stated that, although the actual decision in *Morris* was correct, it was unnecessary and erroneous to suggest that an authorised act could never amount to an appropriation. His Lordship quoted, with approval, a passage from the judgment of Lord Parker in *Dobson v General Accident Fire and Life Assurance Corp plc* (1990) in which it was stated that appropriation can occur even if the owner consents and that it is no defence to say that the property passed under a voidable contract. It was felt to be wrong to introduce into this branch of criminal law questions whether particular contracts are voidable on the ground of fraud.

This decision means that practically all cases of obtaining by deception also amount to theft. Thus, if Colin, prior to consuming the meal, intended not to pay for it, he is guilty of both offences.

By s 7 of the Act, as substituted by s 26 of the Criminal Justice Act 1991, the maximum penalty is seven years imprisonment. The maximum punishment for obtaining property by deception is a term of imprisonment not exceeding ten years (s 15(1)); and for obtaining services by deception a maximum of five years and/or a fine (s 4 of the 1978 Act) (4).

The minicab office: obtaining a pecuniary advantage by deception contrary to s 16

Section 16(2) defines the situations in which a pecuniary advantage is to be regarded as having been obtained and these include where the defendant is given the opportunity to earn remuneration in an office or employment.

In *Callender* (1992) the Court of Appeal held that the term 'office or employment' in s 16 was not restricted to contracts of service and would cover situations, such as the present one, where the defendant enters into a contract for services.

It must be shown of course that the opportunity was obtained *by deception*.

Tom falsely stated that the car was his. There is, however, no deception if the prosecution fail to prove that Harry believed that representation or at least accepted it as the truth (*Hensler* (1870)).

Nor would it amount to an obtaining *by* deception if Harry was indifferent as to the truth or falsity of the representation (see eg *Clow* (1978)).

The offence under s 16 carries a maximum punishment of imprisonment not exceeding five years (s 16(1)).

Minicab office: obtaining services by deception

The supply of the radio equipment to provide information regarding customers is a 'service' for the purposes of s 1 of the 1978 Act. Assuming the deception was operative, and assuming the obtaining was dishonest, Colin is guilty of this offence.

(Tom's obtaining of the services may be regarded as dishonest despite the fact that he has paid for them as required (see *Potger* (1970)). The issue of dishonesty would be a matter for the jury directed in accordance with *Ghosh* (above).)

Franco: obtaining property by deception, theft

It would appear from the facts of the problem that, although initially deceived as to Tom's intention to charge a 'reasonable' fare (see *Silverman* (1987)), Franco was aware at the end of the trip that the fare requested was not the proper fare for the journey.

Thus, it might be argued, on behalf of Tom, that Franco did not part with the money as a result of a deception practised on him. At the crucial moment, ie when he parted with the property Franco was not deceived. As explained above, there is no deception unless the victim believes that the representation made is false.

However, in *Miller* (1992), a case involving similar facts to the present problem, the Court of Appeal held that the question whether there has been a deception is one for the jury to decide and, in coming to their decision, they are entitled to look to the whole course of events to determine whether the deception induced the victim to hand over the money.

The decision may be criticised - the Court of Appeal overlooked the requirement of a causal link between the obtaining and the deception. It is submitted that the accused should be convicted of an *attempt* to obtain property by deception, contrary to s 1(1) of the Criminal Attempts Act 1981 if, at some stage in the proceedings, he knew that the victim was deceived. (If the Court of Appeal's decision in *Khan* (1990) is taken to be of general application then recklessness as to the victim being deceived would suffice.)

Blackmail

Colin might also be guilty of blackmail, contrary to s 21 of the 1968 Act. The *actus reus* of the offence is the making of a 'demand with menaces'.

Even though he may have expressed himself in the *form* of a request, Colin made a 'demand' for the £180 (*Studer* (1915))It is the present of a threat or a menace - explicit or implicit - which determines whether a statement, couched in terms of request is, in reality, a demand.

In this case, Colin's statement that he would call the police, probably amounted to a menace (5).

The general rule is that a menace is a threat of any action which might influence the ordinary person of normal stability to accede unwillingly to the demand (*Clear* (1968)). Where, however, the threats would not have affected the ordinary person they may still be regarded as amounting to menaces if the person addressed was influenced and D was aware of the likely effect of his threats upon V (*Garwood* (1987)). Thus, even though a person of 'normal stability' might not ordinarily be expected to give way to a threat to call the police, Colin was aware of the special circumstances that rendered Franco - a newly arrived foreigner -more vulnerable to the threat.

There is no suggestion in the facts of the problem that Colin believed his demand with menaces to be 'warranted'. It is inconceivable that he believed he had reasonable grounds for making the demand and that the menaces were a proper means of reinforcing the demand (s 21(1)a and b) and, as he made the demand with the necessary view to gain (s 34(2)a)he is guilty of blackmail.

The punishment is a term of imprisonment not exceeding fourteen years (s 21(3)).

In addition, as Franco appears to have parted with the money as a result of intimidation then Colin may be convicted of theft. It is submitted that the effect of the intimidation was to negative any apparent intention to transfer ownership in the money. As Colin presumably was aware, of this he 'dishonestly appropriated property belonging to another etc' when he received the money (see *Lovell* (1881)) (6).

Notes

1 The defendant has an evidential burden in relation to a s 12(6) defence but the prosecution have the burden of proving that he did not have the specified belief (*Gannon* (1987); *MacPherson* (1973)).

2 As Professor Smith points out it would be strange were a person to be convicted of the offence under s 13 in these circumstances as they would have committed a more serious offence in switching the car on than driving it. The offence under s 13 carries a maximum punishment of five years whereas taking a conveyance contrary to s 12 is punishable with a term of imprisonment not exceeding six months and/or a fine of £2000 (s 12(2) T A 1968; s 37 Criminal Justice Act 1988).

3 See, for example: J C Smith, *Law of Theft* (1989) 6th ed p 22; *Corcoran v Whent* (1977).

4 In *Gomez* counsel for the respondent pointed to the difference in maximum terms for the offences under ss 1 and 15 in support of his submission that the offence of obtaining by deception was not submerged in theft. However, bearing in mind that the offence under s 15 carries the greater maximum penalty, this argument is not particularly strong.

5 It has been held that 'menaces' is an ordinary word. The jury generally require no direction with respect to it (*Lawrence* (1971)).
6 If *Miller* is correctly decided and Colin obtained the money by deception then he may be convicted of theft without reference to 'difficult questions of civil law' concerning the passing of property (see *Gomez* above).

Question 35

(a) Critically evaluate the *Ghosh* test of dishonesty
(b) Swoop was walking along the empty pier at Mudpool when she found a $50 note. She was delighted and decided to celebrate by having a meal at 'El Caro' a posh restaurant on the front. Sitting back, having consumed her meal, she overheard an American lady at an adjacent table say to her husband that she had lost $50. Swoop nevertheless decided to keep the money

Discuss Swoop's liability.

Answer plan

A popular form of question in which the second part relates to the first.

(a) The question requires a *critical* evaluation of the *Ghosh* test. A simple account of the test and its application is necessary but not sufficient. The main criticisms of the test are based on the perceived dangers of leaving the matter of 'dishonesty' to the jury. As the *Ghosh* test is a development from earlier decisions, a critical review of its predecessors is helpful.
• the role of the jury in cases where the issue of dishonesty is raised
• the two part test enunciated in *Ghosh*
• the problems of leaving questions of dishonesty to the jury

(b) A relatively straightforward problem centering on the meaning of dishonesty.
• application of s 2(1)c
• the later assumption principle in s 3(1) of the Theft Act 1968

Answer

(a) Many of the offences under the Theft Acts 1968 and 1978 require the prosecution to prove that D's 'appropriation', 'obtaining' or 'receiving' etc was 'dishonest'.

For the purposes of theft only, s 2 (1) of the Act specifies three instances of states of mind which as a matter of *law* are to be regarded as honest. The burden is on the prosecution to prove that D did not have one of the specified beliefs. If the jury have a reasonable doubt that D was dishonest - if P have failed to disprove the absence of an honest belief- then the jury *must* acquit.

Section 2(1) was intended to be only a *partial* (negative) definition of dishonesty. The Criminal Law Revision Committee recognised that it would be unwise to attempt an exhaustive list of those states of mind which, in law, might be regarded as honest. The assumption in their Eighth report seems to have been that, in cases not covered by s 2, the issue of dishonesty would be left to the jury to determine as a question of fact.

And, in *Feely* (1973), this course was accepted as correct by the Court of Appeal. The court held that, as dishonesty was an 'ordinary' word, the jury did not require assistance from the judge as to its meaning. According to the court, the jury would be expected to decide the issue by reference to the 'current standards of ordinary decent people'.

This approach has been criticised by most academic writers as the jury are not only given the task of deciding questions of primary fact, (ie what did the accused believe or intend etc) but are also left the responsibility of evaluating those beliefs and intentions. In a sense, where dishonesty is a 'live' issue, the jury decide the limits of liability for theft. The *Feely* approach appoints the jury to the role of 'mini-legislators'.

Some subsequent cases went even further than *Feely*. In these cases the accused was made his own legislator. In *Gilks* (1972), for example, the judge directed the jury to consider whether the defendant *himself* thought he was acting honestly. This implies that the defendants own standards are to applied (see also *Boggeln v Williams* (1978); *McIvor* (1982); *Landy* (1981)).

In *Ghosh* (1982) the Court of Appeal held that, in determining whether the prosecution has proved that the defendant was acting dishonestly, a jury must first of all decide whether, according to the ordinary standards of reasonable and honest people, what was done was dishonest. If it was not dishonest according to those standards, the prosecution fails.

If it was dishonest by those standards, then the jury must consider whether the defendant himself realised that what he was doing was, by those standards, dishonest. It is dishonest for the defendant to act in a way which he knows ordinary people consider to be dishonest. If the defendant did not know that, the prosecution fails.

This means that a person is not dishonest if what he did was in accordance with the jury's understanding of ordinary standards or he mistakenly believed that what he did was in accordance with those standards.

The first part of the test corresponds to the *Feely* principle. And, of course the *Ghosh* test preserves the principle that the issue of dishonesty is a matter of fact for the jury and not the judge.

There are a number of dangers with this approach. There may be considerable variation in standards from one jury (or bench of magistrates) to the next. The jury may consist of people who have quite low standards. They may believe for example that it is not dishonest to help oneself to the property of an employer. This would mean that some peoples property rights would be less well protected than others.

The second limb of *Ghosh* presents further problems. Fortunately, it does not go as far as *Gilks*. The defendant is no longer his own legislator. He is not to be judged by his own standards. However, it does mean that a person who has got a low opinion (whether mistaken or not) of the general morality of the community will escape liability for theft. The person who has taken his employer's property and 'genuinely' believes that 'everybody thinks it is all right to steal from their employer' is not dishonest according to *Ghosh*. Again, this means that the proprietary rights of some individuals or groups are, potentially at least, accorded less protection in law than others.

And, although much of the criticism regarding *Ghosh* warns that the jury may apply terribly low standards, there is also the danger that they might apply excessively high standards. In crimes of dishonesty other than theft, the issue of dishonesty is exclusively one for the jury - s 2 applies only to theft. Thus, for example, the jury might conclude that a defendant who practised a deception to obtain money to which he mistakenly believed he was entitled was dishonest (cf theft where a mistaken belief that one is legally entitled to the property appropriated is an honest state of mind, *as a matter of law*).

Also it is debatable whether juries find the test easy to understand. (They must acquit unless they think that the defendant thought that ordinary reasonable and honest people (like themselves?) would think that what he did, believed and intended was dishonest!) In *Green* (1992) the Court of Appeal held that it is a misdirection to use a witness as a measure of the objective standard of honesty.

The task of the jury is made a little easier by the fact that, if it is accepted that what D did was dishonest according to ordinary standards, the judge need direct the jury only by reference to the second limb (*Thompson* (1988)). But if D raises the issue of dishonesty by claiming, for example, that he thought what he was doing was not dishonest according to ordinary standards, the judge should direct the jury in accordance with *Ghosh*, even if it is clear to the judge that D was dishonest (*Price* (1989); *Green* (1992)).

It is submitted that the definition of dishonesty should be a matter of law for the judge applied, in the ordinary way, by the jury to the facts as they believe them. The virtue of this approach would be that the concept might then be refined and developed by analogy with the states of mind specified in s 2 - each of which implicitly recognises the proprietary rights of the owner. This would have the virtue of directing attention towards the victims property rights and the defendants attitude towards those rights. This, it is submitted, is preferable to the current approach based on the vague standards of so called 'ordinary people'.

(b) When Swoop discovered the money on the pier, she probably did not commit theft. By virtue of s 2(1)c, a person does not appropriate property dishonestly if they believe that the person to whom it belongs cannot be found by taking reasonable steps.

However, she may have committed theft, when having overheard the conversation between the Americans, she decided to keep the money.

By virtue of s 3(1) a person who originally came by property innocently may be guilty of stealing it on the basis of a later dishonest assumption of a right to it.

Swoop having heard the conversation cannot conceivably rely upon s 2(1)c. If, however, she contends that she thought that keeping the money in those circumstances was in 'accordance with ordinary standards' then the judge would be required to direct the jury in accordance with the *Ghosh* test explained above (*Price* (1990)).

Question 36

(a) Samantha borrowed Rachel's personal stereo player without permission. She returned the player when the batteries were practically exhausted. Rachel would not have consented to Samantha's borrowing of the player.

Discuss Samantha's criminal liability.

(b) Mark took Henry's cat. He hoped and believed that Henry would assume the cat had strayed and that he would offer a reward to anyone finding it. He intended to return the cat to Henry after a few days even if no reward was offered.

Discuss Mark's criminal liability.

Would your answer differ if Mark had planned to let the cat go free were no offer of reward made for its return?

(c) Dick took Fob's watch and pawned it. He intended to redeem and return it to Fob the following week.

Discuss Dick's criminal liability.

Answer plan

A three part problem question involving similar issues and dealing with the offences of theft (s 1), and abstraction of electricity (s 13). The most important issues involve s 6(1) (extended meaning of intention to permanently deprive) and s 4 (property) and, in particular:

- the circumstances in which a borrowing is 'equivalent to an outright taking'
- the meaning and application of the phrase ' an intention to treat the thing as his own to dispose of regardless of the others rights'
- the meaning of 'property'
- the parting of property under a condition as to its return (s 6(2))

Answer

(a) Theft

It is proposed to consider, firstly, Samantha's liability for theft, contrary to s 1 of the Theft Act 1968. The punishment for theft is a term of imprisonment not exceeding seven years (s 7 of the 1968 Act as substituted by s 26 of the Criminal Justice Act 1991).

As Samantha only intended to borrow the stereo player she cannot be convicted of stealing it. Theft requires an 'intention to permanently deprive'. Nor can she be charged with stealing the 'use' or 'enjoyment' of the player. Theft is the dishonest appropriation of *property* belonging to another with the intention of permanently depriving the other of *it*. The use or enjoyment of a thing is not 'property'.

It is, however, *arguable* that she is guilty of stealing the batteries despite the fact that she did not intend to keep them. Section 6 of the Theft Act 1968 provides that, if certain conditions are satisfied, a person may be *regarded* as having appropriated the property with the necessary intent even though, *in a literal sense*, they did not intend to permanently deprive.

The necessary conditions are that the accused appropriated the property, intending to borrow it for a period and in circumstances *equivalent* to an outright taking.

When might these conditions apply?

In *Duru* (1976), the Court of Appeal held that if D borrowed a thing intending to return it in a *substantially* different state then he is to be regarded as having had the necessary intent (1).

In *Lloyd* (1985),. Lord Lane CJ stated that a mere borrowing is never enough to constitute the necessary *mens rea* unless the intention is to return the thing in such a changed state that it can be said that *all* its goodness or virtue has gone.

In this case the batteries are returned with 'practically all the virtue drained from them. It is not clear whether this might be regarded as equivalent to an 'outright taking'.

Clarkson and Keating assume that in cases where less than the complete virtue is drained from a thing the question of whether this is to be regarded as amounting to an intention to permanently deprive is a question of fact (2).

Professors Smith and Hogan, on the other hand, contend that to extend the principle to include cases where D did not intend to drain *all* the virtue would create difficulties in drawing the line between theft and mere borrowings (3). It is submitted that, in principle, this is the better approach. To conclude otherwise would mean that the mere use of property might in certain cases amount to theft. On this basis, Samantha is not guilty of theft.

If, however, the assumptions of Clarkson and Keating are correct, then it will be for the jury to determine whether Samantha's intended use was 'equivalent to an outright taking' - in which case Samantha *may* be guilty of stealing the batteries (subject to the question of dishonesty discussed below).

(If the batteries were rechargeable, and Samantha was aware of that fact, then there is no theft).

Abstraction of electricity

Samantha cannot be convicted of 'stealing' the electricity in the batteries. Electricity is not 'intangible property' within s 4 (*Low v Blease* (1975)).

It would appear, however, that whether the batteries are rechargeable or not, Samantha has committed the offence under s 13 of the Act. This prohibits the dishonest use of electricity. The punishment is a term of imprisonment not exceeding five years.

The offence is not restricted to the dishonest use of mains electricity. It covers dishonest abstraction from a dry battery.

The only issue remaining concerns the question of Samantha's dishonesty.

Samantha may have believed, albeit wrongly, that Rachel would have consented to her using the player and the batteries. If that were the case then, for the purposes of *theft* of the batteries, (discussed above), she was not, as a matter of *law*, dishonest (see s 2(1)b).

If, however, she did not believe that but raises evidence that she believed that what she did would not generally be regard as dishonest then the judge should direct the jury (in accordance with what is known as 'the *Ghosh* tests' (*Roberts* (1987)) to consider as a matter of *fact* whether she was dishonest.

In *Ghosh* (1982) the Court of Appeal held that in determining whether the prosecution has proved that the defendant was acting dishonestly, a jury must first of all decide whether *according to the standards of reasonable and honest people* what was done was dishonest. If it was not dishonest according to those standards the prosecution fails.

If it was dishonest by those standards, then the jury must consider whether the prosecution have proved that *the defendant himself realised that what he was doing was, by the above standards, dishonest*. It is dishonest for the defendant to act in a way which he knows ordinary people consider to be dishonest. If the defendant did not know that the prosecution fails.

Section 2 of the Act does not apply to the issue of dishonesty for the purposes of the offence under s 13. Consequently, as far as that offence is concerned, the issue of her dishonesty is exclusively a question of fact for the jury.

(b) Theft

Might Mark be convicted of stealing the cat? He performed the *actus reus* of theft when he took it.

(Although 'wild' animals are generally not protected by the law of theft - they are not 'property' (s 4(4)) - a domestic pet, being a tame animal, is capable of being stolen.)

Mark's dishonesty is not in doubt.

The issue is whether it can be said that *at the time of appropriation* he intended to permanently deprive Henry of the cat. He planned to return the cat in return for a reward, which, he (accurately) predicted, Henry would offer.

Section 6(1) states that a person may be regarded as intending to permanently deprive if *'without meaning the other to lose the thing itself'* he intends to *'treat the thing as his own to dispose of regardless of the others rights'*.

Did Mark intend to treat the cat as his own to dispose of?

It is submitted that he did not.

Mark did not treat the cat *as his own*. Mark did not intend to represent to Henry that he, Mark, was the owner of the cat (see *Holloway* 1849). Nor did he intend to *dispose* of the 'thing' *regardless of the other's rights* (4).

Mark, lacking the necessary intent, is not guilty of stealing the cat.

Alternative facts

It is submitted that even if his plan had been to get rid of the cat had no reward been offered, he would still have lacked the necessary intent for theft. It could not be said that he *intended* to dispose of the thing as his own regardless of the other's rights. He believed a reward would be offered (5).

In *Warner* (1970) it was said that s 6(1) should not be interpreted as 'watering down' the requirement of an intention to permanently deprive in s 1. *'Recklessness'* is not sufficient.

(c) Theft

Again the issue here is whether it can be said that Dick intended to permanently deprive Fob of his watch.

Section 6(2) provides that a person who parts with property under a condition as to its return that he may not be able to perform is to be regarded as treating the property as his own to dispose of.

The pawning of another's property falls within this section.

It is necessary, however, to consider Dick's intentions. Only if he *intended* to part with the property under a condition which he might not have been able to perform would he be regarded as having *intended* to treat it as his own.

Thus, if Dick believed that he would be able to redeem the pledge he cannot be regarded as having had the necessary intent for theft.

Notes

1 The decision centered on the 'ordinary' meaning of an 'intention to permanently deprive' but the Court of Appeal explained that they could have arrived at the same result by applying s 6(1).
2 *Criminal Law, Text and Materials* (1988) 2nd ed p 735.
3 *Criminal Law* (1992) 7th ed p 550.
4 Cf *Scott* (1987) where D took items from a shop. He returned the next day with the items and asked for a refund. He was convicted of theft. Scott intended to treat the items *as his own*.
5 This situation is analogous to cases like *Easom* (1971) where it was held that a 'conditional intention' to steal is not sufficient.

Question 37

Grundy was the manager of the Red Lion public house. Contrary to his contractual obligations and without the knowledge of his customers he sold them whisky he had bought from a local off-licence. He kept the profit made from the sale of the whisky. When he was arrested in the public house, he had two bottles of whisky that he had bought from the off-licence.

Discuss Grundy's criminal liability.

Answer plan

This question raises questions of liability for theft contrary to s 1 of the Theft Act 1968; obtaining property by deception contrary to s 15 of the Act; going equipped contrary to s 25; and false accounting contrary to s 17.

The principal issues are:

- the causal link between the obtaining and the deception
- the meaning and application of property 'received on account under an obligation to retain and deal with the property in a particular way in s 5(3)

Answer

Obtaining property

It is proposed to consider Grundy's liability for the offence of dishonestly obtaining property (ie the money from whisky buying customers) by deception contrary to s 15 of the Theft Act 1968. The maximum punishment is ten years imprisonment.

The principal issue for consideration is whether Grundy practised a deception within the meaning of s 15. By virtue of s 15(4) a deception may be made by conduct, that is, on the basis of an implied representation. In this case, it may be argued that Grundy impliedly represented that the whisky he offered was his employers (*Doukas* (1978)).

In addition, it must be shown that there was an obtaining *by* deception. In other words, the deception must be an operative cause of the obtaining. If P would have acted in the same even if he had known that D's representation was false then D is not guilty of obtaining (*Edwards* (1978)). Thus, only if the customers would not have parted with the money had they known the truth can Grundy be convicted of the s 15 offence.

In *Rashid* (1977) a British rail waiter substituted his own tomatoes for the railway tomato sandwiches. The Court of Appeal, allowing Rashid's appeal against conviction for the offence of going equipped contrary to s 25 of the Theft Act 1968 stated that he could not be guilty of the offence as passengers would be quite indifferent as to the origin of the sandwiches (1).

In *Doukas* (1978) the Court of Appeal distinguished *Rashid*. A hotel waiter found in the hotel with bottles of wine which he intended to sell to make a personal profit was convicted of going equipped. Doukas appealed against the decision of the judge to allow the case to go to the jury. His appeal was dismissed. The Court of Appeal held that there was sufficient evidence of an operative deception to go to the jury. And, in the opinion of Lord Lane , no customer, to whom the true situation was made clear, would willingly make himself a party to an obvious fraud by the waiter upon his employer.

In *Cooke* (1986) the House of Lords held that the question whether there has been an operative deception is one for the jury in the light of all the evidence and in particular that concerning 'the attitude and understanding' of the customers.

Thus, if the jury conclude that the customers of the Red Lion would have been prepared to buy the whisky even if they had known what Grundy was up to, he must be acquitted.

Alternatively, if the evidence reveals that the customers would not have bought the whisky had they known of the 'fiddle' the jury should acquit if Grundy mistakenly believed that the customers would not have minded. A deception for the purposes of s 15 must be made 'deliberately or recklessly', (s 15(4)).

Going equipped

Grundy may also be charged with the offence of going equipped contrary to s 25 of the Theft Act 1968.

Sections 25(1) and 25(2) provides that a person is guilty of an offence punishable with a maximum of three years imprisonment if, when not at his place of abode, he has with him any article for use in the course of or in connection with any burglary, theft, or cheat. By virtue of s 25(5) 'cheat' means an offence under s 15.

Clearly, in the light of the discussion above, it must be shown that Grundy intended to practise a deception which would have been operative. The question here is not whether anyone was actually deceived (*Whiteside & Antoniou* (1989)) but whether a hypothetical reasonably honest customer would have bought the whisky if he had known the truth (*Cooke* (1986)).

Theft

The difficulty in convicting Grundy of theft of the money or the secret profit made from the sale of the whisky consists of showing that he appropriated property '*belonging to another*'.

By virtue of s 5(3), property is to be regarded as belonging to another where it is received on account of another and the recipient is under an obligation to retain and deal with the property or its proceeds in a particular way.

However, in *Attorney-General's Reference No 1 of 1985* (1986), the Court of Appeal held that an employee who makes a secret profit from his position does not receive the money 'on account of another' and is not under an obligation to 'retain and deal with the property' within the meaning of s 5(3).

Further, although s 5(1) states that property is to be regarded as belonging to any person who has '*any* proprietary right or interest in it', the Court of Appeal held that even if an employee holds a secret profit on constructive trust for his employer this does not amount to a proprietary interest for the purposes of s 5(1) (2).

False accounting

Section 17 of the Theft Act 1968 provides that where a person dishonestly and with a view to gain or intent to cause loss falsifies any account or any record or document made for any accounting purpose he commits an offence punishable with a maximum of seven years imprisonment.

A person is not guilty of the s 17 offence unless the transactions are recorded in or omitted from his employer's account or other document made for accounting purposes (*Cooke* (1986)). The section does not, however, impose any duty to account.

In *Keatley* (1980) a Crown Court judge held that the offence was not committed where D, an employee, failed to reveal secret profits. The judge held that D was not a constructive trustee of the profits and, therefore, was not under a duty to account for them.

The question whether there is a duty to account is determined by reference to the terms of the employee's contract of employment. If Grundy was under a contractual duty to account for *all sales and receipts*, his omission to account for the money received for the whisky would amount to a falsification of an account (*Lee Cheung Wing & Lam Man Yau* (1992); s 17(2)).

In addition, the prosecution must prove that Grundy was 'dishonest' and that he falsified the account with a 'view to gain' or 'intent to cause loss' to another. A 'gain' includes a gain by keeping what one has, (s 34(2)a), and therefore, there may be a view to gain where the falsification of the account *follows* the making of a personal profit (and see *Lee Cheung Wing*).

But, if Grundy did not know that he was obliged to account for the personal profit made from sales of the whisky, he could not be convicted of the offence under s 17. There would not, in those circumstances, be a dishonest *view* to gain.

If Grundy raises evidence that he thought that what he was doing was not dishonest the judge must direct the jury with respect to the meaning of the term (*Price* (1990); *O'Connell* (1992)).

In *Ghosh* (1982) the Court of Appeal held that, in determining whether the prosecution has proved that the defendant was acting dishonestly, the jury must first of all decide whether, according to the ordinary standards of reasonable and honest people, what was done was dishonest. If it was not dishonest according to those standards, the prosecution fails.

If it was dishonest by those standards, then the jury must consider whether the defendant himself realised that what he was doing was, by those standards dishonest. It is dishonest for the defendant to act in a way which he knows ordinary people consider to be dishonest. If the defendant did not know that, the prosecution fails.

Notes

1 *Rashid* is criticised by Professors Smith and Hogan. They contend that the origins of the sandwiches could not be a matter of indifference to the customer. They maintain that, although he may not consciously think about whether a seller is authorised to sell, the customer proceeds on the assumption that he is and would not willingly participate in a fraud against the employer. *Criminal Law* (1992) 7th ed p 566.

2 Doubt is cast on the decision in the Attorney-General's Reference by that of the Court of Appeal in *Shadrokh-Cigari* (1988) the Court of Appeal held that an equitable interest arising under a constructive trust was a 'proprietary right or interest' under s 5(1).

Question 38

(a) Michael lived in London. From David he borrowed a car to take his friend, Charlie, to Liverpool Street railway station. Charlie intended to take the train to Chelmsford where he lived. David agreed to lend Michael the car on condition that he brought the car back immediately after taking Charlie to the station. When, however, Michael and Charlie arrived at the station the last train had departed. Michael tried to telephone David to ask his permission to drive Charlie to his destination but David's telephone was out of order. Michael believed that, in the circumstances, David would probably not mind him taking Charlie to his destination. Michael drove Charlie to Chelmsford, a distance of 35 miles from London. Michael then returned the car to David.

Discuss Michael's criminal liability.

(b) The following day Michael asked Sean if he might borrow his car. Michael said that he needed the car to drive to Leeds with his friend Peter to visit Peter's sick mother. In fact he wanted the car to go to Leeds to watch a football match. Sean agreed to lend the car to Michael. Michael collected Peter and they drove off to Leeds. Michael boasted to Peter that as he had a spare set of keys for Sean's car he had simply taken it without consulting Sean. Peter was impressed. After their trip to Leeds, Michael returned the car to Sean.

Discuss Michael's criminal liability

Would your answer differ if, instead of going to Leeds, Michael and Peter had gone to Edinburgh (a further 200 miles from London) to watch a football match?

Answer plan

This question concerns the offences of taking a conveyance without authority and driving or allowing oneself to be carried in a conveyance taken without authority contrary to s 12(1) of the Theft Act 1968.

The principal issues are:
- what constitutes a 'taking' for the purposes of s 12?
- the effect of a misrepresentation as to purpose or destination upon consent.
- the *mens rea* requirement for s 12(1) and the meaning and application of s 12(6)

Answer

(a) Section 12 (1) and (2) of the Theft Act 1968 provide that a person is guilty of an offence punishable, on summary conviction, with a fine of £5000, imprisonment for up to six months, or both, if, without having the consent of the owner or other lawful authority, he takes any conveyance for his own or another's use or, knowing that any conveyance has been taken without such authority, drives it or allows himself to be carried in or on it.

The section creates two offences - (1) taking a conveyance and (2) driving, or allowing oneself to be carried in, a taken conveyance.

For both offences, the prosecution must prove that the conveyance was taken without the consent of the owner or other lawful authority. Neither offence is committed if the owner has given his consent to the taking.

There may be a taking without consent, however, despite the fact that D initially took possession of the conveyance with the permission of the owner, if he uses it for a purpose in excess of that for which he was given permission.

In *Phipps v McGill* (1970) D was given permission by the owner of a car to use it to take D's wife to Victoria station in London on the express condition that he brought it straight back. D did not return the car immediately. His wife having missed her train, D drove her to Hastings and returned the car two days later. The Court of Appeal held that the use of the car after the express purpose of the borrowing was completed amounted to a taking.

Thus, when Michael drove to Chelmsford he acted in excess of the permission. He took the conveyance for his own use without consent or authority.

We are not told how David reacted on discovering that Michael had acted in excess of the permission. He may not have minded. According to the Court of Appeal in *Ambler* (1979), however, if the owner had not given his consent *at the time of the taking* the fact that he would have consented had he been asked is not a defence. Thus, Michael has committed the *actus reus* of the offence.

With respect to the *mens rea*, s 12(6) provides that there is no offence if the accused believed, at the time of the taking, that the owner would have consented had he known of the circumstances.

The accused has an evidential burden in respect of a s 12 (6) defence (*Gannon* (1987)). The prosecution, however, have the burden of proving that D did not have the specified belief (*MacPherson* (1973)) The test is subjective.

Michael believed that David would *probably* not mind. This is not the same as a positive belief that the owner would consent and, therefore, Michael committed the offence under s 12 when he drove to Chelmsford.

With respect to Charlie's liability for 'allowing himself to be carried in a conveyance taken without consent' the prosecution must prove that, when they set off for Chelmsford, he knew that the vehicle was taken without consent.

If he mistakenly believed that Michael had been granted permission to drive him to Chelmsford he would not be guilty of an offence.

If he was aware that Michael had only been given permission to drive to Liverpool Street, but believed that David would have consented to Michael driving to Chelmsford had David known of all the circumstances then, presumably, he is not guilty of an offence. Section 12(6) states that a person does not commit an offence if he believes that *he* would have the owner's consent if the owner knew the circumstances. Presumably, the secondary offence is not committed where D allows himself to be carried in a conveyance taken by E if D believes that the owner, V, would have consented to E's taking had V been aware of the circumstances.

(b) In *Whittaker v Campbell* (1984) the Divisional Court held that consent obtained by means of a deception or fraudulent misrepresentation is nevertheless a valid consent for the purposes of the offence under s 12(1).

The Court of Appeal reached a similar conclusion in the case of *Peart* (1970). D had obtained the consent of the owner of a van in Newcastle to lend him it by pretending that he needed it for an urgent appointment in Alnwick - a town not too far from Newcastle. In fact his intention from the outset was to drive to Burnley, a much greater distance from Newcastle. He knew that the owner would not have lent him the van if he had known of his real intentions. Despite this it was held that the taking was with the owner's consent. Consequently, Michael is not guilty of an offence (1).

Neither is Peter. Although he believed that Michael had taken the car without consent, Peter did not commit the subsidiary offence under s 12(1) as it had not, in fact, been taken without consent. Nor can he be convicted of an attempt. By virtue of s 1(4) of the Criminal Attempts Act 1981 it is not an offence to attempt to commit a summary offence.

Alternative facts

Had they driven to Edinburgh the answer would be different.

In *Peart*, the Court of Appeal restricted themselves to considering whether there had been a taking without consent when, in Newcastle, the D initially took possession of the vehicle. For technical reasons concerning the grounds of appeal, the court did not consider whether there had been a fresh taking without consent when he deviated from the route to Alnwick and made for Burnley.

In *McKnight v Davies* (1974) it was held that, where there is a wholly unauthorised deviation from an authorised route, there is, at that point, a 'taking without consent'.

When Michael deviated from the route to Leeds and set course for Edinburgh, he 'took the conveyance without consent'.

As Peter knew the conveyance was taken without consent, and allowed himself to be carried in it, he is guilty of the subsidiary offence.

Minor liabilities for theft and abstraction of electricity

Where Michael is guilty of the offence under s 12(1) he may also be convicted of theft of the petrol contrary to s 1 of the Theft Act 1968. If, however, he replaced the petrol used then the jury may conclude that he was not dishonest.

In *Ghosh* (1982) the Court of Appeal held that, in determining whether the prosecution has proved that the defendant was acting dishonestly, a jury must first of all decide whether according to the ordinary standards of reasonable and honest people what was done was dishonest. If it was not dishonest according to those standards, the prosecution fails.

If it was dishonest by those standards then the jury must consider whether the D himself realised that what he was doing was, by those standards, dishonest. If the D did not know that, the prosecution fails.

In addition it is conceivable that he may be convicted of the 'dishonest use without authority ... of electricity (in the car battery)' contrary to s 13 of the Act, despite the fact that the electricity stored in the battery at the end of the trip is probably the same as when he started. The jury might conclude, however, that where there is no intention to cause loss the use is not 'dishonest' (2).

Notes

1   The decision in *Peart* has been criticised. Commentators point to the discrepancy between it and *Phipps v McGill* (above). Professor Smith argues that if, as in *Phipps v McGill* there is a 'taking' when, after completion of an authorised purpose the car is then used for a further unauthorised purpose, it is difficult to accept that there is no 'taking' when, *from the outset*, the car is used, as intended, for an unauthorised purpose. *Law of Theft* (1989) 6th ed p 152.

2   Professor Smith points out that it would be strange were a person to be convicted of the s 13 offence in these circumstances as they would have committed a more serious offence when switching the car on than driving it. The offence under s 13 carries a maximum punishment of five years - *Law of Theft* (1989) 6th ed p 157.

Question 39

John took his video recorder to be repaired by Fred, a video repairman. John explained that the video recorder would neither record nor play videotapes. Fred agreed to examine the recorder. He told John that he would telephone him later when he had discovered the fault. Later that afternoon Fred phoned John and told him that the heads needed to be replaced at a total cost of £100. In fact all that was required was a slight adjustment to the existing heads.

John agreed to the fitting of the new heads.

Fred fitted the new heads and then went to collect his car which was being serviced at a local garage. His car was ready. The total cost of the service was £75. He paid for the service by cheque backed by a cheque guarantee card, valid up to £100. Fred had no funds in his account and his bank had instructed him not to use his cheque book and cheque card.

John returned later to collect his video recorder. He paid the £100.

John asked Fred to carry the video recorder to his car for him. John falsely stated that he had a bad back. Fred was reluctant to assist him as he was very busy. He instructed his employee, Dupe, to take the recorder to John's car which was parked about a mile from the shop.

Discuss the criminal liability of the parties.

Answer plan

This question concerns a number of offences involving deception - obtaining property by deception contrary to s 15 of the Theft Act 1968; obtaining a pecuniary advantage by deception contrary to s 16 of the same Act; and obtaining services by deception contrary to s 1 of the Theft Act 1978.

The principal issues are:

• the representations made when using cheques and cheque cards
• the meaning and application of 'dishonesty' in cases of obtaining
• the obtaining of gratuitous services
• the meaning and application of 'property belonging to another' for the purposes of s 15

Answer

Fred - obtaining property by deception - s 15 of the Theft Act 1968

Firstly, it is proposed to consider Fred's liability under s 15 of the Theft Act 1968 for the offence of obtaining property, ie the £100, by deception. This offence is punishable with a maximum of ten years imprisonment.

According to s 15(4), any false representation of fact, made deliberately or recklessly, amounts to a deception. Assuming therefore that Fred knew that his statement that the heads needed replacement was false, or he was aware that it might have been false, he practised a deception. On the other hand, if Fred genuinely believed that the heads did need to be replaced he practised no deception (*Jeff & Bassett* (1966)).

Assuming he practised a deception, it must be proved that he obtained the money by virtue of the deception; in other words, that John was induced to part with the money on the strength of Fred's false statement. The deception must be a cause of the obtaining and must not be too remote.

In *King & Stockwell* (1987) the appellants persuaded a lady to hire them to cut down her trees. They represented, falsely, that the trees were in such a dangerous state that cutting them down was necessary. The appellants argued that had money been paid pursuant to this agreement it would have been paid because the agreed work had been performed and not as a result of the deception. The argument was rejected. The court held that, in such cases, the issue whether the deception is an operative cause of the obtaining is to be left to the common sense of the jury.

Provided the above requirements are satisfied and that Fred had a dishonest intention to permanently deprive John of the money, he may be convicted of the offence under s 15.

If Fred is guilty of the s 15 offence then he may, in addition, be convicted of stealing the money, contrary to s 1(1) of the Theft Act 1968. In *Gomez* (1992) the House of Lords held, by a majority, that an appropriation of property belonging to another can occur even if the owner consents to what D does and even if ownership in the property transfers to D, and, therefore, the fact that John gave Fred the money does not preclude a conviction for theft.

Obtaining a pecuniary advantage by deception - s 16 of the Theft Act 1968

The maximum penalty for this offence is a term of imprisonment not exceeding five years.

By virtue of s 16(2)(c) a pecuniary advantage is obtained where D is given the opportunity to earn remuneration or greater remuneration in an office or employment.

In *Callender* (1992) the Court of Appeal held that 'employment' was wide enough to include contracts made with independent contractors.

Provided, therefore, that Fred practised a deliberate or reckless deception (discussed above) and that he was dishonest he may be convicted of the s 16 offence.

He may also have committed this offence when he paid using his cheque and card for the repairs to his car. By virtue of s 16(2)(b) a pecuniary advantage is obtained where the D is allowed to borrow by way of overdraft.

In *Charles* (1977) the House of Lords held that a person who draws a cheque supported by a cheque card impliedly represents that he has authority from the issuing bank to use the card so as to create a contractual relationship between bank and payee; and, if he does not have that authority - ie if the cheque would not be met but for the use of the card - a deception is practised. This rule applies even where the payee did not consider whether the drawer of the cheque was exceeding his authority (1).

Provided the conditions on the cheque card are satisfied the bank will honour the cheque. In Fred's case this will result in his account being overdrawn. In *Waites* (1982) the Court of Appeal held that in these circumstances a person has been 'allowed to borrow by way of overdraft' - even though the drawer has been expressly forbidden to write any more cheques! (see also *Bevan* (1986)).

Both *Waites* and *Charles* make it clear that for liability under s 16(2)(b) it is not necessary that the person deceived suffers financial loss nor that the pecuniary advantage is obtained from that person. Provided that Fred was aware that he lacked the authority and assuming he was dishonest, he is guilty of the offence under s 16(2)(b).

Evasion of liability by deception -
s 2(1) of the Theft Act 1978

The offence under s 2(1)(b) of the Theft Act 1978 requires *an intention to make permanent default* of an existing liability and clearly Fred incurs no liability for this offence.

For the same reason he cannot be convicted of the offence under s 3 of the 1978 Act (see *Allen* (1985)).

Obtaining property by deception

Was Fred guilty of obtaining property ie *the car* by deception?

The facts raise two issues:

(i) Did Fred obtain property *belonging to another* when he collected his car?

For the purposes of s 15, property belongs to any person having possession or control of it or having any proprietary right or interest in it (s 5(1); s 34(1)).

In these circumstances the repairer has what is known as a 'lien' over the car. The repairer has the right to retain the car until payment is made. Thus, although Fred owns the car it belongs to the garage for the purposes of s 15.

(ii) It must be shown, however, that Fred was dishonest in obtaining the car.

In *Ravenshad* (1990) the Court of Appeal suggested that where D has practised a deliberate deception it may not always be necessary to give a direction on the issue of dishonesty. It is submitted that the issues of deception and dishonesty are quite separate and that where D raise evidence that he may have believed that he was acting honestly according to ordinary standards then dishonesty is a 'live' issue (*Price* (1989)) and the jury should be directed along the lines required by the Court of Appeal in *Ghosh* (1982) to consider whether Fred was dishonest.

In *Ghosh* (1982) the Court of Appeal held that D is not dishonest if what he did was, in the opinion of the jury, not dishonest according to the ordinary standards of reasonable and honest people or he mistakenly believed that it was not dishonest according to those standards.

As Fred presumably had no intention to cause any loss to the garage - (if the conditions on the guarantee card were satisfied the cheque would be met) - the jury might conclude that he was not dishonest *vis-a-vis the repairer* and therefore did not dishonestly obtain the car. If, on the other hand, the jury conclude that Fred was dishonest, then he is not only guilty of obtaining the car by deception contrary to s 15 but also of stealing it contrary to s 1. The car 'belonged to another' (see s 5 above) and the fact that the garage proprietor allowed D to drive off with the vehicle does not preclude a conviction for theft (see *Gomez* above).

John - obtaining services by deception - s 1 of the Theft Act 1978

Although John practised a deception by falsely representing that he was unfit to carry the video recorder and although Fred, by virtue of that deception, 'caused some act to be done' ie he has instructed his employee, Dupe, to carry the recorder to John's car, there was no obtaining of services contrary to s 1 as the benefit was not conferred 'on the understanding that it (had) been or (would) be paid for'. Section 1 does not apply to gratuitous services.

Note

1   The decision in *Charles* has been criticised on two grounds.
     Firstly, it is submitted that it is not accurate to suggest that card-holders act as agents for the issuing bank.
     Secondly, the decision appears to overlook the requirement of a causal link between the obtaining and the deception. Although P stated in evidence that he would not have accepted the cheques had he known D's lack of authority, he also said that he accepted cheques with a guarantee card because in those circumstances the bank takes the risk. Thus he had no real interest in whether D had authority to use the card. How can it be said that D obtained *by* deception if, in effect, P was indifferent as to the truth of the apparent representation?
     The decision in *Charles* means that an operative deception is practised even if the garage proprietor did not care whether Fred had authority. Only in the unlikely event that the jury are not convinced that the proprietor would have refused the cheque, had he known that Fred had no authority to use the card, can it be said that there was no obtaining *by* deception.

Question 40

Chump caught a rabbit on Adolf's land. He took it to his houseboat. Flash, who had been observing Chump, followed him. Whilst Chump had a nap, Flash, intending to take the rabbit, boarded the houseboat. Flash was about to leave with the rabbit when Chump started to wake up. Flash picked up Chump's walking stick, hit Chump over the head with it, and left with the rabbit.

Discuss the criminal liability of the parties.

Answer plan

This question raises issues of theft contrary to s 1 of the Theft Act 1968, burglary contrary to s 9(1)(a) and s 9(1)(b) of the Act, aggravated burglary contrary to s 10. Minor questions of liability for criminal damage and the offence of 'going equipped' are raised.

Flash's liability for 'aggravated assaults' is fairly 'open' - ie we are not told the extent of the injuries sustained nor his *mens rea* at the relevant time. Thus, a full discussion of the ingredients of liability for each of the various offences - under ss 18, 20 and 47 of the Offences Against the Person Act 1861 - is required.

Principal issues:

- the meaning and application of s 4(4) of the Theft Act 1968 - theft of 'wild animals'
- liability under s 9(1) of the Theft Act - burglary
- the meaning and application of the expression 'has with him' in s 10 - aggravated burglary - and s 25 - going equipped.
- the ingredients of liability for aggravated assaults

Answer

Whilst Chump may be guilty of an offence of poaching under the Game Acts and Poaching Acts he is not guilty of theft, contrary to s 1 of the Theft Act 1968.

The common law rule that wild creatures could not be stolen because they were not regarded as property is preserved by s 4(4) of the Act. This provides that a person cannot steal a wild creature unless it has been reduced into possession by or on behalf of another person and possession of it has not since been lost or abandoned. The owner of the land on which the animal is found is protected by the criminal law relating to poaching but not by the law of theft.

Neither may Chump be charged with criminal damage contrary to s 1 of the Criminal Damage Act 1971. The definition of 'property' in s 10 of the 1971 Act is very similar in this respect to the definition in s 4(4) of the 1968 Act.

As, however, the rabbit *has been reduced into, and remains in, the possession* of Chump, it is capable of being stolen from him. Therefore, as the facts indicate that Flash had a dishonest intention to permanently deprive, he is guilty of stealing the rabbit from Chump.

The maximum punishment for theft is seven years imprisonment (s 7 of the TA 1968 as amended by s 26 of the Criminal Justice Act 1991).

Moreover, by virtue of s 9(1)a, a person is guilty of burglary if he enters any building as a trespasser intending to commit one of a number of offences including theft, and, by virtue of s 9(3) Chump's houseboat -an 'inhabited vessel' - is a building for the purposes of this offence.

As a matter of civil law, a person enters as a trespasser if he enters without the possessor's consent. For the purposes of burglary the prosecution must prove, in addition, that, at the time of entry, the accused knew that he was entering without permission or was reckless with respect to that fact (*Collins* (1973)). As Flash intended to steal the rabbit when he boarded the boat, the above criteria are satisfied.

He may also be convicted of two counts of burglary contrary to s 9(1)(b). This sub-section provides that a person is guilty of burglary if, *having entered* any building as a trespasser, he steals anything in the building or inflicts or attempts to inflict grievous bodily harm on any person in the building.

The ingredients of liability - that D entered as a trespasser and that, at the time of the theft, he knew or was reckless as to the facts which made his entry a trespass - were present when he appropriated the rabbit.

He also may have committed burglary under s 9(1)b when he struck Chump on the head. However, the facts of the problem are 'open'. Neither the extent of any injuries suffered by Chump nor Flash's *mens rea* is disclosed. Thus:

(i) Assuming that the injuries amounted to 'grievous bodily harm'(1).

In *Jenkins* (1983) the Court of Appeal appeared to accept that, for the purposes of s 9(1)(b), the infliction of grievous bodily harm need not, in itself, amount to an offence of any kind (2). (The House of Lords (1984) allowed *Jenkins* appeal on another ground and made no comment on this issue.)

The better view, it is submitted, is that the serious offence of burglary requires a *mens rea* beyond that relating to the trespassory entry and that the prosecution are required to prove that D's conduct amounted to an offence under either s 18 or s 20 of the Offences Against the Person Act 1861.

The s 18 offence - causing grievous bodily harm with intent - carries a maximum penalty of life imprisonment.

The *mens rea* requirement is an intention to cause gbh. If it was his aim or purpose to cause gbh then Flash intended it. If it was not his aim or purpose, but the jury are satisfied that gbh was a virtually certain consequence of his actions, then they may infer that gbh was intended (*Bryson* (1985)).

For the offence under s 20 - which carries a maximum punishment of five years imprisonment - the prosecution must prove that Flash foresaw the risk of causing some harm, albeit not serious harm (*Savage; Parmenter* (1991)).

(ii) Assuming the injuries amounted to 'actual bodily harm'.

If the injuries sustained are not serious, Flash may be guilty of the lesser offence of assault occasioning actual bodily harm contrary to s 47 of the OPA 1861. The maximum punishment for this offence is five years imprisonment.

'Actual bodily harm' means 'any hurt or injury calculated to interfere with the health or comfort of the victim' provided it is more than transient or trifling (*Miller* (1954)). There is no need for a physically discernible injury (*Reigate Justices ex p Counsell* (1983)).

It is unnecessary to prove that the accused intended or was reckless with respect to causing actual bodily harm (*Savage;*

Parmenter). The offence is committed where, as in this case, he intentionally (or recklessly) applied unlawful force to another, who, as a consequence, suffered harm, as defined above.

Assault occasioning actual bodily harm is not a specified offence for burglary under s 9(1)(b).

(If Flash intended grievous bodily harm but the injuries sustained were less serious then he may be convicted of an attempt to cause gbh contrary to s 1(1) of the Criminal Attempts Act 1981. An attempt to cause gbh is a specified offence for the purposes of burglary contrary to s 9(1)(b).)

Finally, it is proposed to consider whether Flash committed the offence of aggravated burglary, contrary to s 10 of the Theft Act 1968.

Section 10 provides that it is an offence, punishable with a maximum of life imprisonment (s 10(2)), if a person commits any burglary and at the time has with him , among other things, any 'weapon of offence'.

If Flash intended to use the stick to cause injury to or incapacitate Chump then it was a 'weapon of offence', (s 10(1)(b)).

However, to be guilty of the offence under s 10 the accused must have the article with him at the time of committing the burglary. Where the accused is charged with burglary contrary to s 9(1)(a) this is the time of the trespassory entry. Where the charge is burglary contrary to s 9(1)(b) the relevant time is the time of commission of the specified offence.

Clearly Flash did not commit aggravated burglary at the moment of entry. Did he commit aggravated burglary when he struck Chump?

Smith and Hogan suggest that, by analogy with decisions concerning s 1 of the Prevention of Crime Act 1953 (possession of an offensive weapon), 'has with him' should be interpreted to imply a degree of continuous possession (see, for example *Ohlson v Hylton* (1975)).

In *Kelly* (1992), however, the Court of Appeal held that s 1 of the 1953 Act and s 10 of the 1968 Act are directed at entirely different mischiefs. Potts J, delivering the judgment of the court, stated that whereas the former is directed at the carrying of a weapon with intent to use it if the occasion arises, the latter is directed at the actual use of articles which aggravate the offence of simple burglary.

Similarly, in *Minor* (1988), the Divisional Court held that, for the offence of going equipped contrary to s 25, it was sufficient that D had the article with him prior to the commission of a burglary, theft or cheat. If this decision is correct then, Flash may be convicted of going equipped with the stick provided he intended to use it to cause Chump grievous bodily harm (3). He was not at his place of abode and he had (although only for a matter of moments) the article for use in the course of a burglary (4).

Notes

1   This was defined by the House of Lords in *Smith* (1961) as 'really serious bodily harm'. In *Saunders* (1985) the Court of Appeal held that the adverb 'really' is superfluous. The question whether Chump's injuries amounted to grievous bodily harm is for the jury.

2   If this were accepted it would mean that the prosecution would not have to prove that the accused inflicted gbh with the *mens rea* necessary for a conviction under either s 18 or s 20 of the Offences Against the Person Act 1861.

3   In *Ellames* (1974) The Court of Appeal held that the intention to use the article must relate to the future. Presumably, therefore, there can be no liability for the offence under s 25 in relation to the theft of the rabbit.

4   Professor Card has criticised the decision in *Minor*. He suggests that 'it cannot be said in common sense terms that D has the thing with him, nor that he was going equipped for stealing etc' (which is the description of the offence given by the marginal note to the section); Card Cross and Jones *Criminal Law* (1992) 12th ed p 337.

Question 41

George agreed to paint Liam's flat for £500. He gave George an advance of £50. Having painted the flat George was given a roll of notes by Liam's wife, Margaret, in payment. George put the money in his pocket without counting it. When he got home he discovered that Margaret had given him £500. George decided to keep the excess. Later that evening Liam, having discovered his wife's mistake, visited George to request the return of the £50. George was not at home but his wife, Lucy, who was aware that Liam had been overpaid, persuaded Liam that her husband had been given £450 by Margaret.

Discuss the criminal liability of George and Lucy.

Answer plan

This problem is fairly intricate. It involves liability for theft contrary to s 1 of the Theft Act 1968; obtaining property by deception contrary to s 15 of the Theft Act 1968; and evasion of liability by deception contrary to s 2(1) of the Theft Act 1978.

As there are issues relating to the liability of Lucy as an accessory, George's liability should be discussed first.

Note that the facts of the problem are 'open' with respect to the question of George's dishonesty.

The most important issues are:

- the meaning and application of 'dishonesty' for the purposes of theft
- property got by another's mistake - s 5(4)
- accessorial liability
- was assistance given at the time of the theft?
- enabling another to retain as a basis of liability for s 15
- evasion of liability under s 2(1)(b)

Answer

George - theft contrary to s 1 of the Theft Act 1968

Theft is defined as the 'dishonest appropriation of property belonging to another with the intention of permanently depriving the other of it'.

George did not commit theft when Liam's wife handed over the money. Clearly, as he was unaware of the extra £50, he did not dishonestly appropriate it.

He may have been guilty of theft, however, when, on discovering that he had been overpaid in error, he decided to keep the excess. Although he originally came by the property innocently, appropriation is defined to include any later assumption of a right to property by 'keeping or dealing with it as owner' (s 3(1)). Therefore George, by keeping the £50, may be said to have appropriated it.

Did he, however, appropriate 'property *belonging to another*'?

Section 5(1) provides that 'property shall be regarded as belonging to any person having possession or control of it or having in it any proprietary right or interest' ...

And, s 5(4) provides that where a person gets property by another's mistake, *and* is under an obligation to make restoration (in whole or in part) of the property then the property (or part) shall be regarded as belonging to the person entitled to restoration.

In *Gilks* (1972) the Court of Appeal held that 'obligation' in s 5(4) means 'legal' obligation.

Where D is overpaid in error, although, as a matter of civil law, the ownership in the money passes to him, he is under a quasi contractual legal obligation to make restoration (*Moynes v Coopper* (1956); *Davis* (1988)). Therefore, for the purposes of theft, the £50 belonged to another. (It is not clear whose money was used to pay George, but, as far as George's liability is concerned, it is immaterial whether it belonged to Liam or Margaret.)

(It may be unnecessary for the prosecution to rely on s 5(4) to attribute a 'notional' proprietary interest to Liam or his wife. In *Chase Manhattan Bank NA v Israel-British Bank (London) Ltd* (1981) it was held that where an action will lie to recover money or other property paid or transferred under a mistake of fact, the payer or transferor retains an equitable proprietary interest. Applying this rule to the law of theft, the Criminal Division of the Court of Appeal in *Shadrokh-Cigari* (1988) held that the property paid in such circumstances is property belonging to another within s 5(1).)

Therefore either by virtue of s 5(4) or the rule in *Chase Manhattan* George may be convicted of stealing the £50 if the remaining conditions of theft are satisfied.

Section 5(4) provides that an intention not to make restoration is to be regarded as an intention to permanently deprive. Thus, the only point remaining which requires consideration is whether George was dishonest in keeping the excess.

Section 2(1) of the Act provides that certain beliefs are, *as a matter of law*, honest beliefs. Where one of these beliefs is alleged, the judge must instruct the jury that the defendant is to be acquitted if he had or may have had one of the defined states of mind. The reasonableness of the belief is not legally relevant. The only issue is whether it was genuinely held but, of course, the unreasonableness of a belief is some evidence that it was not genuinely held (*Holden* (1991)).

When George discovered the extra £50 he may have believed that it was a bonus or tip, in which case his decision to keep it would have been an honest one, by virtue of s 2(1)(b).

Alternatively, he may have been aware that Liam or Margaret made a mistake but believed that, despite the mistake, he was legally entitled to keep the money; in which case he would be able to take advantage of s 2(1)(a). This provides that a person is not dishonest if he believes, albeit mistakenly, that he has in law the right to deprive the other of the property.

If George was aware that he had no legal right to retain the money but alleges that he believed he was morally entitled to retain it then, according to the Court of Appeal in *Price* (1989) and *O'Connell* (1991), the issue of his dishonesty should be left to the jury instructed in accordance with the principles expounded in *Ghosh* (1982).

The jury must decide whether according to the ordinary standards of decent and honest people keeping the extra money was dishonest. If it was not dishonest by those standards, the prosecution fails.

If, on the other hand, the jury decide that it was dishonest according to those standards then they should consider whether George realised that keeping the money was, by the above standards, dishonest. If he did not realise that, then the prosecution fails.

Accessorial liability of Lucy

Provided George was dishonest and is guilty of theft, his wife Lucy may be guilty as an accomplice to the theft. By virtue of s 8 of the Accessories and Abettors Act 1861 a person who aids, abets, counsels or procures the commission of an offence is liable to be tried and punished for that offence as a principal offender.

Lucy may have aided the commission of the theft.

Although accessorial liability attaches only where assistance is given *before* the conclusion of the offence (*King's* case (1817)), it could be argued that where, as in this case, the appropriation consists of *'keeping* or *dealing* with the property as owner', the act of theft is a continuing one; in which case, the question whether George was still in the course of committing the offence is, presumably, a question of fact for the jury (1).

The fact that George was unaware of Lucy's assistance is, it is submitted immaterial (2).

With respect to the *mens rea*, the prosecution must prove that Lucy intended to assist and that she knew the essential matters ie the circumstances which must be proved in order to constitute the offence (*Johnson v Youden* (1950)). The facts of the problem clearly support this conclusion. She had been informed that her husband had been overpaid and was aware that this was in error.

In addition it must be shown that Lucy was either aware that George was acting with *mens rea* ie that he was dishonest as discussed above or, if she did not know that, she was aware that he may have been acting dishonestly (*Carter v Richardson* (1976)).

Handling - s 22 of the Theft Act 1968

If the theft was concluded prior to Lucy's involvement, then, as explained above, there can be no accessorial liability. In those circumstances, however, Lucy - assuming she *knows* or *believes* the money to be stolen - could be convicted of handling stolen goods contrary to s 22 of the Theft Act 1968. Lucy assisted George to retain the stolen money by persuading Liam that no money was owing (see *Kanwar* (1982)).

Conspiracy

There is no question of liability for conspiracy (even if George and Lucy had dishonestly agreed to keep the money). By virtue of the Criminal Law Act 1977 s 2 (2)a a person is not guilty of statutory conspiracy if the only other person with whom he or she agrees is his or her spouse. The same rule applies to common law conspiracy to defraud (*Mawji v R* (1957)).

Obtaining property by deception - s 15 of the Theft Act 1968

Lucy may be guilty of obtaining property by deception contrary to s 15(1) of the Theft Act 1968.

Clearly, she practised a deliberate deception when she falsely told Liam that George had received £90 (see s 15(4)). And, although Lucy does not , by deception, obtain property for herself, there is , by virtue of s 15(2) an obtaining of property for the purposes of this offence where the accused by any deception dishonestly 'enables another to ... retain'.

The property obtained must, at the time of the obtaining, belong to another. By virtue of s 34(1) the definition of 'belonging to another' in s 5(1) applies to s 15. However, s 5(4) does not apply and therefore the prosecution will have to rely upon the principle expressed in the *Chase Manhattan* case (above).

In addition, the prosecution must prove that Lucy was dishonest. The partial definition in s 2 does not apply to s 15. The judge must direct the jury in accordance with *Ghosh* (above). For a charge brought under s 15 he need not expressly direct them that claim of legal right is a defence as, according to the Court of Appeal in *Woolven* (1983), such a defence is incorporated within *Ghosh*.

Evasion of liability by deception - s 2(1) of the Theft Act 1978

Finally, Lucy may be guilty of evading liability by deception contrary to s 2(1) of the Theft Act 1978 (3).

Section 2(1)(b) provides that a person commits an offence where, by deception, he dishonestly induces a creditor to wait for payment or to forgo payment of an existing legally enforceable liability to make a payment. In addition, D must either intend to make permanent default of an existing liability of his own or intend to to let another, X, make permanent default of a liability owed by X (*Attewell-Hughes* (1991)).

It covers the situation where a debtor, by telling lies, persuades the creditor that there never has been a debt.

Provided Lucy was dishonest, and that she knew that George wished to avoid the debt, she is guilty of this offence. She has, by deception, induced Liam to forgo payment of an existing liability, ie £50, and did so with intent to let another ie George make permanent default.

It is immaterial whether the money is owed to Liam or Margaret as the offence is committed where the creditor or *a person claiming payment on behalf of the creditor* is induced by a deception to forgo payment.

If, however, Lucy did not know that George wished to default then she did not *intend to let* him make permanent default, and, therefore, would not be guilty of the offence under s 2(1)(b).

Notes

1   In *Hale* (1978) CA it was held in a case involving robbery that it was for the jury to decide whether or not the act of appropriation was at an end.

2   The Court of Appeal in *Attorney-General's Reference No 1 of 1975* stated, that D may 'procure' the commission of an offence even though the principal is unaware of D's involvement. The court stated, obiter, that the other forms of accessorial liability will *'almost inevitably'* involve the knowledge of the principal. Lord Widgery said that he found it difficult to think of a case of aiding, abetting or counselling when the parties have not discussed the offence which they have in mind. However, the court did not expressly state that the knowledge and/or agreement of the principal is a prerequisite of liability for the aider. Lord Widgery also stated that the words 'aid, abet etc' should be given their ordinary meaning. It is submitted that the ordinary meaning of the word 'aid' does not imply consensus see Smith and Hogan *Criminal Law* (1992) 7th ed p 128.

3   There is no liability under 2(1)a as there is no remission of liability when the creditor is deceived into believing that no debt exists.

Question 42

Tony, the tenant of 23 Railway Cuttings

(i)   removed the lead from the roof;

(ii) dug up a rose bush in the garden and gave it to his uncle, Sidney;

(iii) offered to sell the living room fireplace to his friend, Hattie. She declined the offer;

(iv) picked mushrooms from a neighbouring field intending to sell them to Luigi, the owner of a local restaurant;

(v)   agreed that his girlfriend, Lolita, could take a cherry tree growing in the garden when she visited the following day.

(Tony knew that his landlord would not have approved of any of the alterations or planned alterations to the house or garden.)

Discuss the criminal liability of the parties.

Answer plan

This question involves consideration of the meaning of 'property' for the purposes of the Theft Act 1968 and, in particular, the situations in which a person may be guilty of theft contrary to s 1 where they appropriate things forming part of the land.

The following points need to be discussed:

- theft of 'things forming part of the land'
- an 'offer to sell' as appropriation
- conspiracy where one party 'exempt'
- attempting the impossible
- the wider meaning of property for the purposes of criminal damage

Answer

The situations in which a person may be convicted of theft where they have appropriated 'something forming part of the land' are defined in s 4(2)(b) and s 4(2)(c) of the Theft Act 1968 (1).

Section 4(2)cc)is somewhat narrower than s 4(2)(b). Whereas the non possessor can be guilty of stealing *anything* forming part of the land, a tenant can be guilty only where he appropriates a *fixture* or *structure*.

(i)&(ii)

Thus, Tony by virtue of s 4(2)(c) may be convicted of stealing the lead contrary to s 1 but he is not guilty of stealing the rose bush. Consequently, his Uncle Sidney cannot be guilty of handling stolen goods contrary to s 22 of the Theft Act 1968. The goods are not stolen.

(iii)

With respect to the fireplace, s 4(2)(c), unlike s 4(2)(b), does not require that the fixture be severed to amount to an appropriation of property; and in *Pitham & Hehl* (1976) the Court of Appeal held that an offer to sell is an assumption of the owner's right to sell and hence an appropriation. Thus, provided, as the facts imply, Tony had a dishonest intention to permanently deprive, he may be convicted of theft.

Pitham has been criticised by leading academics. Professor Williams argues that the purported exercise of a power is not an assumption of a right of the owner. He points out that a person who purports to sell property belonging to another does not commit a civil wrong against the owner if there is no subsequent taking of possession and he insists there is no reason why he should be convicted of stealing it (2).

Attempt

Tony may be guilty of attempting dishonestly to obtain property, viz the money for the fireplace, by deception contrary to s 1(1) of the Criminal Attempts Act 1981.

Section 1(1) provides that, if with intent to commit an offence an indictable offence, a person does an act which is more than merely preparatory to the commission of the offence, he is guilty of attempting to commit the offence.

The question whether an act is 'more than merely preparatory' is a question of fact (s 4(3)). Thus where there is evidence on the basis of which a jury could reasonably conclude that the accused had gone beyond mere preparation, the judge must leave the issue to the jury (*Gullefer* (1990)). It is submitted that, in this case, there is clear evidence that Tony has done an act that is more than merely preparatory.

The above analysis is based on the assumption that the accused intended to practice a deception. Where a person offers goods for sale he impliedly represents that he has a right to sell those goods (see *Edwards* (1978)) but the facts of the problem are unclear as to whether Tony intentionally practised such a deception. He may have made it clear to Hattie that he had no right to sell the fireplace or he may have assumed that she knew he had no right to sell it in which case there can be no liability for attempting to obtain by deception.

What would the position be if Tony had intentionally made a false representation, either impliedly or expressly, that he had a right to sell the fireplace but Hattie had known that the representation was false?

Section 1(2) of the Criminal Attempts Act provides that a person may be guilty of attempting to commit an offence even though the facts are such that the commission of the offence is impossible. This is reinforced by s 1(3) which provides that D is to be judged according to his intentions and understanding of the facts.

In *Shivpuri* (1987) the House of Lords interpreting these two provisions held that in such cases it must be proved, firstly, that the accused had an intention to commit the crime in question and, secondly, that the conduct of the accused would have been more than merely preparatory to the commission of the offence if the facts had been as D believed them to be.

Thus, if Tony intentionally represented, falsely, that the fireplace was his to sell, he can be convicted of attempt, even if Hattie knew that he had no right to sell it.

(iv)

It is arguable that Tony is guilty of stealing the mushrooms. Although, in general, the person who picks wild mushrooms or flowers from wild plants growing on another's land is, by virtue of s 4(3), exempt from the provisions of 4(2)(b) the exemption does not apply where it is done for reward or sale or other commercial purpose.

Professor Smith argues that an isolated small scale case of picking might be held not to amount to a 'commercial' purpose.

The wording of the sub-section implies that sales must be 'commercial' and suggests therefore that the protection of the sub-section would be unavailable to Tony only if he had been making a business of dealing in the mushrooms (3).

(v)

Tony and Lolita may be guilty of statutory conspiracy to steal contrary to s 1(1) of the Criminal Law Act 1977.

The relevant part of the section provides that a person is guilty of conspiracy if he agrees with another that a course of conduct shall be pursued which if carried out would necessarily amount to the commission of an offence by one of the parties to the agreement.

There is no requirement that both parties are capable of committing the agreed offence as principal. Tony and Lolita made an agreement to dig up the tree which if carried out would amount to the commission of an offence by one of them (*Lolita*) and that constitutes a conspiracy. The fact that s 4(1) would exempt Tony from liability as a perpetrator does not exempt him from liability for conspiracy. And the exemptions to liability for *conspiracy* in s 2 of the 1977 Act are not relevant.

Section 4 of the 1968 Act would not exempt Lolita from liability for theft. And the exemptions in s 2(2) of the 1977 Act do not apply (4).

The above analysis is based on the assumption that Lolita had a dishonest intent. If, however, she mistakenly believed that Tony had the authority to allow her to remove the tree then her intended taking of the tree would not be 'dishonest' (s 2(1)(a) of the 1968 Act). And thus as both parties to the agreement must have *mens rea* there would be no conspiracy (s 1(1) and s 1(2) of the 1977 Act).

Criminal damage

The definition of 'property' for the purpose of criminal damage is in s 10 of the Criminal Damage Act 1971. It is broadly similar to the definition in s 4 of the Theft Act but, whereas there can be no theft of land or a building, criminal damage can be committed in respect of land or a building.

Thus, Tony may be convicted of criminal damage contrary to s 1(1) of the Act for damaging the roof and digging up the rose bush.

The *mens rea* requirement, which appears to be satisfied in both cases, is intention or *Caldwell*-type recklessness with respect to the risk of damage.

As he knew his landord did not approve of alterations, he cannot take advantage of the defence of 'lawful excuse' in s 5(2)(a) of the 1971 Act.

Tony and Lolita may be guilty of conspiracy to cause criminal damage (see above).

Section 5(2)(a) of the 1971 Act provides, however, that D has a lawful excuse to criminal damage if he damages property with the consent of a person who D mistakenly believed was entitled to consent. And thus there was no conspiracy if Lolita mistakenly believed that Tony was entitled to authorise the removal of the cherry tree (5).

(No offence would be committed if the agreement was carried out in accordance with *their* intentions.)

Finally the mushrooms cannot be the subject of criminal damage (s 10(1)(b) of the CDA 1971).

Notes

1   The relevant provisions are:-
    Section 4(2)(b) which provides that a person may be convicted of theft if, when not in possession of the land he appropriates anything forming part of the land by severing it or causing it to be severed and,
    Section 4(2)(c) which provides that a person in possession under a tenancy may be convicted of theft if he appropriates any fixture or structure let to be used with the land.
2   Professor Williams argues that it is 'jurisprudentially preposterous' to say that a person may be guilty of theft merely by making an offer. He contends that the error in the reasoning of the Court of Appeal lies in their failure to distinguish between the rights of an owner like the right to possession and the powers of an owner including the power to sell. An assumption of the rights of an owner is clearly an appropriation. Textbook of Criminal Law (1983) pp 763 - 766.

3   *The Law of Theft* (1989) 6th ed p 55.
4   (See also *Whitchurch* (1890) and *Duguid* (1906); *Sockett* (1908) is
    authority for the proposition that Tony might have been guilty
    as an accomplice had Lolita carried out the agreement.)
5   It is immaterial whether this belief is justified or not so long as
    it is honestly held (s 5(3); *Jaggard v Dickinson* (1981).

Question 43

Does a person who obtains property by deception contrary to s 15
of the Theft Act 1968 also thereby commit theft contrary to s 1?

Answer plan

This question requires a discussion of the (often conflicting)
authorities concerning the overlap between theft and obtaining
property by deception.

The principal issues are:

- the question whether a person may be said to 'appropriate
  property belonging to another' if the owner has been induced
  to part with ownership and/or possession as a result of a
  deception practices upon him
- issues of civil law concerning the passing of property

Answer

In general the question whether a person who is guilty of
obtaining by deception can also be convicted of theft depends on
whether it can be said that they have appropriated property
belonging to another.

If the nature of the transaction between D and P was such that,
although P has been induced to transfer *possession* of the property,
the *ownership* in the thing remained with P, then there is nothing
to prevent a conviction for theft should D dishonestly appropriate
the thing. On the other hand, if the victim of the deception
transferred his entire proprietary interest in the thing prior to any
act of appropriation by the defendant then it would seem to
follow that the defendant cannot be guilty of stealing it.

(It should be noted that, as a matter of civil law, the question whether ownership is transferred is answered by reference to the intention of the parties. Further, the effect of fraud (ie a deception) upon a contract of sale or a gift is not to prevent the passing of ownership. Under the civil law, fraud renders a contract voidable not void. Ownership transfers to the cheat but will revert to P if and when he rescinds the transaction.)

Consider the following example devised by Professor Smith as an illustration of an obtaining by deception which, he suggests, should not amount to theft:

D lies to P by saying that he requires a bottle of brandy to treat his sick mother. P goes round to D's house and in the latter's absence leaves the brandy. P intends to make a gift of the brandy to D. Consequently, as a matter of civil law, the ownership in the brandy is transferred to D. D returns and consumes the brandy. Although he has obtained the brandy by deception he has not appropriated property *belonging to another* (1).

Professor Smith contends that even if the transfer of ownership is practically simultaneous with the alleged appropriation there should be no liability for theft, although of course the defendant would be guilty of obtaining by deception.

There are a number of authorities, including the most recent decision of the House of Lords in *Gomez*, however, which decide that there is an appropriation of property belonging to another even where D, by deception, obtains the entire proprietary interest in the thing.

In *Lawrence* (1972) a newly arrived Italian student asked Lawrence a taxi driver to take him from Victoria station to Ladbroke Grove. The student gave Lawrence £1. Lawrence indicated that the fare was more than that and took a further £5 from the student's wallet. The student made no protest at this. The proper fare was approximately fifty pence.

Lawrence was convicted of stealing the approximate sum of £6. He appealed arguing that there was no theft as the Italian consented to the taking of the money.

The appeal was unsuccessful. The House of Lords rejected the contention that s 1(1) of the Theft Act should be construed as though it contained the words 'without the consent of the owner'.

Viscount Dilhorne, giving the judgment of the House, pointed out that the money in the wallet belonged to the Italian when Lawrence appropriated it.

Professor Smith does not agree that *Lawrence* is a clear authority for the proposition that a person appropriates property belonging to another where ownership passes simultaneously with the appropriation. He refers to those passages in the decision which indicate that the Lords were not convinced that the student consented to the taking of the excess fare and that therefore the property in the money did not pass to Lawrence (2). According to this analysis the decision in *Lawrence* is unremarkable. The theft was committed by the act of Lawrence in taking the money from the wallet without consent.

Professor Griew, however, argues that the decision read as a whole appears to say that the ownership in the money may not have passed but *even if it did pass* Lawrence was guilty of theft (3). This approach to *Lawrence* was adopted by the Court of Appeal in *Dobson v General Accident Fire and Life Assurance Corp plc* (1990).

The plaintiff had advertised a watch and ring for sale. A rogue answered the advertisement and agreed to buy the goods, payment to be made by building society cheque the following day. He collected the goods the following day in return for the cheque. The cheque had been stolen and was worthless.

The issue was whether the plaintiff was entitled to claim on his insurance policy for 'loss or damage caused by theft'.

The insurance company contended that although there was an offence under s 15(1) there was no theft. They submitted two arguments to support their contention that there was no appropriation of property belonging to another:

(i) firstly, the ownership in the watch had passed to the rogue prior to any act that conceivably amounted to an appropriation. The defendant insurance company argued that the ownership in the watch and ring transferred to the rogue either at the time of contracting but in any case before the possession of the articles was transferred to the rogue

(ii) and, secondly, because the plaintiff had consented to the rogue taking the watch there was no appropriation.

The Court of Appeal disagreed. They held that even if the ownership in the goods passed on the making of the contract there was an appropriation of property belonging to another. According to Parker LJ *the making of the contract* in these circumstances constitute the appropriation. That is, the transfer of ownership by contract may amount to an appropriation of property belonging to another. This analysis, if correct, would result in an almost complete overlap between theft and obtaining property by deception. Moreover, it would mean that a person might be convicted of both offences although he had not yet taken possession of the property.

(Note: a person may be regarded as obtaining property if he obtains ownership possession or control of it (s 15(2)).

The court also stated that, if the ownership in the articles passed on delivery, theft was committed at that moment. At the instant of delivery the plaintiff still owned the goods and the rogue appropriated property belonging to another.

In any case, the Court of Appeal took the view that probably the property was not intended to pass without a valid building society cheque in payment. If this analysis is correct then the conviction for theft is straightforward. However, it is submitted, that the normal civil law analysis of this type of fraud is that a voidable title is transferred to the fraudster.

Another criticism of the cases of *Lawrence* and *Dobson* concerns the effect of the apparent consent of the owner upon the question of whether there was an appropriation.

An appropriation is defined in s 3 as the assumption of the rights of an owner. And, until recently, the balance of authority supported the view that a person did not assume anothers rights if those rights were conferred upon him. The general view was that if the owner of the property consented to what the defendant did or otherwise authorised the acts of the defendant then although the latter may have had a secret dishonest intention he did not appropriate the property until he did something inconsistent with the consent of the owner.

In *Skipp* (1975), for example, the defendant pretended to be a haulage contractor. He was instructed to collect a number of loads from various sites in London and deliver them to Leicester. He absconded with the loads. The Court of Appeal held that even though Skipp had intended from the outset to steal the goods he did not appropriate the loads until he acted inconsistently with the instructions. Up until that point he had not assumed the rights of the owner.

In *Morris* (1984) the House of Lords held that an appropriation involves an act done which usurps the rights of an owner and there is no usurpation of those rights if the owner consents or otherwise authorises the actions.

In *Fritschy* (1985) the defendant, as instructed, took Krugerrands to Switzerland. He then absconded with them. Although he had intended to steal the Krugerrands from the outset he had not commited theft within the jurisdiction of the English courts as he had acted as authorised until he arrived in Switzerland.

In *Lawrence*, however, the House of Lords held that the defendant had appropriated the money. As mentioned above the House decided that to secure a conviction of theft there was no need to prove that the taking was without the consent of the owner. Rather confusingly, Lord Roskill in *Morris* thought that Lawrence had appropriated the money. His Lordship was not prepared to overrule *Lawrence*. It is possible that Lord Roskill thought that the Italian student had not consented to the taking of the £5.

The Court of Appeal in *Dobson* took the view that following *Lawrence* an act done with consent can amount to an appropriation. The court held that *Morris* had not overruled the 'very plain decision' in *Lawrence* that there may be an appropriation even if the owner consents. In an attempt to reconcile the various decisions the court drew a distinction between cases (eg *Skipp*; *Fritschy*) where D's dealing with the goods was 'authorised' and those where D merely had 'consent' to do what he did (eg *Lawrence*). The court held that an act done with consent may amount to an appropriation whereas an act done with authority could not.

The decision was clearly inconsistent with *Morris* in which Lord Roskill drew no distinction between consent or authority whether express or implied. He used the expressions interchangeably.

In *Gomez* (1992) the unworkable distinction between authority and consent was rejected by the Court of Appeal. D1, an assistant manager of a shop, obtained authority from his manager, P, to supply goods to D2 in return for a cheque. D1 knew that the cheques were worthless. The Court of Appeal held that as P had authorised the transaction there was a voidable contract and a transfer of ownership to D2. Therefore there was no appropriation of the goods and the defendants convictions for theft were quashed although clearly they were guilty of obtaining property by deception.

Lord Lane concluded that if there was a conflict between *Lawrence* and *Morris* then *Morris* should be followed. And in Lord Lane's view *Morris* decided that when D by deception induces the owner P to transfer his entire proprietary interest that is not theft because when D takes possession of the goods he is entitled to do so by virtue of the, admittedly voidable, contract of sale.

The House of Lords, by a majority, allowed the prosecutors' appeal. Lord Keith stated that, although the actual decision in *Morris* was correct, it was unnecessary and erroneous to suggest that an authorised act could never amount to an appropriation and, whilst he rejected the distinction drawn in *Dobson* between consent and authority, he agreed with much of Lord Parker's judgment including the opinion that *Morris* could not be regarded as having overruled the decision in *Lawrence*.

However, although he concluded that there was no significant distinction between the facts in *Dobson* and in the case before him, Lord Keith did not express any opinion on the suggestion made by Lord Parker in *Dobson* that the appropriation consisted of the making of the contract which resulted in ownership transferring under a voidable title. Indeed, he remarked that in the three cases, *Lawrence*, *Dobson* and *Gomez*, 'the *taking* amounted to an appropriation'.

Lord Keith referred to the cases of *Skipp* and *Fritschy* (discussed above), and concluded that, as they were both inconsistent with *Lawrence*, they were wrongly decided.

Lord Lowry, dissenting, referred to the *Eighth Report of the Criminal Law Revision Committee, Theft and Related Offences* (1966), and concluded that whilst the framers of the Theft Act recognised that there would be some overlap between theft and obtaining property by deception, it was intended that the statute recognise the distinction between obtaining *possession* by deception, and obtaining *ownership* by deception (3).

In the former case, Lord Lowry argued, the offender does appropriate the property because although the owner has handed over possession by consent (obtained by deception) the offender appropriates the thing by the unilateral act of dishonestly treating it as his own. In the latter case, however, the offender does not appropriate property belonging to another because the ownership is transferred with the owner's consent, albeit by deception.

In Lord Lowry's opinion, the statement made by Viscount Dilhorne in *Lawrence* that Parliament, by omitting the words 'without the consent of the owner' from s 1(1) of the Act 'has relieved the prosecution of the burden of establishing that the taking was without the owner's consent', was quite clearly wrong. It was based on the misconception that an appropriation was a neutral expression and not one which implied the sense of taking property for oneself without authority (4).

In addition, he criticised the supporters of *Lawrence* approach for choosing to ignore the civil law concerning the transfer of ownership (5) and pointed out that the interpretation adopted by the majority would mean that s 15 was strictly unnecessary and 'must have been included in the Act as a mere matter of convenience'. He rejected the view that s 15 'merely describes a particular type of theft' and that all stealing by means of deception can be prosecuted under s 1 as well as under s 15.

Lord Browne-Wilkinson did not agree that the decision of the House rendered s 15 otiose. As he correctly observed, if the subject matter of the obtaining is land then this may amount to an offence under s 15 but, in general, one cannot be guilty of stealing land (6).

Furthermore, as a result of the extended meaning of 'obtaining property' in s 15(2) a defendant who, by deception, 'enables another to retain property' belonging to another commits the offence under s 15 but, presumably, will not ordinarily be guilty of theft contrary to s 1, as he will not have done anything amounting to an appropriation, even in the extended 'neutral' sense.

It is rather hard to accept that s 15 was included in the Act to cover only these cases and that all other forms of obtaining are included within theft, but that is the conclusion that logically follows from the decision of the House in *Gomez*.

As Lord Lowry pointedly observed:

'A possible alternative theory is that the Committee, the responsible Government Department and the learned Parliamentary Draftsmen all thought that s 15 was needed, which turns out to be a mistaken view when s 1 is properly understood.'

Notes

1   *Law of Theft* (1989) 6th ed p 20.
2   *The Theft Acts 1968 and 1978* (1990) 6th ed p 56.
3   Lord Lowry quoted, with approval, a passage from the speech of Viscount Dilhorne in *Black-Clawson International Ltd v Papierwerke Waldhof-Aschaftenburg AG* (1975) AC 591 at p 63d said:
    'While I respectfully agree that recommendations of a Committee may not help much when there is a possibility that Parliament may have decided to do something different, where there is no such possibility, as where the draft Bill has been enacted without alteration, in my opinion it can safely be assumed that it was Parliament's intention to do what the Committee recommended and then to achieve the object the Committee had in mind. Then in my view the recommendations of the Committee and their observations on their draft Bill may form a valuable aid to construction which the courts should not be inhibited from taking into account.'
    In *Kassim* (1992) 1 AC 9 at p 16, Lord Ackner turned to the Eighth Report to ascertain the intended meaning of s 20 of the Theft Act.
    In *Gomez*, Lord Keith, on the other hand, thought that 'it serves no useful purpose at the present time to seek to construe the relevant provisions of the Theft Act by reference to the Report which preceded it, namely the Eighth Report ... The decision in *Lawrence* was a clear decision of this House upon the construction of the word 'appropriate' in s 1(1) of the Act, which had stood for twelve years when doubt was thrown upon it by obiter dicta in *Morris*'.
4   1972 AC 626 at p 632a.

5   Lord Keith, in *Gomez*, referred, with approval, to the following
     passage from the speech of Lord Roskill in *Morris* (1984) AC 320
     at p 334:
     'Without going into further detail I respectfully suggest that it is
     on any view wrong to introduce into this branch of the criminal
     law questions whether particular contracts are void or voidable
     on the ground of mistake or fraud or whether any mistake is
     sufficiently fundamental to vitiate a contract. The difficult
     questions should so far as possible be confined to those fields of
     law to which they are immediately relevant and I do not regard
     them as relevant questions under the Theft Act 1968.'
6   Section 34(1) of the Act applies sub-section (1) of s 4 to s 15. This
     defines property to include 'all ... property, real or personal'.
     Section 4(2) does not apply to s 15. It provides that, generally,
     'a person cannot steal land, or things forming part of the land ...'

Question 44

Dodger was a pickpocket. He entered a branch of the Mid west
bank and waited for a customer to make a large withdrawal of
cash. Mrs Pendlebury entered the bank and withdrew £500. She
put the money in an envelope and put the envelope into her bag.
Whilst she was distracted, Dodger picked the envelope from her
bag. Mrs Pendlebury realised what had happened and screamed
for assistance. Dodger dropped the money and ran out of the
bank. Trevor, an employee of the bank tried to block Dodger's
escape. Dodger pushed Trevor who fell and suffered slight
bruising. Dodger hailed a taxi and asked the taxi driver to take
him to the station. When they arrived at the station, Dodger asked
if he could pay by cheque. The taxi driver reluctantly agreed.
Dodger 'paid' the fare with a stolen cheque.

   Discuss Dodger's criminal liability.

Answer plan

This question involves a number of offences contrary to the 1968
and 1978 Theft Acts. Although it does not raise any particularly
difficult issues, it is important to be methodical about answering
this question. It is advisable in a question of this type for your
answer to mirror the sequence of events.

Particular issues to be considered:

- burglary: did D 'enter the bank as a trespasser'?
- robbery: was force used in order to steal?
- assaults: only minor injuries are suffered and therefore only liability under s 47 of the OAPA 1861 needs to be considered
- obtaining services by deception: was there a causal link?
- evasion of liability by deception - representations made when drawing cheques
- eaking off without payment. Does a person make off if they leave with permission?Is payment made 'as expected or required' when a stolen cheque is given

Answer

Burglary s 9(1)(a)

Dodger may be convicted of burglary contrary to s 9(1)(a) of the Theft Act 1968. This provides that a person commits burglary if he enters a building as a trespasser with intent to commit one of a number of specified offences, including theft (s 9(2)).

A person enters as a trespasser if he enters without consent or permission. Although there is an implied permission to enter a bank this is restricted to particular lawful purposes. As Dodger entered the building intending to steal, he entered in excess of the implied permission (*Jones & Smith* (1976)) and as he knew of the facts that made his entry trespassory he entered with the appropriate *mens rea* (*Collins* (1973))).

Dodger did not intend to steal specific property from a particular individual when he entered the bank. This, however, does not present a problem. A person may be convicted of burglary contrary to s 9(1)(a) if he intended to steal something in the building even though at the time of entry he had no specific item in mind. In the *Attorney-General's References Nos 1 and 2 of 1979* (1979) it was held that an intention to steal, conditional on there being money in the building, would suffice for burglary. The indictment should be framed in general terms alleging an 'intent to steal' without reference to specific property or victim.

Theft

When Dodger took the money from Mrs Pendlebury's bag, he committed theft contrary to s 1 of the Theft Act 1968. In *Corcoran v Anderton* (1980) two youths snatched a bag from a woman. The Divisional Court held that the appropriation took place at the moment they snatched it from her grasp.

The fact that Dodger did not manage to keep possession of the money makes no difference to his liability. Theft requires an intention to permanently deprive; there is no requirement of permanent deprivation in fact.

Burglary s 9(1)(b)

At this point he also committed burglary contrary to s 9(1)(b) of the 1968 Act.

This provides that a person is guilty of burglary if, having entered a building as a trespasser, he commits one of a number of specified offences, including theft.

It must be shown that the defendant entered as a trespasser (see discussion of this point above) and that *at the time of the theft* he knew or was at least reckless with respect to the facts that made his entry trespassory (*Collins* above).

Robbery

It would appear that Dodger is not guilty of robbery contrary to s 8 of the Theft Act 1968.

Robbery under s 8 requires the use or threat of force on any person in order to steal. There is no evidence in this case that he used force on Mrs Pendlebury when he stole the envelope from her bag. And, although for the purposes of robbery the force may be used on *any* person and not necessarily the person from whom the property was stolen, the force used against Trevor, it is submitted, would not suffice for robbery. Section 8 requires that the force is used 'immediately before or at the time of the theft' and 'in order to steal'. Dodger applied force to Trevor after the theft and did so in order to escape and not to steal.

In *Hale* (1978) it was said that an appropriation is a continuing act and that a person may be guilty of robbery when he uses force as he makes off with the property. The Court of Appeal held that the question whether the theft has come to an end is one for the jury. In *Hale*, however, the D's still had possession of the property as they made their getaway. In the case of Dodger the theft clearly came to an end when he dropped the envelope.

Assaults

Dodger may be convicted of assault occasioning actual bodily harm contrary to s 47 of the Offences Against the Person Act 1861.

The section requires that the defendant committed an assault or a battery which resulted in actual bodily harm (*DPP v Little* (1991)).

A battery is the intentional or reckless infliction of unlawful personal force on any person (*Faulkner v Talbot* (1981)).

When Dodger pushed Trevor in order to escape he committed a battery.

'Actual bodily harm' was defined in *Miller* (1954) to include any hurt or injury which interferes with the health or comfort of the victim and this would include even minor bruising.

Although the *actus reus* of the offence under s 47 requires that actual bodily harm be occasioned, the House of Lords held in *Savage* (1991) that, as far as the *mens rea* for the offence is concerned, it is not necessary to prove that the accused intended or foresaw actual bodily harm; all that is required is intention or recklessness with respect to the application of force (Recklessness in this context bears a 'subjective' meaning ie '*Cunningham*-type' recklessness is required (*Spratt* (1991)).

Thus, as he intentionally applied force to Trevor, and Trevor suffered actual bodily harm as a result, Dodger may be convicted of the offence under s 47 punishable with a maximum of five years imprisonment.

To amount to a 'wound' the inner and outer skin must be broken (*JCC v Eisenhower* (1983)) - a bruise is not a wound - and so, as the injuries suffered by Trevor were not serious, there is no liability under either ss 18 or 20 of the 1861 Act.

Obtaining services by deception

Dodger may be guilty of the offence of 'obtaining services by deception' contrary to s 1 of the Theft Act 1978.

If, when he hired the taxi, Dodger intended to use the stolen cheque to pay the fare, then he practised a deception which induced the taxi driver to 'confer a benefit by doing some act ... on the understanding that the benefit ... will be paid for' (1).

(A deception is a false statement made deliberately or recklessly s 15(4). A person hiring a taxi impliedly represents that he intends to pay the appropriate fare at the destination and thus if he intends to avoid payment he practises a deception.)

Evasion of liability

When he induced the taxi driver to accept the cheque, Dodger evaded liability by deception contrary to s 2(1)(b) of the Theft Act 1978.

He practiced a deception which induced the taxi driver to wait for payment of an existing liability.

In *Gilmartin* (1983) it was held that the giver of a cheque impliedly represents that it will be honoured. Dodger knew the cheque would not be met and consequently he practised a deception. And, s 2(3) provides that, for the purposes of 2(1)(b), a person induced to take a cheque in payment is not to be regarded as having been paid but as being induced to wait for payment.

As Dodger intended to make permanent default he is guilty of the s 2(1)(b) offence (2).

Making off without payment

Whether Dodger might be convicted of 'making off without payment' contrary to s 3 of the 1978 Act is not clear.

It remains to be authoritatively decided whether a person can be said to have 'made off without having paid as required or expected' if he left with the consent of the creditor, that consent having been obtained by deception.

A circuit judge at Lincoln Crown Court held that there is no 'making off' if the creditor consents to the defendant's leaving in circumstances such as those in the present problem (*Hammond* (1982)). It was said that a person who takes a cheque without a cheque card is aware of the risk of non payment and as he allows D to leave it cannot be said that D 'makes off'.

It is submitted that this interpretation of the section is wrong. The section is aimed at the bilking customer - it should not matter whether the D leaves with stealth or openly with or without the apparent consent of P.

If this latter view is correct, Dodger committed the s 3 offence on leaving the taxi. A stolen cheque does not operate as a conditional discharge of his liability to pay. Dodger made off *without having paid as expected or required.*

Going equipped

Section 25 of the Theft Act 1968 provides that a person is guilty of an offence if:

- when not at his place of abode
- he has with him any article
- for use in the course of or in connection with any burglary, theft or *cheat.*

By virtue of s 25(5) a 'cheat' is an offence under s 15 of the 1968 Act.

Although Dodger has not actually used the stolen cheques for a specified offence, he may be convicted of the s 25 offence if it could be proved that he *intended* to use them to obtain property, if and when the opportunity arose (*Ellames* (1976)).

Notes

The facts raise no issue of dishonesty and so this element has not been discussed. However, it is, of course, an ingredient of the *mens rea* for each of the Theft Acts offences (except s 25). If the issue is raised the prosecution must prove beyond reasonable doubt that the appropriation, obtaining or evasion was dishonest.

1   If his decision to avoid payment was only made when he reached the destination then the vital causal link between the deception and the obtaining would be lacking (see eg *Collis-Smith* (1971)).

2   There was no remission of the liability nor did the taxi driver
     agree to extinguish the debt and therefore there can be no
     liability under s 2(1)(a) of the 1978 Act.

Question 45

Arnold met George and told him that, unless George gave him a
video recorder from the shop in which George worked, Arnold's
brother, Malcolm would come round later and beat up George's
wife when she returned from shopping. George took a video
recorder from the stockroom and gave it to Arnold.

Arnold swapped the video recorder with his friend, Barry, for
a compact disc player which Barry had lawfully purchased.

Barry was pretty sure that the video recorder was stolen.

Barry sold the video recorder for £280 to Charlie, a bona
fide purchaser.

Barry gave the £280 to Mike.

Later that evening, Charlie learned that the video recorder had
originally been stolen. The following day, he sold it for £300 to
Eric, a bona fide purchaser.

Arnold who had become bored with the compact disc player
sold it to David. David was aware of all the circumstances.

Discuss the criminal liability of each of the parties.

Answer plan

This question is factually fairly complex. Liability for a number of
offences must be discussed in relation to each of the parties.

The principal issues are:
•   the meaning of 'stolen goods'
•   the effect of s 3(2) upon liability for theft

Answer

Theft (George)

George may be charged with theft of the video recorder, contrary to s 1 of the Theft Act 1968.

However, he may be able to take advantage of the defence of duress. This applies where the accused is compelled to commit an offence as a result of threats.

In *Ortiz* (1986) the Court of Appeal held that, as in George's case, threats to injure one's spouse will amount to duress provided the tests in *Graham* (1982) are satisfied.

That is, if George was compelled to steal the video recorder because he had good cause to fear that if he did not do so Malcolm would cause his wife serious injury and a sober person of reasonable firmness sharing the characteristics of the accused would have responded in a similar fashion then the defence will be made out. If, however, George failed to take a reasonable opportunity to escape the threat then duress can not be relied on (see *Hudson & Taylor* (1971)).

Duress, if successfully pleaded, is a complete defence absolving the accused of criminal liability. There is an evidential burden on the accused but the burden of disproving the defence lies with the prosecution (*Gill* (1963)).

Theft (Arnold)

Arnold appropriated property belonging to another and as he had a dishonest intention to permanently deprive the shop owner of it he is guilty of theft, contrary to s 1.

Robbery (Arnold)

Although Arnold has stolen and employed threats in order to effect the theft he cannot be guilty of robbery contrary to s 8 of the Theft Act 1968 because he did not 'put or seek to put any person in fear of being then and there subjected to force'. George was not in fear of being subject to force. Neither was his wife. She was not present at the time the threats were made.

Blackmail (Arnold)

However, Arnold may be guilty of blackmail, contrary to s 21 of the Theft Act 1968.

He made a 'demand' viz that George give him the recorder.

The demand was made with 'menaces' viz that Malcolm would beat up George's wife.

'Menaces' include 'threats of any action detrimental to or unpleasant to the person addressed' (*Thorne* (1937)). Provided the threat would have moved an ordinary person of normal stability and courage to accede unwillingly to the demand it will suffice for blackmail (*Clear* (1968)).

It is immaterial that the threat related to action to be taken by Malcolm and not Arnold, the person making the threat (s 21(2)). Nor does it matter that the victim of the blackmail, George, was not the individual to whom the threatened action was directed, George's wife.

The requirement that demand was made with ' a view to gain' in terms of property (s 34(2)(a)) is satisfied.

Whether or not the demand with menaces was unwarranted is a question of *mens rea*. There is nothing in the facts to suggest that Arnold believed that he had reasonable grounds for making the demand and that the menaces were a proper means of reinforcing the demand, and, therefore, it would appear he is guilty of blackmail.

Theft and handling (Barry)

If Barry knew or believed that the video recorder was stolen then he is guilty of theft, contrary to s 1 and handling stolen goods by receiving them, contrary to s 22 of the Theft Act 1968. Handling stolen goods is punishable with imprisonment for a maximum of 14 years.

By virtue of s 24 'stolen goods' means goods which have been stolen contrary to s 1 of the Act or obtained by deception contrary to s 15 or by blackmail contrary to s 21.

It must be shown that, at the time Barry came into possession of the recorder, that is, at the time he received it, he had the relevant *mens rea* ie he knew or believed it to be stolen.

Suspicion that the goods were stolen is not sufficient (*Grainge* (1974)). Nor is a belief that it is more probable than not that the goods are stolen (*Reader* (1978)).

On the other hand, if he did not know for certain that the goods were stolen but he was aware that on the basis of the circumstances as he knew them there was no other reasonable explanation then he would be guilty of receiving them believing them to be stolen (*Hall* (1985)).

Attempt to obtaining property by deception (Arnold)

In *Edwards* (1978) the Court of Appeal held that where a person purports to sell property he impliedly represents that he has a right to sell it. If he mistakenly thought that Barry believed the goods to be lawfully his, Arnold may be convicted of attempting to obtain property, ie the compact disc player, by deception contrary to s 1(1) of the Criminal Attempts Act 1981 (see s 1(3)).

Obtaining property by deception (Barry)

As Barry knew that the recorder might be stolen he recklessly represented that he had a right to sell it. As that representation was false, and as a deception made recklessly will suffice for liability (s 15(4)), Barry obtained the £280 by deception, contrary to s 15(1).

Handling the £280 (Mike)

If Barry was a handler, the £280, being the proceeds of stolen goods (the video recorder)in the hands of a handler (Barry), was itself 'stolen goods'(s 24(2)(b)). Thus Mike, provided he was both aware of the provenance of the money and was dishonest, may be convicted of handling by receiving.

Theft and handling (Charlie)

Charlie, as he was bona fide, was not guilty of theft when he took possession of the video recorder. Nor, on discovering that it was stolen, was he guilty of theft by 'keeping or dealing with it as owner'. Section 3(2) operates as an exception to the later assumption principle in s 3(1). The sub-section protects - from a conviction for theft - the innocent purchaser of stolen goods who later discovers they are stolen and decides to keep them or otherwise dispose of them.

As he had no *mens rea* when he took possession he cannot be convicted of handling by receiving. Nor, when he sold it, did he commit handling by undertaking or assisting in the retention, removal, disposal or realisation of the goods by or for the benefit of another. It was held in *Bloxham* (1983) that a person who sells stolen goods on his own behalf does not undertake nor assist in the realisation or disposal by or for the benefit of another. Their Lordships held that a person who sells an article does not assist the buyer to dispose of it since the buyer does not dispose of it nor does the seller undertake the realisation or disposal for the benefit of another as he sells it for his own benefit. The buyer benefits from the purchase but not from the realisation.

However, Charlie may be convicted of obtaining property viz £300 by deception, namely, by representing that the goods were his to sell (see *Edwards* and discussion above). Section 3(2) does not affect the principles of civil law concerning ownership nor does it provide protection from the offence in s 15.

Handling (David)

By virtue of s 24(2)(a) the compact disc player amounted to 'stolen goods' since it directly represented the goods originally stolen (the video recorder) in the hands of the thief (Arnold) as the proceeds of a disposition of then.

The problem states that David knew the circumstances. If this means he knew the history of the goods - how Arnold came by the video recorder and the compact disc player - then he is guilty of handling by receiving the player.

Question 46

(a) Albert approached Mrs Bennett as she was walking in the park with her sixth month old baby, Edgar. Albert threatened to hurt Edgar unless Mrs Bennett handed over some money. Mrs Bennett took a £50 from her purse and gave it to Albert. Discuss Albert's criminal liability.

(b) Michael was owed £30 by Thomas. When Michael asked for the return of the money owing, Thomas told him that he was unable to pay until the end of the month. Angered by this, Michael told Thomas that unless he hand over his watch in satisfaction of the debt he would beat him up. Reluctantly, Thomas handed over the watch.

Discuss Michael's criminal liability.

Answer plan

A two-part problem question concerning the (incomplete) overlap between robbery and blackmail.

The following points, in particular, need to be discussed:

- the meaning of 'puts or seeks to put any person in fear of being then and there subjected to force' in s 8 of the Theft Act 1968
- the meaning of 'menaces' in s 21 of the 1968 Act
- the difference between the meaning of 'dishonesty' for the purposes of theft and 'unwarranted' for the purposes of blackmail

Answer

(a) Theft

Albert has committed theft of the £50 contrary to s 1 of the Theft Act 1968 , an offence carrying a maximum of seven years imprisonment. Although Mrs Bennett gave him the money it was obviously not intended as a gift and thus it can be said that he 'appropriated property belonging to another', and the facts imply that he had the *mens rea* for theft ie a dishonest intention to permanently deprive Mrs Bennett of the money.

Robbery

A person is guilty of robbery, according to s 8, if he steals, and immediately before or at the time of doing so, and in order to do so, he uses force on any person or puts or seeks to put any person in fear of being then and there subjected to force.

The offence is punishable with life imprisonment.

However, although for the purposes of robbery, threats of force used on *any* person in order to steal will suffice, s 8 requires that the accused puts or seeks to put that person *in fear of being then and there subject to force.*

This requirement is not satisfied in the current problem. Albert did not put nor seek to put Mrs Bennett in fear of being subject to force because the threat was to hurt Edgar. Neither did he put, nor presumably seek to put, Edgar in fear of being subject to force. Edgar was, of course, unaware of Albert's threats.

For similar reasons, Albert may not be convicted of common assault nor assault with intent to rob contrary to s 8(2) of the Theft Act 1968.

A person is guilty of an assault if he intentionally or recklessly causes another to apprehend immediate and unlawful personal violence. In other words the victim must anticipate the application of immediate and unlawful force to his or her body. For the reasons explained above neither Mrs Bennett nor Edgar anticipated or apprehended such force (*Fagan v Metropolitan Police Commissioner* (1969)).

Blackmail

Section 21 of the Theft Act 1968 provides that a person is guilty of blackmail if, with a view to gain for himself or another or with intent to cause loss to another, he makes any unwarranted demand with menaces. Blackmail is an offence triable only on indictment and punishable with imprisonment for a maximum of 14 years.

Albert has made a demand for £50.

A 'menace' includes threats of any action detrimental to or unpleasant to the person addressed. It is not restricted to threats of violence directed at the victim of the demand (Lord Wright in *Thorne v Motor Trade Association* (1937)). Provided the threat is of such a nature and extent that the ordinary person of normal stability and courage would be influenced to accede unwillingly to the demand, the threat amounts to a menace (*Clear* (1968)).

Albert's threat to hurt Edgar would appear to amount to a menace. It is an issue for the jury but one might reasonably expect them to conclude that a threat to hurt a baby would move a mother to accede unwillingly to a demand to hand over money.

The demand must be made with a view to gain or intent to cause loss in terms of money or other property (s 34(2)(a)). In this case, Albert made the demand with a view to gain money.

Provided the prosecution can prove that Albert either did not believe that he had reasonable grounds for making the demand or that he did not believe that the menaces were a proper means of reinforcing the demand - and from the facts there appears to be no reason to doubt this - Albert's demand with menaces was 'unwarranted and he may be convicted of blackmail (see below for a fuller discussion of the meaning of 'unwarranted').

(b) Theft

Michael has committed the *actus reus* of theft ie he has 'appropriated property belonging to another'.

If, however, he genuinely, albeit mistakenly , believed that he was legally entitled to take the watch in satisfaction of the debt then, in accordance with s 2(1)(a) of the Theft Act 1968, his appropriation was not dishonest and therefore he did not commit theft. Furthermore, if Michael believed he had the legal right to deprive he cannot be convicted of either theft or robbery even if he knew that he had no legal right to use nor threaten force (*Robinson* (1977)).

Section 2 (1)(a) is limited to the situation where the accused believes he has a *legal* right to deprive another of property. If Michael knew that he had no legal right to the watch but considered himself to be *morally* entitled to take it then the question of his dishonesty would be determined by the jury directed in accordance with the test expounded by the Court of Appeal in *Ghosh* (1982).

According to the Court of Appeal the jury should be instructed, firstly, to determine what the accused's beliefs and intentions were and then, having done so, to decide whether what the accused did was dishonest according to the ordinary standards of reasonable and honest people. If they were not dishonest according to those standards the prosecution fails.

However, if the accused's actions were dishonest according to the ordinary standards of reasonable and honest people, the jury must consider whether the accused realised that what he did was dishonest according to those standards. If the accused did not realise that then he was not dishonest and the prosecution fails.

If the jury conclude that Michael was not dishonest then he is neither guilty of theft nor robbery. On the other hand, if the court concludes that he was dishonest he will be guilty of theft and as he put Thomas in fear of being subjected to force in order to steal, he will also be guilty of robbery.

With respect to Michael's liability for blackmail, he made a demand with menaces (as explained above) when he threatened to beat up Thomas unless he paid the money owing.

In addition, he acted with a view to gain. In *Parkes* (1973) it was held that the repayment of a debt is a gain. Whether he is guilty of blackmail will, therefore, depend upon whether his demand with menaces was unwarranted.

This is a question of *mens rea*. The onus is on the prosecution to prove *either* that Michael did not believe that he had reasonable grounds for making the demand for the return of the money *or* that he did not believe that the use of the threat to beat Thomas was a proper means of reinforcing the demand.

Albert might have believed he had reasonable grounds for making the demand but unless he also believed that the threat employed was morally and socially acceptable he will be guilty of blackmail. The test is subjective but the word 'proper' refers to general standards. A person believes a threat to be 'proper' not merely by believing that it is in accordance with his own standards. The test is whether he believes that the use of the threat would be regarded as proper by people generally (1).

In *Harvey* (1981) the Court of Appeal held that, in general, where the accused knew that the act threatened was unlawful it will not be possible for him to contend that he thought it was proper.

Therefore it is unlikely that Michael's demand with menaces was 'warranted' and thus he may be convicted of blackmail.

Note

1   But see *Lambert* (1972) where it was accepted that menaces were warranted if D believed that *by his own standards* what he threatened was proper.

Question 47

Plug went in to a supermarket belonging to Beefy intending to do some shopping and to steal some Forest lager. When Plug arrived at the beer counter he discovered that Forest lager was out of stock. He put a bottle of sherry in the trolley provided by the supermarket intending to steal it at some later stage. Plug continued with his shopping. He selected a bottle of his favourite wine He did not notice that the particular bottle he chose was underpriced. Plug then removed a 30p label from a tin of peas and put it on a £1 tin of salmon. He was about to take the underpriced salmon from the shelf and place it in the trolley when he noticed that he was being observed by a shop assistant. He left the salmon on the shelf and also returned the bottle of sherry to its shelf. At the checkout, as he gave the bottle of wine to the shop assistant Plug noticed that it was underpriced. He said nothing. The shop assistant rang up the price marked on the bottle. In addition, the assistant gave Plug too much change. Plug did not notice the excess until after he had left the supermarket. He decided to keep it.

Discuss Plug's criminal liability.

Answer plan

This question concerns the familiar problem of theft from supermarkets and the question of whether there is an appropriation where D does an act expressly or impliedly authorised by the supermarket owner. You should consider separately his liability for theft of each of the various items. The question also raises issues concerning liability for burglary where D enters premises in excess of an implied permission. The offence of obtaining property by deception is also discussed with reference to the obtaining of the wine at a reduced price.

The principal issues are:

- burglary under s 9(1)(a) of the Theft Act 1968; entry in excess of implied permission
- theft of the sherry, salmon and wine; appropriation and consent - the decision of the House of Lords in *Gomez* (1992)
- obtaining property, ie the wine, by deception - does silence constitute deception?
- section 5(4) of the Theft Act 1968 - property got by another's mistake - and theft of the excess change

Answer

Burglary

By virtue of s 9(1)(a) of the Theft Act 1968 a person is guilty of burglary if he enters a building as a trespasser intending to commit one of a number of offences. By virtue of s 9(2) the offences specified include theft contrary to s 1 of the Act.

The penalty for burglary in a building other than a dwelling is a term of imprisonment not exceeding ten years (s 9(3)(a) as substituted by the Criminal Justice Act 1991).

The *actus reus* of burglary contrary to s 9(1)(a) consists of entering a building as a trespasser. A person enters as a trespasser if he enters without the consent or permission of the occupier. Furthermore, it was decided in *Jones & Smith* (1976) that a person is a trespasser for the purposes of s 9 if he enters premises in excess of the permission that has been given to him - provided that he knows that he is entering in excess of the implied permission or at least is reckless with respect to that fact (see *Collins* ((1973)).

As Professor Williams has pointed out, the decision implies that a person who enters a building intending to commit one of the specified offences is a trespasser at the moment of entry; and, thus, a person who enters a supermarket intending to steal items within the shop is a burglar. The shopkeeper's invitation to enter the premises does not extend to those who enter for the purpose of stealing, and it is submitted that an entry is trespassory where, as in Plug's case, a person enters partly for lawful purposes, ie to do their shopping and partly for unlawful purposes, ie to steal (1).

As Plug entered intending to steal he was aware of the facts that made his entry trespassory and therefore may be convicted of burglary.

It is immaterial for liability under s 9(1)(a) that he failed to get his hands on any lager. He *intended* to steal and that is sufficient.

Theft

Section 1 of the Theft Act 1968 provides that a person is guilty of theft if he dishonestly appropriates property belonging to another with the intention of permanently depriving the other of it.

The maximum punishment for this offence is a term of imprisonment not exceeding seven years (s 7 of the Theft Act as substituted by s 26 of the Criminal Justice Act 1991).

(i) the sherry

In *Morris* (1984) Lord Roskill stated that appropriation involved an usurpation of the rights of an owner and therefore a person did not appropriate an article if he did an act which was expressly or impliedly authorised by the owner.

The House approved the decision of the Divisional Court in *Eddy v Niman* (1981) where D, a shopper, intending to steal, had put items in the basket provided by the supermarket. The Divisional Court held that, despite D's secret dishonest intention there was no theft at that stage as D had acted within the scope of the authority granted to shoppers.

Lord Roskill also referred to *MacPherson* (1973) where D removed two bottles of whisky from a shelf in a supermarket and put them in *her own shopping bag*. It was held by the Court of Appeal that there had been an appropriation. Lord Roskill regarded the decision as wholly consistent with the principles he had expressed regarding the nature of an appropriation. In his view, the appropriation was effected by the combination of the acts of removing the goods from the shelf and of concealing them in the shopping bag.

In *Gomez* (1992), however, the House of Lords preferred a broader more 'neutral' view of appropriation. Lord Keith, delivering a speech in which the majority concurred, stated that, although the actual decision in *Morris* was correct, it was erroneous and unnecessary to state that an authorised act could never amount to an appropriation. He referred, with approval to a passage from the judgment of Lord Parker in *Dobson v General Accident Fire and Life Assurance Corp plc* (1990) in which it was observed that the transcript of the judgment in *McPherson* revealed that the bottles of whisky were appropriated *when they were taken from the shelves*.

Lord Keith observed that by taking the article from the shelf the shopper gained control of the article and acquired the capacity to exclude other shoppers from taking it, and thus could be said to have assumed some of the rights of an owner over it.

Thus, as Plug had a dishonest intention to steal when he removed the sherry from the shelf he committed theft then and there and the fact that he returned the sherry to the shelf is legally immaterial (2).

(ii) the salmon

In *Morris* it was held that a person who exchanges labels on items in a supermarket intending to buy the more expensive article for the cheaper price appropriates the more expensive article. According to Lord Roskill in *Morris* the assumption of any of the rights of the owner amounts to an appropriation.

In *Gomez*, Lord Keith said that the switching of price labels on an article for sale is, in itself, an appropriation, whether or not it is accompanied by some other act such as removing the article from the shelf and placing it in a basket or trolley. He stated that no one but the owner has the right to remove a price label from an article or to place a price label upon it.

Thus, provided, as the facts imply, that Plug had a dishonest intent, he stole the salmon when he changed the label and the fact that he did not remove the salmon from the shelf is legally immaterial.

Furthermore, Plug may be convicted of burglary contrary to s 9(1)(b). This provides that a person is guilty of burglary if, having entered a building as a trespasser, he steals anything therein. Plug intended to steal when he entered the shop and therefore his entry was trespassory and he was aware of that fact when he appropriated the sherry and the salmon (see the discussion above; *Jones & Smith; Collins*).

Although, following *Gomez*, Plug appropriated the peas, he did not steal them as he had no dishonest intent in respect of them.

(iii) the wine

Although Plug may be said to have appropriated the bottle of wine when he removed it from the shelf he had no dishonest intention to steal and therefore he did not commit theft at that point.

Nor, it is submitted, did he commit theft when he took possession of the bottle, the incorrect price having been rung up by the cashier. In *Dip Kaur* (1981) it was held that a mistake as to price does not render a contract void. The ownership in the goods transfers to the buyer who, therefore, cannot be said to appropriate property *belonging to another* when he pays for and takes possession of the goods.

Doubt was cast on the decision in *Kaur* by Lord Roskill in *Morris*. His Lordship did not fully explain why he considered *Kaur* to be wrongly decided but said that he did not consider fine points of civil law regarding void and voidable contracts to be relevant issues as far as theft was concerned.

Although *Kaur* was not discussed in *Gomez*, Lord Keith agreed that it was wrong to introduce into this branch of criminal law questions whether particular contracts are void or voidable on the ground of mistake or fraud

It is respectfully submitted that it is not possible to avoid recourse to the civil law when the facts raise the issue of whether the property belonged to another at the time of the alleged appropriation. And, indeed, in *Walker* (1984) the Court of Appeal allowed D's appeal against conviction for theft where the trial judge had failed to direct the jury with respect to the relevant issues of civil law contained in the Sale of Goods Act 1979.

In addition - although the point was not argued in *Kaur* - Plug may contend that taking the incorrectly priced wine was not dishonest.

If Plug mistakenly believed that he had a right in law to take the wine at the price indicated then, as a matter of law, he was not dishonest (s 2(1)(a)). Alternatively, even if he knew that he had no legal right to the wine at the wrong price, he may raise evidence that he believed that it was not dishonest by ordinary standards to take advantage of a pricing error made by a supermarket. If so, the judge should direct the jury in accordance with what is known as the '*Ghosh* tests' to consider as a matter of fact whether he was dishonest (*Roberts* (1987)).

In *Ghosh* (1982) the Court of Appeal held that an appropriation of property belonging to another is not dishonest if what the defendant did was in accordance with the ordinary standards of reasonable and honest people or the defendant mistakenly believed that what he did was in accordance with those standards. (The burden of proof is on the prosecution to prove that the appropriation was dishonest.)

Obtaining property by deception

Did Plug obtain the wine by deception?

The Divisional Court in *Kaur* held that D in that case had used no deception to obtain the goods. In general, in criminal law and civil law, silence constitutes neither fraud nor deception and the answer to the question posed above is, therefore, 'no' (3).

Theft of the change

Plug did not steal the excess change when he was given it by the cashier. As he was unaware of the excess he did not dishonestly appropriate it.

Section 3(1) provides, however, that a person appropriates property on the basis of a later assumption of a right to it 'by keeping or dealing with it as owner'. And although the ownership in the money passed to Plug on delivery, the excess change is regarded as belonging to Beefy. The conditions in s 5(4) apply. The money was 'got by another's mistake' and Plug is 'under an obligation to make restoration' (in quasi-contract).

Again, Plug may contend that keeping excess change is not dishonest, in which case the jury should be instructed to resolve the issue in accordance with the *Ghosh* tests discussed above.

Notes

1   *Textbook of Criminal Law* (1983) 2nd ed p 848.
2   It is extremely unlikely, however, that the offence would be detected as Plug's *behaviour* corresponds to the terms of the implied consent granted to shoppers in supermarkets to remove goods from the shelf.
3   *DPP v Ray* (1974) is distinguishable from the present facts. In that case the restaurant customer was taken to impliedly represent on ordering a meal that he intended to pay for it which he continued to make throughout. A shopper, on the other hand, does not impliedly represent the accuracy of the prices displayed on goods for sale. Nor if he remains silent does he do anything positive to induce a false belief in the accuracy of the price.

Question 48

Simon checked in at the Shilton Hotel. He produced a forged membership card of the Travel Club. Membership of the Club entitled clients of the hotel to a 20% discount off the price of a room. In addition, Travel Club guests receive a complimentary bottle of wine in their rooms. He decided that, before going to his room, he would have a drink in the hotel lounge. He entered the lounge, but found it to be empty. He noticed that the bar till was open. He went behind the bar, intending to take any cash he found in the till. The till was empty so he left the lounge. He went to his room and consumed the wine. The following morning he checked out of the hotel. He paid the discounted price for the room. He then went to the hairdressers to have his haircut. He paid with a stolen credit card.

Discuss Simon's criminal liability.

Answer plan

This question requires consideration of a number of offences found in the Theft Acts 1968 and 1978 (principally those involving deception).

Principal issues:

- the requirement of a 'causal link' in deception offences
- does a person 'make off' if they have (fraudulently obtained) consent to depart
- burglary and conditional intent
- evasion of liability - s 2 of the Theft Act 1968

Answer

Evasion of liability

It would appear that when Simon checked in to the hotel presenting a forged Travel Club card he committed the offence of 'evasion of liability by deception' contrary to s 2(1)(c) of the Theft Act 1978.

Section 2(1)(c) is not restricted to the evasion of an existing liability. It also covers the situation where, as in this case, the accused practices a deception to obtain an abatement of a prospective liability (1).

Section 5(1) of the Theft Act 1978 provides that 'deception' bears the same meaning for the purposes of s 2 as it does for s 15 of the Theft Act 1968 ie a deliberate or reckless deception by words or conduct as to fact or law.

Simon represented by his conduct (the presentation of the card) that he was a member of a club entitled to a discount. He obtained the abatement of liability by virtue of that deception. Therefore, provided that Simon was dishonest at the time he checked in, he is guilty of the offence in question (2).

Obtaining services

In addition, it would seem that Simon has, by deception, dishonestly obtained services from another contrary to s 1(1) of the Theft Act 1978. The maximum punishment for this offence is also five years imprisonment.

The comments made above regarding the issues of 'deception' and 'dishonesty' apply equally to the offence now under discussion.

Simon was permitted to enjoy the services of the hotel on the understanding that they would be paid for, albeit at a reduced rate and thus, there was an 'obtaining of services from another' (3).

Obtaining property

With respect to the free bottle of wine, Simon may be charged with the offence of obtaining property by deception contrary to s 15 of the Theft Act 1968. The maximum punishment is ten years imprisonment.

Simon has, by the false representation that he was a member of the Travel Club induced the hotel to make him a gift of the wine. By virtue of s 15(2) he has obtained property ie the ownership of the wine by deception and, provided he was dishonest, he is guilty of the offence. In addition, he may be convicted of stealing the wine contrary to s 1 of the Theft Act 1968. In *Gomez* (1992) the House of Lords held, by a majority, that an appropriation of property belonging to another can occur even if the owner consents to what D does and even if ownership in the property transfers to P.

Burglary

Did Simon commit burglary contrary to s 9 of the Theft Act 1968 when he went behind the bar intending to steal any cash he found in the till?

According to s 9(1)(a) a person is guilty of burglary if he enters any building or part of a building as a trespasser with intent to commit one of a number of specified offences. These include theft of anything in the building or part of the building (s 9(2)).

The maximum punishment is 14 years imprisonment.

Trespass in the law of tort refers to presence on property without legal right. In general, presence on the property without the consent of the possessor is a trespass. Thus a person enters a building or part of a building as a trespasser if he enters without permission and where permission to enter is limited to certain parts of the premises, there is a trespassory entry where that permission is exceeded.

Whether the area behind the bar constituted a separate 'part' of the building from which Simon was excluded is a matter for the jury (*Walkington* (1979)). If they are satisfied that the hotel management had impliedly prohibited customers from that area and that Simon knew of (or was reckless in respect of) that prohibition then he may be convicted of burglary (*Collins* (1973)).

The fact that Simon intended to steal 'any cash that he found' does not preclude a conviction for burglary. In *Attorney-General's References Nos 1 and 2 of 1979* it was held that where D is charged with entry into a building or part of a building with intent to steal, and the indictment does not allege an intent to steal a specific object, he can be convicted if at the time of entry he intended to steal *something* in the building or part of a building.

This applies even though he merely intended to steal anything that he may find worth stealing and even though there was, as in this case, nothing that he regarded as being worth stealing. Where D intends to steal anything of value or worth stealing at the time he commits the *actus reus*, he has the necessary 'intention to steal' for the purposes of s 9(1)(a) burglary.

Evasion of liability

When Simon checked out, continuing the deception that he was entitled to a discount he committed the offence under s 2(1)(b) of the Theft Act 1978 (3).

The receptionist has been induced to forbear from demanding the full price by Simon's continuing representation that he was entitled to a discount and he intended to make permanent default in *part* on the still existing liability to make a payment.

The maximum punishment is five years imprisonment.

Making off without payment

Whether Simon may be convicted of the offence of 'making off without payment' contrary to s 3 of the Theft Act 1978 is more controversial. It remains to be authoritatively decided whether a person can be said to have 'made off without having paid as required or expected' if he leaves with the consent of the creditor, the consent having been obtained by deception. In *Hammond* (1982) a circuit judge held that there is no 'making off' if the creditor consents to D leaving.

It is submitted that this interpretation of the section is wrong. The section is aimed at the bilking customer - it should not matter whether D leaves with stealth or openly, with or without the apparent consent of the creditor.

The punishment for contravention of s 3 is a term of imprisonment not exceeding two years.

The barber shop

Provided Simon intended to use the stolen credit card prior to asking the hairdresser to cut his hair, he committed the offence of obtaining services by deception contrary to s 1 of the 1978 Act. In *Lambie* (1982) it was held that the user of a credit card impliedly represents that he has authority to use it.

In addition, whether or not he intended to use the card from the outset, he is guilty of the offence of evasion of liability contrary to s 2(1)(a) of the Act. By tendering a stolen credit card in 'payment' for the haircut, he, by deception, secured the remission of an existing liability to make a payment (*Jackson* (1983)).

Notes

1 The sub-section provides that a person commits an offence if, by any deception, he dishonestly obtains any exemption from or abatement of liability to make a payment. The maximum punishment is five years imprisonment.

2 Although there is nothing in the facts of the problem to raise the issue of dishonesty, there are some general observations that may be made in respect of this element of the *mens rea*. Firstly, dishonesty is a question of fact for the jury. Secondly, the partial negative definition of dishonesty in s 2 of the Theft Act 1968 does not apply to the various offences of deception. Finally, it is only where there is evidence that the accused was not dishonest on the basis of the tests in *Ghosh* (1968) that the judge must leave the issue to the jury. As the facts do not raise any issues of dishonesty, it has been assumed throughout that Simon was dishonest.

3 Section 1(2) provides that there is an obtaining of services from another where the other is induced to confer a benefit by doing some act, or causing or permitting some act to be done on the understanding that the benefit has been or will be paid for.

4 According to this sub-section a person commits an offence where by any deception he dishonestly and with intent to make permanent default, in whole or in part, on any existing liability to make a payment induces a creditor to forgo payment.

Question 49

(a) Stanley, a schizophrenic, received what he believed were instructions from 'God' to destroy all 'places of sin'. Stanley explained to 'God' that it was a crime in England to destroy property. 'God' reassured Stanley that, if he did as he was instructed, no human life would be endangered and informed him that unless Stanley set about the task immediately the towns of England would be destroyed in alphabetical order. Stanley who lived in Accrington, responded straightaway. He went out and threw a petrol bomb through the window of a betting shop. The shop was completely destroyed. Although there were a number of people in neighbouring buildings, no-one was injured.

Discuss Stanley's criminal liability.

(b) Optic lived at No 11 Acacia Avenue. One night he arrived
home drunk. By mistake he attempted to get in to No 13. As
his key failed to open the door, he assumed that the lock was
broken. He went to the back of the house and, to gain entry,
smashed the window of the back door.

Discuss Optic's criminal liability.

Would your answer differ if No 11 had been the house of one of
Optic's friends with whom Optic had been spending a few days?

Answer plan

Although both parts of this question contain elements of liability
for criminal damage, they deal with quite different issues. The
first part focuses on the defence of insanity. The second part
involves analysis of the contrasting treatment of, on the one hand,
drunken mistakes going to the *mens rea* and, on the other,
drunken mistakes going to a 'defence' of 'lawful excuse'.

Particular issues:

- the meaning of 'recklessness'
- the meaning and application of 'lawful excuse' in s 5(2)(b) of
the Criminal Damage Act 1971 - protection of property
- the defence of insanity - nature and quality of act; insane
delusions
- drunkenness and '*Caldwell* recklessness'
- the meaning and application of 'lawful excuse' in s 5(2)(a) -
belief in consent; mistake induced by drunkenness and s 5(2)(a).

(a) Stanley may be charged with criminal damage contrary to
s 1(1) of the Criminal Damage Act 1971 ('simple damage')
and damaging property being reckless as to whether the
life of another would be endangered contrary to s 1(2)
('dangerous damage').

Where the offence is committed by fire then it is charged as
arson (s 1(3)). Arson is punishable with life imprisonment (s 4(1)).

Clearly, Stanley committed the *actus reus* of both offences
('Property' includes land - s 10(1) of the 1971 Act).

In the case of simple damage, the *mens rea* is satisfied on proof
of an intention to damage/destroy property belonging to another
or recklessness with respect to that. The facts of the problem
indicate that he intended to destroy the building.

Section 5(2)(b) of the 1971 Act provides that a person has a lawful excuse for the purposes of 'simple damage' if he destroyed property to protect other property which he believed to be in need of immediate protection. (This 'defence' does not apply to 'dangerous damage).

In *Hunt* (1978) however, the Court of Appeal held that whether property was in need of protection involves an objective question - whether in fact the action taken might protect property (1).

Undoubtedly the court would take the view that destroying a betting shop could not protect Accrington, and thus Stanley committed 'simple damage' (subject to the defence of insanity discussed below).

For dangerous damage the prosecution would have to prove that he was at least reckless with respect to the prospect of the life of another being endangered.

This requires proof that (1) by setting fire to the betting shop Stanley created an obvious risk that life would be endangered and that (2) Stanley had either (a) not given any thought to the possibility of there being any such risk, or (b) having recognised that there was some risk went on to take it (*Caldwell* (1982)).

Whether a risk is 'obvious' is determined by reference to whether the reasonable prudent person would have appreciated it as such. It is immaterial that D failed to appreciate the risk. This rule applies even if D was incapable, for whatever reason, of appreciating the risk. The first part of the definition is entirely objective (*Elliott v C* (1983)).

Let us assume that in this case the risk of life being endangered was 'obvious', as defined. That is not the end of the matter. The prosecution must prove, in addition, that Stanley had one of the alternative 'states of mind' (2a or 2b) described in the second limb of the *Caldwell* formula.

The facts state that Stanley considered the risk of human life being endangered and acted on the assurance of God that it would not be. Thus Stanley lacked both of the alternative 'states of mind' required by the second limb of the test. He falls within the so-called loophole in the *Caldwell* test (see *Reid* (1992)) (2).

Thus, as he has neither intentionally nor recklessly endangered life he cannot be convicted of the offence under s 1(2).

Insanity

According to the *McNaghten Rules* (1843) a person is legally insane if at the time he committed the act he was suffering from:

1 a defect of reason caused by disease of the mind
2 (a) as not to know the nature and quality of his act
    or
    (b) if he did know that he did not know he was doing what was wrong.

There is a presumption of sanity in English law. The burden of proving insanity is, therefore, on Stanley. He must prove his case on a balance of probabilities (*McNaghten Rules*; *Bratty v Attorney-General for Northern Ireland* (1963)).

Whether a condition amounts to insanity is a question of law (*Bratty v Attorney-General for Northern Ireland* (1963)).

In *Sullivan* (1984) Lord Diplock explained that disease of the mind in the Rules refers to an impairment of the faculties of reason, memory and understanding. It is unnecessary to show that the brain is diseased - the disorder may be functional.

The condition from which Stanley suffered is clearly capable in law of amounting to a disease of the mind.

The judges in the *McNaghten* case said that, in cases of insane delusion, the defendant is to be considered in the same situation as to responsibility, as if the facts were as he perceived them to be.

His delusion that God was going to destroy other property unless he destroyed the places of sin falls within this rule. If the facts had been as he believed, he would have had a lawful excuse. He believed that the property was in immediate need of protection, (see s 5(2)(b)(i)) and that the means adopted were reasonable, and, therefore, the proper verdict on a charge of simple damage is 'not guilty by reason of insanity'.

As explained above, Stanley apparently lacked the *mens rea* for 'dangerous damage'. However, again, he is entitled only to a qualified acquittal. Where the defendant has put his state of mind in issue the judge may rule that he has raised the defence of insanity (*Bratty v the Attorney-General for Northern Ireland* (1963)); *Sullivan* (1984)) (3).

As Stanley understood his act to be legally wrong the case for insanity must be based on the 'nature and quality' limb. This refers to whether Stanley knew what he was doing. It has not been authoritatively decided whether this would apply to the situation where D dismisses a risk that the reasonable man would recognise as 'obvious', but, it is submitted, the foreseeable consequences of an act are an element of the nature and quality of the act - and that this interpretation is supported by the rule regarding insane delusions (4).

Where a defendant is found not guilty by reason of insanity, the judge must make one of a number of orders including a hospital order with or without restrictions on discharge (s 5 of the Criminal Procedure (Insanity) Act 1964 as substituted by the Criminal Procedure (Insanity) Act 1991 Sched 1).

(b) Optic may be guilty of 'simple damage' as defined in s 1(1) of the Criminal Damage Act 1971 (see above).

He has damaged property ie the window belonging to another.

Clearly Optic on the facts did not *intend* to damage property *belonging to another*. But he may have been reckless. If, in the light of all the evidence, the jury conclude that the risk that the property might belong to another was 'obvious' (as explained above) then Optic will be liable if he failed to give any thought to the risk that the property belonged to another. The fact that he thought it was his, does not necessarily mean, it is submitted, that he put his mind to the *risk* of it belonging to another (5).

If he thought about the risk but because he was drunk he concluded, wrongly, that there was no risk then although not reckless (6) he may be convicted of 'simple damage'. Where D is alleged to have 'recklessly damaged property belonging to another' the offence is one of 'basic intent' (*Caldwell*). A lack of *mens rea* caused by drunkenness is no defence to a crime of basic intent (*Majewski* (1977)).

Alternative facts

In this situation Optic will have a 'lawful excuse' if he believed that the person *whom he believed to be entitled* to consent to the damage (ie his friend) would have consented to the damage (s 5(2)(a)) of the 1971 Act (7).

In similar circumstances, the Divisional Court in *Jaggard v Dickinson* (1981) held that D could rely on her intoxication to explain her mistaken belief. The Divisional Court considered that the *Majewski* rule was inapplicable. This was not a case where the D's 'drunken mistake' went to the *mens rea*.

The Divisional Court were influenced by the fact that s 5(3) provides that, for the purposes of s 5(2), it is immaterial whether the belief is justified or not so long as it is genuinely held.

Notes

1 This decision ignores the clear subjective terms in which the sub-section is expressed. The use of the expression *'in order to protect property'* implies a subjective test. *Hunt* was followed, however, in the cases of *Ashford & Smith* (1988) and *Hill & Hall* (1989).

2 In *Reid* Lord Browne-Wilkinson appeared to suggest that the loophole applies in situations where 'despite D being aware of the risk and deciding to take it, he does so because of a reasonable misunderstanding' (at p 696 f).
   There are two objections to this:
   (i) if D takes a risk of which he is aware he is reckless. As explained above the lacuna in *Caldwell* applies where D has considered whether there is a risk and concluded there is *none*.
   (ii) there is no justification for narrowing the lacuna to the situation where D *reasonably* concludes there is no risk. As Lord Goff pointed out both limbs of the *Caldwell* test of recklessness are tests of *mens rea* and that a bona fide mistaken belief that there was no risk will excuse. The reasonableness of the mistake is merely evidence that it was genuinely held (at p 690 f-h).

3 According to Lord Denning in *Bratty* (1963) the prosecution may adduce evidence of insanity when the defendant puts his state of mind in issue. Professor Williams argues that this is not limited to cases of automatism and would apply where the defendant as in this case alleges a mistake of fact. *Textbook of Criminal Law* (1983) 2nd ed p 664.

4 Williams, *Textbook of Criminal Law*, p 657.

5 In *Pigg* (1982) the Court of Appeal held that *Caldwell* recklessness applies to the circumstances of an offence as well as the consequences.

The prosecution may give evidence that Optic was drunk in support of their case that he had not thought about the risk or that he had consciously taken a risk that he would not have had he been sober (*Griffiths* (1989); *Clarke* (1990)).

6 See the explanation of the '*Caldwell* loophole' in part (a) above.
7 The D has an evidential burden in relation to a s 5(2) defence; *Gannon* (1988) CA.

Question 50

(a) George telephoned Paul and said that, if Paul did not destroy some compromising photographs of George with Patti, he would set fire to Paul's shop. In fact Paul's telephone was faulty with the result that he did not hear the message.

   Discuss George's criminal liability.
(b) John, a farmer, noticed that a large dog, Martha, belonging to Stuart was attacking his sheep. He asked Ringo, who was shooting grouse in a neighbouring field, if he would lend him his shotgun. Ringo refused. John wrenched the gun from Ringo's grasp and pushed Ringo to the ground. John shot and killed Martha.

   Discuss John's criminal liability.

Answer plan

The first part of the question is concerned with the offences of blackmail contrary to s 21 of the Theft Act 1968 and threats of damage to property contrary to s 2 of the Criminal Damage Act 1971. The second part concerns issues of liability for criminal damage and to a minor extent, battery.

Particular issues:

(a)

• whether a 'demand with menaces' is 'made' for the purposes of blackmail if the intended recipient does not hear it (s 21 of the Theft Act 1968)
• the meaning and application of 'view to gain' or 'intent to cause loss' in s 21
• whether a 'threat of damage' is 'made' if the intended recipient does not hear it (s 2 of the Criminal Damage Act 1971)

(b)

- the meaning and application of 'lawful excuse' in s 5(2)b of the CDA 1971
- the availability of the defence of 'duress of circumstances'

Answer

(a) Blackmail

George may be guilty of blackmail contrary to s 21 of the Theft Act 1968, an offence punishable with a term of imprisonment not exceeding fourteen years.

The *actus reus* of blackmail is a 'demand with menaces'.

In *Treacy v DPP* (1971), the House of Lords held by a majority that a demand contained in a letter is made when it is posted irrespective of whether it arrives or is read by the the person to whom it is addressed. Lord Diplock was influenced by the fact that the person who makes an uncommunicated demand is no less wicked or less in need of deterrence than the person whose demand is received.

The same may be said of the person who makes an oral communication which is not heard and thus, it is submitted, George made a demand viz that Paul give him the photographs.

A threat of any action detrimental to or unpleasant to the person addressed is capable of amounting to a menace so long as the threat is of sufficient strength or intensity that it would move the ordinary person of normal stability and courage to accede unwillingly to the demand (*Thorne v Motor Trade Association* (1937); *Clear* (1968)). Thus, it is unnecessary to know how Paul would have reacted to the threat to demolish his shop. The question is whether the *ordinary person* would be influenced by the threat.

The demand must be made with a 'view to gain' *or* 'intent to cause loss' in terms of money or other property (s 34(2)(a)). In this case George intended to cause Paul the loss of property ie the photographs.

The prosecution must prove that the 'demand with menaces' was unwarranted. This is a question of *mens rea*. Section 21(1) provides that D's demand with menaces is unwarranted unless D made it in the belief (a) that he had reasonable grounds for making the belief and (b) that the use of the menaces was a proper means of reinforcing the demand. The facts of the problem suggest that George's demand with menaces was unwarranted. Even if he believed that he had reasonable grounds for demanding the photographs it is improbable that he believed the use of the menaces was a proper means of reinforcing the demand. If George knew that what he threatened to do was unlawful his demand with menaces was unwarranted (*Harvey* (1981)).

Threats to destroy property

It is an offence contrary to s 2 of the Criminal Damage Act 1971 to threaten to destroy or damage property belonging to another intending that the person threatened would fear that the threat would be carried out.

The offence is not limited to written threats. And, although there is no direct authority on the point, it is submitted that, by analogy to blackmail, a threat is made even if it is not received.

(b) Criminal damage

John may be charged with criminal damage contrary to s 1(1) of the Criminal Damage Act 1971, an offence which, by virtue of s 4, is punishable with a maximum of ten years imprisonment.

The offence is committed where D intentionally or recklessly damages property belonging to another.

Tame animals or animals reduced into possession amount to 'property' for the purposes of this offence (s 10(1)(a)). And the killing of an animal constitutes destruction of the animal.

His *mens rea* is not in doubt - John intentionally destroyed property belonging to another.

Section 1(1) however provides that no offence is committed if D had a 'lawful excuse'. And, s 5(2)(b) provides that a D has a lawful excuse if he destroyed the property in order to protect property belonging to himself which he believed to be in immediate need of protection.

For the reasons explained above the sheep are 'property' belonging to John.

Although the defence in s 5(2)b is expressed in 'subjective' terms the Court of Appeal in *Hunt* (1978) held that the defence will be denied it is proved that what was done could not amount, objectively, to something done in protection of property.

It is submitted that in this case the objective requirement is satisfied. If, as the facts imply, John believed that his sheep were in immediate need of protection and he believed that shooting the dog was a reasonable means of protecting his property then he has a 'lawful excuse'. It is immaterial whether those beliefs were justified. All that matters is that they were genuinely held (s 5(3)).

Battery

John may be charged with the battery of Ringo.

Battery is a summary offence. The maximum punishment is a fine not exceeding £5000 and/or a term of imprisonment not exceeding six months (s 39 of the Criminal Justice Act 1988).

A person commits a battery where he intentionally or recklessly inflicts unlawful personal violence upon another (*Rolfe* (1952)). The slightest degree of force will suffice (*Cole v Turne*r (1704); *Collins v Wilcock* (1984)).

It is clear from the facts that John intentionally applied force. The issue is whether he did so 'unlawfully'.

Section 5(2) only provides a defence of 'lawful excuse' to a charge of criminal damage. It does not apply to other offences. And, it would appear that there is no other defence of which John may take advantage.

The newly recognised defence of 'duress of circumstances' applies only where the D can be said to be acting reasonably and proportionately in order to avoid a threat of death or serious injury to himself or another person (*Martin* (1989)).

Although there is some weak authority for the proposition that a defence of necessity might be available in cases where a lesser danger threatens (see eg *Conway* (1988) per Woolf LJ), there is no modern authority in which a threat of damage to property has been allowed.

Index